ABOUT PINTER: The Playwright and the Work

Mark Batty is a senior lecturer in Theatre Studies at the Workshop Theatre, University of Leeds, and researches Twentieth Century drama, translation for the stage and the history of the stage director. He is the author of *Writers and their Work: Harold Pinter* (Northcote House, 2001) and has published articles on the work of Pinter and Beckett.

Series Editor: Emeritus Professor Philip Roberts was Professor of Drama and Theatre Studies, and Director of the Workshop Theatre in the University of Leeds from 1998 to 2004. Educated at Oxford and Edinburgh, he held posts in the Universities of Newcastle and Sheffield before arriving in Leeds. His publications include: *Absalom and Achitophel and Other Poems* (Collins, 1973), *The Diary of Sir David Hamilton, 1709–1714* (Clarendon Press, 1975), *Edward Bond: A Companion to the Plays* (Theatre Quarterly Pubs, 1978), *Edward Bond: Theatre Poems and Songs* (Methuen, 1978), *Bond on File* (Methuen, 1985), *The Royal Court Theatre, 1965–1972* (Routledge, 1986), *Plays without Wires* (Sheffield Academic Press, 1989), *The Royal Court Theatre and the Modern Stage* (CUP, 1999).

Series Editor: Richard Boon is Professor of Performance Studies at the University of Leeds. He is the author of a number of studies of modern British political theatre, including *Brenton the Playwright* (Methuen, 1991), and is co-editor of *Theatre Matters: Performance and Culture on the World Stage* (CUP, 1998). He is also author of *About Hare: The Playwright and the Work* (Faber and Faber, 2003).

in the same series

ABOUT PINTER

The Playwright and the Work

Mark Batty

Para mi querido
Papa.

Te quiero
mucho.
18th May 2005

ff

faber and faber

Rhang + Peeko

First published in 2005
by Faber and Faber Limited
3 Queen Square London WC1N 3AU

Typeset by Faber and Faber Limited
Printed in England by Bookmarque Ltd, Croydon

A CIP record for this book
is available from the British Library

ISBN 0-571-22005-3

2 4 6 8 10 9 7 5 3 1

For Juliette

Contents

Editors' Note

There are few theatre books which allow direct access to the playwright or to those whose business it is to translate the script into performance. These volumes aim to deal directly with the writer and with other theatre workers (directors, actors, designers and similar figures) who realise in performance the words on the page.

The subjects of the series are some of the most important and influential writers from post-war British and Irish theatre. Each volume contains an introduction which sets the work of the writer in the relevant historical, social and political context, followed by a digest of interviews and other material which allows the writer, in his own words, to trace his evolution as a dramatist. Some of this material is new, as is, in large part, the material especially gathered from the writers' collaborators and fellow theatre workers. The volumes conclude with annotated bibliographies. In all, we hope the books will provide a wealth of information in accessible form, and real insight into some of the major dramatists of our day.

Abbreviations

P1: Harold Pinter, *Plays 1*
P2: Harold Pinter, *Plays 2*
P3: Harold Pinter, *Plays 3*
P4: Harold Pinter, *Plays 4*
VV: Harold Pinter, *Various Voices: Poetry, Prose, Politics 1948–1998* (an updated edition is planned for 2005)
MB: Michael Billington, *The Life and Work of Harold Pinter*
MG: Mel Gussow, *Conversations with Pinter*

All other references are given in endnotes on pages 223–8.
For full references, see the bibliography on page 229.

A Chronology

1930   Born in Hackney, East London.

1948–9 Studies acting for two terms at RADA.

1949   'Kullus' written

 –   Tried as a conscientious objector.

1950   Two poems, 'New Year in the Midlands' and 'Chandeliers and Shadows', published in *Poetry London*.

1951–3 Following a term at Central School of Speech and Drama, five seasons acting under Anew McMaster, including tour of Ireland, and one season acting under Donald Wolfit.

 –   The novel *The Dwarfs* composed.

1954–7 Under the name of David Baron, works as an actor in regional repertory companies.

1956   Marries Vivien Merchant.

1957   *The Room* is performed at Bristol University.

1958   *The Dumb Waiter* is first performed in February in the Kleines Haus in Frankfurt.

 –   19 May: *The Birthday Party* is performed at the Lyric Opera House, Hammersmith.

      Daniel Pinter born.

1959   9 July: *A Slight Ache* is broadcast by the BBC Third Programme.

 –   *The Hothouse* is written, but shelved.

 –   Contributes sketches to two revues, 'The Black and White' and 'Trouble in the Works' as part of *One to Another* at the Lyric Hammersmith and 'The Last to Go', 'Request Stop' and 'Special Offer' as part of *Pieces of Eight* at the Apollo Theatre.

1960 21 January: *The Dumb Waiter* performed in double bill with *The Room* at the Hampstead Theatre Club.

– 1 March: *A Night Out* Broadcast on BBC radio, and then televised (24 April) as part of ABC's *Armchair Theatre* series.

– 22 March: *The Birthday Party* broadcast by Associated Rediffusion TV.

– 27 April: *The Caretaker* is premièred at the Arts Theatre.

– 27 July: *Night School* is broadcast by ARTV.

– *The Dwarfs* broadcast by the BBC Third Programme (2 December).

1961 11 May: *The Collection* broadcast by ARTV. Staged on 18 June 1962 by the Royal Shakespeare Company.

1963 *The Lover* broadcast by ARTV on 28 March, then staged in double bill with the *The Dwarfs* on 18 September.

– 3 September: *The Servant* released.

1964 February: *The Caretaker* film released.

1965 25 March: *Tea Party* teleplay broadcast by BBC.

– 3 June: *The Homecoming* premièred at the Aldwych by the RSC.

1966 Appointed CBE.

1967 20 February: *The Basement* broadcast by BBC TV.

– February: *Accident* released.

1968 *Poems* published.

– 25 April: *Landscape* broadcast on BBC radio.

1969 2 July: *Landscape* and *Silence* performed together at the Aldwych.

1970 Directs James Joyce's *Exiles*.

– Awarded the German Shakespeare Prize.

1971 1 June: *Old Times* presented at the Aldwych.

– *The Go-Between* released.

– Directs Simon Gray's *Butley*.

1972 The year is dedicated to the writing of the unfilmed *Proust Screenplay*.

1973–83 Associate director of the National Theatre.
1973   13 April: *Monologue* broadcast on BBC TV.
1975   23 April: *No Man's Land*, starring Ralph Richardson and John Gielgud, premières at the National Theatre.
1976   Directs Noel Coward's *Blithe Spirit* at the National Theatre.
1978   15 November: *Betrayal* performed at the National Theatre.
1980   24 April: *The Hothouse* finally staged at the Hampstead Theatre.
  –   Divorces Vivien Merchant. Marries Lady Antonia Fraser.
1981   22 January: *Family Voices* broadcast by BBC Radio.
  –   The film *The French Lieutenant's Woman* released.
1982   14 October: *Other Places*: *A Kind of Alaska*, *Victoria Station* and *Family Voices*, staged at the National Theatre.
1984   13 March: *One for the Road* premièred at the Lyric, Hammersmith.
1988   20 October: *Mountain Language* staged at the National Theatre.
1989   The film *Reunion* released.
1990   The novel *The Dwarfs* published.
1991   31 October: *Party Time* staged at the Almeida Theatre.
1992   *The Trial* filmed and released.
1993   7 September: *Moonlight* premièred at the Royal Court.
  –   Directs David Mamet's *Oleanna* for the Royal Court Theatre.
1995   Awarded the David Cohen British Literature Prize.
  –   Directs Ronald Harwood's *Taking Sides*.
1996   12 September: *Ashes to Ashes* staged at the Almeida.
  –   Rejects offer of a knighthood extended by Prime Minister John Major.
1997   Awarded a Molière d'honneur in Paris, the *Sunday Times* Award for Literary Excellence and given a BAFTA Fellowship.

1998   *Various Voices: Prose Poetry, Politics 1948–1998* is published.

–   Made a Companion of Literature by the Royal Society of Literature.

2000   16 March: *Celebration* is performed in double bill with a revival of *The Room* at the Almeida, directed by the author.

–   23 November: *Remembrance of Things Past* premières at National Theatre.

–   Awarded the Critics' Circle Award for Distinguished Service to the Arts.

2001   Awarded The S. T. Dupont Golden Pen Award 2001 for a Lifetime's Distinguished Service to Literature.

–   Diagnosed with cancer of the oesophagus.

2002   8 February: Performs in première of *Press Conference* at National Theatre.

–   Survives surgery for cancer.

–   Made Companion of Honour at a ceremony at Buckingham Palace.

2003   17 April: New adaptation of *The Dwarfs* staged at the Tricycle Theatre.

–   *War* (a collection of war poems) published.

2004   Directs Simon Gray's *The Old Masters*.

–   Awarded the Wilfred Owen Prize for poetry opposing the Iraq conflict.

Preface

Harold Pinter has attracted a good deal of critical attention over a span of five decades. Of all the playwrights of his generation, only Samuel Beckett has had more written and published about him. It is an inevitable but curious consequence of this ever-growing body of analysis and commentary that much more has ever been written about Pinter than he himself has put down in ink. To add another book to the bookshop and library shelves on this subject, then, is a challenging task. Whilst going over some of the ground already well-trodden by many who have responded to Pinter's life and works previously, this book aims to provide a survey of his achievement in an original, readable and useful manner.

The book is divided into three roughly equal parts. The first third is a concentrated survey of Harold Pinter's life and work, and aims to place the writer's output within the social, theatrical and political contexts from which it grew and into which it was delivered. There is an extended consideration of his place in the growing and rapidly changing British theatrical landscape of the 1950s which strives, in part, to clarify the significance of his contribution to the latest wave of writing that was being generated by the new artistic climate. Whilst most studies of Pinter concentrate wholly on his work and reputation as a dramatist, the unfolding discussion of his career here attempts to embrace all aspects of his artistic ambition, and reveals his temperament and the specific fascinations of his creative imagination by considering his work as a screenplay writer, actor and director alongside his better-known output as a world-renowned playwright. His later engagement in political activism is considered in the final section of this book's commentary.

Throughout the first section, as much as possible, Pinter's own voice is interjected to clarify his intent or illustrate points raised. The second section, though, is dedicated wholly to Pinter's own words, and represents the largest and most varied compilation of the writer's thoughts and opinions ever to be printed. Again, rather than concentrating wholly on his responses to his own plays, and to the craft of playwriting, the selection of interviews has been arranged to bring together the writer's thoughts on writing for film, and his political opinions, alongside his reflections on some of his drama, the manner in which it has been produced and the effect it has upon its audiences. From his memories of evacuation to Cornwall as a child to his latest politically charged expression, the material gathered in this section, when digested together, reveals a great deal about Pinter's beliefs and his relationship with artistic endeavour. It is prefaced with a brand new interview from 2004, granted specifically for this book, which offers something of an overview of his career as a writer.

The final section is dedicated to interviews with those who have known and worked most closely with Pinter over the past fifty years. Writers, actors, designers, film and stage directors and friends discuss the nature of their collaboration with him, and collectively reveal further information about his attitude to his work in the contexts in which his writing is put most firmly to the test – in the rehearsal rooms and film studios in which his dramatic worlds have been discovered, tried out and brought to life. Four of these interviews are original, and reproduced here for the first time.

A book of this size must, of necessity, rely on brevity and concise phrasing to cover substantial material, themes and events. The interviews reproduced are, for the most part, abridged versions of more complete and, often, much longer originals. An annotated bibliography is provided to guide those who might wish to pursue in more detail specific aspects of, or detailed approaches to, the various facets of Pinter's career, and includes a list (as comprehensive as possible) of the published interviews that Pinter has given since his first in 1959.

Mark Batty (*aboutpinter@mac.com*)

2005

East End to West End

In September 2001 Harold Pinter launched his own website. It was to act as a repository for facts and information on his career and, more importantly, provide him with a forum where he might express his concerns, unhindered by the limitations and agendas of conventional media outlets. The first words to be seen at the head of the home page were and remain:

> In 1958 I wrote the following:
> 'There are no hard distinctions between what is real and what is unreal, nor between what is true and what is false. A thing is not necessarily either true or false; it can be both true and false.'
> I believe that these assertions still make sense and do still apply to the exploration of reality through art. So as a writer I stand by them but as a citizen I cannot. As a citizen I must ask: What is true? What is false?

Introducing Noam Chomsky as 'the leading critical voice against the criminal regime now running the United States' at the Kurdish Human Rights Project 10th Anniversary Lecture in St Paul's Cathedral on 9 December 2002, Pinter commended the writer's 'fearless, formidable, totally independent voice', and emphasised that which he valued most in Chomsky's approach to international political commentary: 'He does something which is really quite simple but highly unusual. He tells the truth.'[1]

On the walls of Pinter's home studio, where he conducts all his writing and research, two paintings hang which represent these two seemingly opposing attitudes to the 'truth'. As he sits at his desk, positioned in the centre of the room, he faces a sizeable canvas as large as a window, flanked by the book-cases that wrap round the office and surround him. It is a mono-chrome/ brown painting of an empty room. An oval frame painted within the actual wooden frame gives the viewer the illusion of being invited to peer into that room as though through a lens, or in a convex mirror. The depicted room is therefore distorted, its contours and windows warped in a gentle curvature outwards from the centre by the illusionary refraction of light. On the wall directly opposite, behind him as he writes, is a much smaller frame filled entirely by a char-coal-grey face, asexual in aspect and possessing somewhat blurred features, with eyes, brow and jaw in relaxed, neutral, emotionless repose. Where a mouth should be, however, there is a blank space, faintly lighter than the grey face, as though that aperture has been erased. Both paintings are hauntingly appealing, both draw the focus into a void, a space that might be inhabited, that we crave to make more reassuringly human. One painting reflects perhaps Pinter's interest in the unrelia-bility of perspective, in the distorting effect of an appropriat-ing gaze, and in issues of occupancy and the human relationship to domestic space. The other reflects a commit-ment to human dignity, to the right to give voice, and is an appeal to fair and just representation. Like Pinter's own art, they demand an engagement on the part of those who witness them and, through their depositing of some uncanny disrup-tion, require one to respond on a personal level.

These cherished paintings neatly illustrate the two facets of 'truth' which Harold Pinter justifies as his legitimate preoccu-pations, and it is an investigation of what constitutes 'truth' that marks all of his activity as both artist and citizen. As an artist his concerns have involved charting the anatomy of truth as a phenomenon constructed by the individual's perceptions of experience, tempered by the vagaries of memory, by the chal-lenges and invasions of others and by longings and fears coloured by denial, betrayal and anxiety. This is the elusive truth of self-affirmation, an impulse towards manufacturing systems of verification that the experience of being alive often reveals as missing. As an engaged citizen, he strives to keep the truth of the fact of human oppression centre-stage, and his political pronouncements target those who abuse power and manipulate language to keep those truths obscured. This is the truth that must repeatedly be excavated, revealed and presented to those who hold a responsibility to respond to it. Contemplating these two operations of the concept of 'truth', then, has been central to Harold Pinter's activity as a public figure. This book aims to examine these two poles of Pinter's career, first by surveying his output as a creative artist over more than five decades, then within a compilation from amongst the numerous interviews he and a number of his artistic collaborators have given over that time.

Since 1950, Harold Pinter has written twenty-nine plays, thirteen sketches, twenty-one screenplays, one novel, fourteen short works of prose fiction and many poems. He has directed thirty-five productions, one film and six teleplays. He has acted in over eighty plays (his last stage appearance being in 2001), appeared in three films (and made cameo appearances in a few more) and lent his voice to various radio productions. To this activity we might add his numerous speeches, political writings and open letters. Today, ten years past retirement age and after having survived a cancer of the oesophagus (in 2002), he remains relentlessly active. On a daily basis, he strolls through the garden of the Holland Park house he shares with his wife, the celebrated author Lady Antonia Fraser, to enter his one-up one-down mews house studio, climb the stairs and read or write for the afternoon. At either side of his desk, closest to his occasional casual gaze, are two collections of books that represent his most enduring of passions: to his right are bookcases crammed with volumes on cricket and cricketers, including a complete collection of Wisden's Cricketers' Almanacs that date from the creased, brown copies of the 1870s to the latest twenty-first-century brick-thick editions in their bright yellow dust jackets; to his left, between the studio's two windows, stretching from floor to ceiling, is a bookcase full of poetry and poetry magazines.

John Fowles imagines that for Pinter 'all audiences are [. . .] batsmen to be dismissed and essentially to be left gasping'.[2] A love of cricket – an engaging, social game of gentlemanly combat – fits understandably well into the psychological make-up of the author of works such as *The Caretaker*, *The Home-coming*, *No Man's Land* and *Ashes to Ashes* in which bluff, double-bluff, manipulation and threat unsettle their audiences with all the force of the feints and charge of a fast bowler. One journalist once also noted that there is 'something of the umpire about Pinter's involvement in politics, calling foul, refusing to be intimidated, insisting on fair play'.[3] It was poetry, though, that captured Pinter's imagination first, as a young boy growing up in Hackney in the East End of London.

The only son of parents descended from East European Ashkenazi Jews who settled in England in the first years of the last century, Pinter enjoyed a contented and comfortable working-class upbringing in Hackney, interrupted only by his being evacuated as a child during the war. His father was a tailor, with a successful firm in Stoke Newington, but no demands or expectations in that direction were made on the young Pinter and his early interest in poetry and literature was encouraged. What is perhaps remarkable about Pinter's reading as a boy and young man is that whilst at school he developed an extra-curricular inclination towards modernist literature in his choices of Dostoevsky, Rimbaud, Eliot and Joyce (whose *Ulysses* he first read aged fifteen and which remains a firm favourite to this day). The names of artists trotted out by the lonely figure in Pinter's *Monologue* (1973), written for and originally performed by his old school friend Henry Woolf, form a list of the reading a teenage Pinter would enthuse to his mates about, or the books that they would cherish and pass on to him: André Breton, Louis-Ferdinand Céline, John Dos Passos, Alberto Giacometti, Cyril Tourneur, Tristan Tzara, John Webster. In *Celebration* (2000) the figure of the waiter, making frequent interjections into the bawdy diners' conversations (much as Pinter did once while working at the National Liberal Club in his twenties, earning him the sack) provides a more exhaustive list, adding Dylan Thomas, W. B. Yeats and Franz Kafka.

These miniature bibliographies of Pinter's reading were, as Michael Billington points out, 'all part of the Hackney gang's cultural trade and mart' (MB, p. 236). Pinter and his school friends also developed a taste for European cinema, such as Louis Buñuel's *Un Chien Andalou*, Marcel Carné's *Le jour se lève* or Robert Wiene's *The Cabinet of Dr Caligari*, and appreciated the openness and expressionism that was less likely to be found in home-grown film-making. Pinter once stated: 'Buñuel was a phenomenon: there was no one like him; nor will there ever be. To say I was influenced by him is to put it much too glibly. He was part of my life' (VV, p. 50), and Linda Renton locates the link between Pinter's awareness of Surrealist ambition and his own writing in his poem *August Becomes*, which he headed with a quotation from André Breton's 1934 essay 'What is surrealism?'

It was in this mixed seedbed of formalist experiment and modernist realignment of subjectivity in linguistic and visual media that the young writer's mind took root. He tried his hand at poetry first, starting around the age of thirteen, and much of his juvenilia shows traces of the influence of Dylan Thomas. In 1950 he had two poems published under the pseudonym Harold Pinta in *Poetry London* magazine: 'New Year in the Midlands' and 'Chandeliers and Shadows'. Around the same time, he began writing prose. The biographical *The Queen of all the Fairies*, which remains unpublished, the short stories 'Kullus', 'Latest Reports from the Stock Exchange', 'The Black and White' and 'The Examination' all date from between 1949 and 1955. In these earliest works, some of the themes and concerns that were later to colour Pinter's plays first became manifest. The figure of Kullus, for example, was an invention that he developed to consider the human impulse towards dominance, psychological game-play and territorial gain. The character appeared in three early pieces of writing: 'Kullus' (1949), the poem 'The Task' (1954) and 'The Examination' (1955) and all demonstrate a fascination with the violating presence of an intruding personality. In all three pieces, Kullus slowly takes control of a room into which he is invited by an unnamed narrating voice. In 'The Task', the dominance is captured in a shift from the passive 'Kullus, seen' to the active 'Kullus saw' (VV, p. 131), and this movement is tracked in detail in the two related prose pieces. 'Kullus', in which the character adopts his host's apartment and occupies it with a girlfriend, provided a scenario which Pinter later revisited in the television play *The Basement* (1967). In 'The Examination' Kullus is called to a room to be interviewed, but by employing silence as a means of dominating the interview, he eventually gains control of both interview and room and the narrator assents to his dominance. Silence as a conversational ploy was to play an important role in Pinter's drama and intruding figures were to form crucial elements of the dramatic apparatus of some of his first plays.

Pinter's only novel, *The Dwarfs*, later to be adapted for radio and then stage, was compiled between 1952 and 1956 but not published until 1990. The key character of Virginia innocently causes a rift between two close friends, Pete and Mark, by casually informing Mark of Pete's true opinion of him. Their mutual friend Len exhibits schizophrenic tendencies and speaks of a group of helpful but domineering dwarfs living beside him in his flat and yard. His obsession with decay and his mental and physical disorders parallel the entropy within friendship, and the novel deals with the modes of often inauthentic behaviour that interfere in the management of relationships. This examination of the dilemmas that arise in maintaining meaningful contact with others, including the need to trust in the authenticity of what people project of themselves, was to inform a great deal of Pinter's subsequent output, from *The Caretaker*, *Old Times* and *Betrayal*, in the sixties and seventies, through to *Moonlight* and *Ashes to Ashes* in the nineties.

Notably, Pinter's intellectual curiosity as a young man had been drawn to literature, poetry and cinema, and not theatre. In his early writing, he demonstrated no ambition to compose plays. Like many of his modest background, he did not frequent theatres other than on the school trips he was taken on, and his exposure to the stage was to be through his experiences as an actor: 'I saw very few plays, in fact, before I was twenty. Then I acted in too many,' he once stated (P2, p. vii). The theatre to which he was to be exposed through his numerous acting roles was far removed in style and intent from the modernism of the novels he devoured or the expressionism of the cinema he was interested in. His first onstage roles were at the Hackney Downs Grammar School, playing the lead in *Macbeth* at the age of sixteen and, a year later, Romeo in *Romeo and Juliet*. Both these productions were directed by Joseph Brearley, his English teacher and eventual close friend. Brearley sought to fill his pupils with an enthusiasm for the vitality of Jacobean verse and took Pinter and his peers to see John Webster's *The White Devil* and Donald Wolfit's productions of *Macbeth* and *King Lear*, the latter production so impressing Pinter that he returned to see it five further times. These few early experiences of dramatic writing and production were enough to convince the young Pinter, once he had ruled out higher education and any nine-to-five job, to pursue a career in acting. He successfully gained a scholarship from the London City Council to pay his fees at the Royal Academy of Dramatic Art and enrolled there in the autumn of 1948. His greatest performance at RADA was that of affecting a nervous breakdown to escape the place, which he very quickly abhorred. The academy was the training ground for the professional stage, which catered to middle-class tastes and the fare of drawing-room dramas that proliferated at the time. The director Joan Littlewood remembered RADA in the fifties as 'posed, static and unexciting', where 'dishonest acting' was taught and 'language [was] despised, all the virility of language'.[4] Pinter's distaste for the place might have been informed by this first exposure to the mid-century stagnation of the British theatre world. The vast majority of the school's students would have hailed from the kinds of families that could well afford the required fees, and mixing with those of a substantially different background might easily have alienated or irritated the young, non-conformist Pinter.

Recognising, nevertheless, the need for a training of sorts, Pinter returned to drama school and endured six months at the Central School of Speech and Drama, in 1951. His first professional engagement as an actor was as a walk-on in *Dick Whittington and his Cat* at the Chesterfield Hippodrome during the winter of 1949–50 and, following his stay at Central, he successfully auditioned for Anew McMaster's company, with which he toured Ireland. From 1951 to 1952 he played numerous second-lead Shakespearean roles with the troupe, alongside the occasional Sophocles or Oscar Wilde. In 1953 he joined Donald Wolfit's company at the King's Theatre in Hammersmith in the final spring season of its sixteen-year existence, this time playing smaller roles in a similar diet of Shakespeare and other classical drama.

McMaster and Wolfit, both of whom had made their names at Stratford in the 1930s, belonged to an older theatrical tradition of the actor-manager that had its roots in the nineteenth century. The notion of 'company' in actor-manager systems was subordinate to the central star actor, who managed the group he employed to play against him in the lead roles. All elements of play production centred around the lead actor: texts were cut to avoid lengthy sections without the star on stage, regardless of any incoherence this might cause; directing, as Pinter recalled, consisted of the occasional, encouraging shout of 'speak up, get on with it';[5] blocking involved the star taking a centre-stage position whilst others adopted positions in a crescent around him; acting involved a demonstration of the controlled use of range, timbre and projection of the voice to capture and mesmerise an audience. All this made for a theatre of bold statements, of exaggerated delivery and resonant bathos – the kind of theatre that might today inspire the emphatically pejorative use of the word 'theatrical', in dismissal of its excesses. In his eulogy 'Mac', written in 1968, Pinter captured his memories of his early master, offering a glimpse of that 'theatricality': '[H]is gestures complete, final, nothing jagged, his movement of the utmost fluidity and yet of the utmost precision: stood there, dead in the centre of the role, and the great sweeping symphonic playing would begin, the rare tension and release within him, the arrest, the swoop, the savagery, the majesty and repose' (VV, p. 23). Actor-managers were a dying breed, and in McMaster and Wolfit Pinter experienced two fine examples of their work and methods before their extinction. They were systematically replaced in Great Britain by the development of repertory theatre in the early years of the twentieth century, and it was to this world that Pinter was to shift.

The term 'repertory' strictly implies the staging of a fixed repertoire of plays, each usually for a week at a time and repeated regularly at irregular intervals, according to public demand. British 'rep' more commonly involved a season of plays running three or four weeks each, with no real 'repertoire' to speak of or any repeated productions. It is, of course, the format commonly adopted today by most playhouses. 'Weekly rep' was a more gruelling format for its actors, involving a seven-day rotation of plays to keep entertained smaller regional audiences, which might readily be exhausted within a week. The demands of such a turnaround of dramatic product upon actors were exigent: six evening and two matinee performances, with rehearsals during the days for the next week's presentation. In 1950 there were ninety-four theatres with permanent rep companies operating in Britain, most of which operated weekly rep systems. As a young actor, the writer John Osborne remembered joining one such company, managed by the notorious Harry Hanson: '[T]he company were docile, like prisoners without heart or spirit [. . .]. The audience was noisy and inattentive. Rehearsals were conducted in a guilty kind of haste and the actors were only given moves where not indicated in the script. No one dared fudge them or forget a move.'[6]

At their worst, regional rep companies produced material that Peter Brook would later identify as 'deadly theatre',[7] offering a fare of West End leavings and a dramatic diet of farces, light comedies, thrillers and romantic dramas. Following his brief stint with Wolfit's company in 1953, this was to be Pinter's daily life for five years, and his prime manner of earning a living alongside stints as a waiter, a postman, a bouncer and snow-clearer whilst all the time harbouring ambitions as a poet and writer. For a stage name he adopted his paternal grandmother's maiden name, and between 1954 and 1959, as David Baron, he acted in excess of eighty plays in rep companies from Whitby to Torquay, Birmingham to Eastbourne.

Regional repertory work may have seemed a hellish way of making a living but it proved an invaluable training ground for many British actors and playwrights of Pinter's generation, including, to name but a very few, Richard Briers, Albert Finney, Ronald Harwood, Peter O'Toole, Paul Scofield and Donald Sinden. For Pinter, too, his time in rep served as a crucial period of schooling, and the significance of his work on innumerable plays during this period has been hypothesised comprehensively in David T. Thompson's *The Players' Playwright*. Pinter's relationship with the work fluctuated. Often he might enthuse over some of the material that came his way, and he certainly enjoyed the opportunities of an itinerant lifestyle (especially his days in Ireland with McMaster). He would, though, frequently be less than enamoured of the toil and once told his friends that acting was a 'shit-house of a profession' (MB, p. 45). A certain weariness with the vocation is present in his poems 'The Second Visit' (*c.*1952) and 'The Drama in April' (1952); in the former, memories of a vital childhood relationship (from his time as an evacuee) with shore and sea are deflated by a flaccid 'Now an actor in this nocturnal sink' (VV, p. 128) and in the latter, Pinter presents a tired view of the drudgery of acting work, offering a world of 'mourning', 'ash' and 'grave unnumbered stones'. 'I move to the interval' says the spectator of the poem in its final stanza, 'Done with this repertory' (VV, p. 123). At the worst of times, acting barely constituted a living, and Pinter remembers getting by on a pitiful 'six shillings a week as an actor and tuppence halfpenny as a poet'.[8] Pinter's first wife, Vivien Merchant, whom he married in 1956, was also an actor (in fact, she was then far more renowned in her career than he in his) and together they struggled to piece together the wherewithal to enjoy married life and bring up their son, Daniel, who was born in 1958. Pinter's playwriting career began modestly in 1957, and it was still to be a few years before success was to help establish a more comfortable lifestyle.

Pinter's name was first made as a dramatist at a time when the British theatre scene was going through what has historically been identified as a crucial period of regeneration. He belonged to a generation of playwrights who, together, were to redefine the very nature of British drama and rewrite the established rules of what constituted appropriate modes and subjects of enquiry. The significance of his eventual contribution to the newly established, mainstream theatre that emerged in the 1960s is best appreciated by considering the culture and environment in which he grew as a playwright, and some of the challenges faced by artists of his generation. Their first challenge was to confront the very fabric of established theatre practice.

2

1956 and All That

In *A Short History of English Drama*, a Pelican paperback for a general readership published in 1948, B. Ifor Evans noted that 'of the English theatre in the twentieth century this at least can be said, that it is better than the English theatre of the nineteenth century'.[1] His despair at the state of contemporary playwriting was an attitude shared by many. As a jobbing actor in the 1950s, Harold Pinter had first-hand experience of the drama and production practices of the times and, as a writer, he is arguably as much a product of the theatre of the 1940s and 1950s as he was a reformer in response to it. For his style and aesthetic approach to have flourished at all, much first needed to be rectified, and, as commentators such as Evans identified, the whole infrastructure of mid-century British theatre practice was in need of an overhaul.

For much of the fifties, theatres in Britain had been run purely on commercial principles and there were very few that might be deemed 'fringe'. The Royal Shakespeare Company was not to be established until 1960, and Britain was without a National Theatre until 1962. The Arts Council of Great Britain, formed in 1946, was offering growing amounts of Treasury funds to promote resident companies, touring work, and to assist established theatres in improving production standards, but it had little to offer towards new writing. What is more, only something short of two-thirds of theatres in Britain in the early fifties actually produced plays – many instead provided twice-nightly collections of revue sketches or variety acts such as that documented and satirised in John Osborne's *The Entertainer* (1957). Cinema was well established and its threat to the mainstream theatre was physically manifested in the

number of Victorian playhouses that had already been converted to cinemas (a third of them by 1952).[2] To add to this assault,
in 1953 television ownership in the UK doubled as a result of
the broadcast of the coronation of Queen Elizabeth II.
Complementing the BBC's output, the entertainment-driven
ITV began broadcasting in September 1955 and as television
variety programming such as *Sunday Night at the London
Palladium* (1955), revue sketch shows such as *The Crazy Gang*
and the appropriately titled *Let's Stay Home* (both 1956), and
the one-off live-broadcast dramas of *Armchair Theatre* (1956)
grew in popularity, many understandably predicted a slow
death for British theatrical traditions. Between 1950 and 1955
the number of theatres with permanent repertory companies
dropped from ninety-six to fifty-five. In such a commercial
environment, what form of live drama might survive?

Mainstream theatrical establishments in London and the
provinces were effectively controlled by a small number of commercial management groups, a situation which did little to promote or permit change to the *status quo*. When seeking material
to be performed, these few managers understandably relied on
tried and tested formulae, seeking plays that offered suitable
vehicles for the audience-attracting talent and charisma of star
actors. Isolated from the formalistic experiments of American
and European drama, and stuck in their self-perpetuating commercial rut, British theatres of the 1940s and 1950s offered a
dramatic diet of the so-called 'well-made play' formula that
was amply supplied by playwrights such as Agatha Christie,
Noel Coward, J. B. Priestley, and Terence Rattigan. One might
still experience a small taste of this mid-twentieth-century fare
in the form of Christie's *The Mousetrap*, which has, extraordinarily, run non-stop in London's West End from 1950 to the
present day.

Though it would be inaccurate to represent the pre-1956
British theatre as a cultural wasteland, the fact remains that
managers had to play safe in an environment where commercial concerns relied upon a returning audience. The plays that

were most frequently performed, therefore, represented the safe, middle-class milieu and world-view or aspirations of the audiences that would come to see them. It was a theatre representing the upper-middle-class comfort of suburbia or the affluent bourgeoisie at leisure, entering the drawing rooms of their country residences through the French windows; a world where servants knew their place and in which regional accents might indicate a bumpkin simplicity or comic disposition.

A commercial dependence upon the tastes of a particular type of theatre-goer was certainly a hindrance to risk and experimentation. In 1953 Rattigan – unwittingly creating a rod for his own back – decried the 'hopeless lowbrow' audiences upon which the British theatre had become dependent and personified their attitudes in the fictional character of Aunt Edna, whom he described as without 'knowledge or discernment'. Dismissive of the contributions made to their disciplines by Franz Kafka ('Why always look on the dark side of things?') or Pablo Picasso ('Why three noses?'),[3] Aunt Edna was intolerant of the modernist impulses that had defined much of twentieth-century European artistic endeavour. The supply-and-demand ethic of the British theatre repertoire that she represented was certainly one of the reasons why such impulses were slow to make their impression upon the British stage despite their growing influence on the European scene. Pinter remembers this audience-centred climate of the 1950s British theatre from his years in rep: 'They didn't want anything else, they were perfectly happy to put their feet up. That was what the theatre was normally about, going and putting your feet up and just receive something, received ideas of what Drama was, going through various procedures which were known to the audience. I think it was becoming a dead area.'[4]

The first serious challenge to this state of affairs was the production of Samuel Beckett's *Waiting for Godot* mounted at the Arts Theatre in 1955 by a young director fresh out of college, Peter Hall. Harold Pinter was something of a fan of Beckett's already. Having come across an excerpt from the novel *Watt* in a poetry magazine in 1953, he had sought out anything the writer had produced at the Bermondsey Central Library and, appalled that the copy of *Murphy* he was handed had not been borrowed for over a decade, decided that he would appropriate it. It still sits on a shelf in Pinter's office alongside other, legitimately purchased, works by the same author. He subsequently devoured Beckett's novels *Molloy* and *Malone Dies* and, in 1954, described the author as 'the most courageous, remorseless writer going' (VV, p. 45). Pinter got wind of Hall's production and, having seen it, considered it a 'revolutionary piece of work'.[5] It nevertheless perplexed a good few theatre-going sensibilities. Having received a harshly dismissive critical response on its opening night, when half the audience left at the interval, the production survived following Kenneth Tynan's and Harold Hobson's praise in their weekend reviews. Considered in Paris as 'knocking the dust off the theatre',[6] the play rejected all hitherto recognised forms of character construction and narrative, thrusting two tramp figures onto a scene of windswept wasteland to pass the time in verbal game-playing as they await the elusive title character, who might provide them with a sense of purpose and self-worth. They return to do the same again in a second act and Godot, of course, never shows his face. Appearing on the British cultural scene with no immediate dramatic precedent, it must perhaps have been too much of 'a curiosity, a four-leafed clover, a black tulip',[7] as Hobson described it, to have been anything other than a powerfully influential marvel.

Perhaps enthused by the promise and adventure of such foreign writing, in 1955 Tynan lamented the lack of 'a native prose playwright who might set the boards smouldering'.[8] He was in effect criticising a system that gave no significant space for such writers to confront the theatre-going audiences, or to discover new audiences of their own. In November 1956 the publication *Encore* held a symposium entitled 'Cause without a Rebel' on the state of British theatre, where the need for precisely such a new production climate was discussed. Tynan, again, bemoaned the lack of a tradition of political theatre in Britain and Arthur Miller offered his impression that 'British theatre is hermetically sealed against the way society moves'. This call for greater social realism in writing was articulated alongside a need for 'some possibility of intelligent planning of productions' and the recognition that 'you can't have an *avant-garde* composed of dramatists only. You've got to have an *avant-garde* on the receiving end as well.'[9] These were the desired prerequisites for a new theatrical climate and, as things turned out, it was not Tynan's new playwright who would deliver a much-needed shot in the arm to the British theatre, but a theatre company that would prove so influential as to slowly engineer a change of mainstream British theatre practice.

Established in 1956, the English Stage Company at the Royal Court Theatre, under its celebrated artistic director George Devine, sought to establish an arts theatre repertoire of contemporary British and international works and create an environment that would encourage and nurture new writing. Its first season, running from April 1956, included Arthur Miller's *The Crucible*, Bertolt Brecht's *The Good Woman of Szechwan*, and a new play by a young actor in the company – John Osborne's *Look Back in Anger*. These plays were typical of the scope and reach of the Royal Court's nascent artistic policy: new, gifted writing, international and home-grown, which sought to address issues of how the individual relates to or is formed by the society in which he or she exists. Osborne's play was to prove as significant an event on the London stage as *Waiting for Godot* had become the year before and was subsequently considered 'arguably the biggest shock to the system of British theatre since the advent of Shaw'.[10] The basic realism of its setting challenged the demureness of traditional theatrical décor and the play gave voice to a frustrated, disenfranchised constituency of lower-middle-class, first-generation graduates of post-war British education policies. Jimmy Porter, the bitter, articulate focus of the drama, rails against a class-ridden Establishment that his education has provided no means to either breach or influence, and bemoans the lack of idealistic purpose. In this way, the play was deemed to represent a prevailing state of mind among the disenchanted youth of the times: 'In that summer of 1955,' Osborne recalled, 'it was still easy enough to identify what we regarded as a permanent Establishment. The continued acceptance of hanging, the prosecution of homosexuals, and censorship in film and theatre made life easy for a liberal conscience.'[11]

The play was the only script selected of the 675 that the ESC had received in response to a previously circulated advertisement for new plays. One early reader of the play, however, had stated that the ESC 'could never put such a thing on in the theatre. One could not insult an audience in this kind of way.' Philip Roberts comments that the 'remark is unintentionally revealing about the expectations of audiences when watching a play. It is a remark about theatre as confirmatory of the audience's *status quo*. The notion that the theatre should be in any way disturbing, let alone bad mannered, was inconceivable.'[12] George Devine and the English Stage Company were to forge an artistic environment where such work *was* conceivable, and as such they might be considered significantly responsible for the subsequent development of British playwriting and related shifts in audience demographics.

Other writers whose work was exposed to the London audiences at the Royal Court include John Arden, Edward Bond, Shelagh Delaney, Ann Jellicoe and Arnold Wesker, all young authors of the same generation as Pinter who, alongside Osborne, were seen to represent the voice of the post-war discontent of their generation. Together, they brought working-class figures, settings and concerns onto the British stage for the first time, earning and embracing the term 'kitchen sink' dramatists. Pinter himself was to develop no significant relationship as a dramatist with the ESC, quite possibly because Harold Hobson, after having seen his first play *The Room* performed in Bristol, in 1957, had inadvertently irritated George Devine – not a man to be told what to do – by asserting: 'The

directors of the London Arts Theatre and the English Stage
Company should be backing Mr Pinter before they eat their
lunch today.'[13] It is without doubt, though, that Pinter was significantly advantaged in his artistic ambitions by the cultural
shift that Devine and the Court had brought about in London
theatres.

If Aunt Edna was displeased at the new, challenging writing
that was emerging, her theoretical nephew (if we might imagine him) was now discovering a gratifying experience in the
theatre. Finally plays began to speak to his generation. The
Royal Court received a letter from a group of young theatre-
goers congratulating them on the production of *Look Back
with Anger*, in which they stated: 'It seems to us the first time
that our home-grown brand of kid has been presented on any
stage.'[14] This is more remarkable than it might now seem. As a
twenty-year-old Briton in the mid-fifties, you would have had a
vivid memory of wartime danger and deprivation (food
rationing, in fact, only ended in 1954) and perhaps a growing
distrust of the systems of resource-annexing Empire that had
led to global conflict. The first of three consecutive
Conservative governments had been elected in 1951, initiating
a period of deflation in the aspirations of the Left. This had
been exacerbated further by the shattering of the hope of egal-
itarian society that Communism had seemingly offered to
many, following the exposure of Stalinist repression and
Khrushchev's expansionist policies. The recent revelations of
the details of the Holocaust would have coloured your
response to the news of the Soviet tanks rolling into Hungary
in late 1956 and the new totalitarian threat that this represented. With the Cold War just establishing itself, and a prevalent
awareness of the all too conceivable threat of a nuclear confrontation between the newly emerged axes of power, your
interest or dismay in the manoeuvres of your politicians would
have been differently informed from those of a young generation living today in a period of relatively stable European
peace. At home, you would have been experiencing the benefits

of significant domestic social reform. The establishment of the
Welfare State in the late 1940s had created a respected
National Health Service and a system of state benefits that
were to protect the poorer elements of society. You would have
been one of the first of a generation of pupils to have benefited
from a free secondary school education and to have been given
greater access to higher education. 'You've never had it so
good,' Prime Minister Harold Macmillan told the nation in
1957, and, certainly, increased employment since the war provided for a growing consumerist economy in which the young
could now participate. The marketing of products specifically
targeting mass teenage consumers dates from this time, taking
the lead from the United States, which exported wholesale to
British shores the rebellious, if seemingly directionless, impulses of its rock-and-roll (Little Richard, in 1956, invited his fellow teens to 'Rip It Up,') and cinema (in *The Wild One* [1953],
when asked what he was rebelling against, Marlon Brando's
character replied, 'Whaddya got?'). As a twenty-year-old, contributing through taxes and the recently applied National
Insurance premiums to a universally endorsed Welfare State,
you might have felt an ambivalence to a society that still considered you a year away from adulthood (the voting age in the
UK was twenty-one until 1969). In short, you would have been
part of the generation that was seeking to explore and define its
identity, shored up by the financial means to enjoy a social existence and a growing variety of cultural outlets for the reflection
or expression of your concerns, ambitions and anxieties.
Whilst Osborne's *Look Back in Anger* would not have been the
definitive answer to this theoretical search, the attraction of all
this noisy 'anger' might well have caught your attention, fired
your imagination and developed your sense of purpose.

Harold Pinter turned twenty-five in 1955, and he manifested
his fair share of anger. He had witnessed the tragic loss caused
by the bombing of his London suburb in the Second World War
and, as a member of a Jewish family and community, felt a personal and complex association with the significance of the

Holocaust. In a bar near the Royal Court theatre, in the late 1950s, he overheard a man proclaiming that Hitler had not gone far enough in dealing with the Jews, and an attempt to confront the man verbally ended with Pinter laying into him quite ferociously. He later recognised that his uncontrolled outburst was 'because he wasn't just insulting me [. . .]. He was insulting people who were dead, people who had suffered.'[15] This awareness of the atrocities of global conflict contributed to his decision, following his 1948 National Service call-up, to register as a conscientious objector. He took his toothbrush with him to two consecutive trials, fully prepared to go to prison for his beliefs. Had he been five years older, he contested, he would unquestionably have signed up, stating to the court: 'I would defend the innocent with my life without hesitation,'[16] but he felt morally obliged to protest against what he perceived as the madness of preparing for another war three years after the end of the previous devastation. He got off lightly with fines amounting to £125, paid for out of his father's pocket. The stand was an extraordinarily brave act in the political climate of Soviet/Western stand-off that had escalated that summer, and is exemplary of Pinter's intransigence in representing his deeply felt beliefs. Later that decade, this anger and resistance towards any authority that would assume command over the individual conscience or consciousness was worded very clearly in a letter to Peter Wood, the director of *The Birthday Party*, in which Pinter defined his characters Goldberg and McCann as 'the hierarchy, the Establishment, the arbiters, the socio-religious monsters' who represent 'the shitstained strictures of centuries of "tradition"'. The inverted commas Pinter places around the word 'tradition' are the interrogative pincers of a modernist temperament, one that questions the social foundations of traditions and sees these as the atrophied indices of a power structure that would use them as motivators of acquiescence and subservience.

It was with *The Birthday Party*, his first full-length play, that Pinter made his London debut as a playwright in April 1958, and offered his own version of an anti-Establishment statement. The play concerns the plight of Stanley Webber, a dishevelled, directionless, unemployed young tenant in a seaside boarding house. He is sought out by Goldberg and McCann, a professional couple on a 'job', which we learn is to admonish him for some past infraction and return him to whatever fold he has abandoned. They book a room in the house, and, once they have an opportunity, confront Stanley and interrogate him. This cross-examination is then adjourned until after a surprise birthday party arranged for Stanley (though he denies it is his birthday) by Meg, his overly affectionate and dim-witted landlady. The party becomes the site of further torment for Stanley as he is obliged to participate in a game of blind man's bluff, and he takes advantage of a power failure to assault Meg and her neighbour Lulu. He is not seen again until later in Act Three, following a night in Goldberg and McCann's hands, and re-enters compliant, mute and neatly dressed to be led out to Goldberg's car and taken away from his indolent haven.

'Don't let them tell you what to do', Meg's ineffectual husband Petey advises Stanley as he is led out of the house (P1, p. 80). 'I've lived that line all my damn life' (MG, p. 71) Harold Pinter later stated. Given the reception the play was to receive, he needed to remain resistant and persist with his vision.

3

First Stages

In early May 1958 Pinter was employed to understudy at the Royal Court for Osborne's *Epitaph for George Dillon*. He had just finished acting (as David Baron) in a run of *Look Back in Anger*, performing the role of Jimmy Porter's mate Cliff Lewis, and had received respectable notices for giving 'a real gem of a performance'.[1] Professionally, it must have seemed to him that all was going in the right direction; he was becoming established in a vibrant new artistic community in London and now looking forward to the debut of what he must have considered his most accomplished piece of writing to date.

The Birthday Party opened in London at the Lyric Hammersmith on 19 May. Following the warm praise the play had been awarded on its regional tour, Pinter was to be bitterly disappointed by the reception it received in London. 'Sorry, Mr Pinter, you're just not funny enough,' sneered the bold typeface of the title to one review; another critic complained that Pinter 'wallows in symbols and revels in obscurity', whilst a third protested that 'his characters speak in non-sequiturs, half-gibberish and lunatic ravings'.[2] Irving Wardle, in *Encore*, summed up the general press response: 'Nowadays there are two ways of saying you don't understand a play: the first is to bowl it out with the word "obscurity", once so popular in poetry reviews; the second way is to say that the seminal influence of Ionesco can be detected. Mr Pinter received the full treatment [. . .] and, within a couple of days of receiving it, *The Birthday Party* was over.'[3]

Its run halted after just eight performances in the wake of this critical panning, the play accumulating poor box-office takings of just £260 11s. 5d. Pinter has kept the receipt for those takings and it now hangs, framed, on the wall above a small washbasin in a snug WC at the top of the stairs that lead to his studio office. It can be viewed directly at eye level from the seated position. The choice of location for this memento may be a self-conscious, private act of considered humility or it may represent a self-confident dismissal of past rejection, but it is without doubt a characteristically casual, witty and self-aware gesture of the writer's own response to his success as an author, and illustrative of his assertion: 'When I was a failure, I wasn't a failure to me. When I'm a success, I'm not a success to me.'[4]

The Birthday Party was the third of three plays that Pinter had written in the space of a year. The first two, *The Room* and *The Dumb Waiter* (both 1957), operated with similar dramatic premises to *The Birthday Party*: mystery surrounds characters' pasts and the reasons why those pasts should invade and infect the present, and no explanations are tendered by character or situation as to why the odd things that occur do so. The room of the title of Pinter's first play is a sparse, humble bed-sitting room in an ample house which is home to Rose and her uncommunicative husband Bert. Rose treasures the little protection and warmth the room affords her. Her secure tenancy of the room, however, is threatened by repeated suggestion, most markedly by a Mr and Mrs Sands who come to view the room having been informed by the mysterious occupant of the blacked-out cellar that the room is soon to be vacant. The cellar dweller, a blind black man named Riley, finally appears and begs her on behalf of her father to return home. Bert comes home and violently murders the envoy from Rose's past and Rose goes suddenly blind as the curtain falls on the violent scene. The working-class London hitmen Ben and Gus in *The Dumb Waiter*, who carry out orders to assassinate people whose transgressions are never clarified, might represent another arm of the organisation from which Goldberg and McCann take their orders. The play opens with them on a 'job' in Birmingham, awaiting the arrival of their latest target in a basement flat. This flat, i would seem, is the converted kitchen of some former restaurant, for between their beds there is a service hatch which eerily and peculiarly trundles to life with orders for food sent down in its dumb waiter. Gus reads this as a test, and he has reason to be concerned, for, unlike Ben, he manifests a weary, questioning and unprofessional attitude to his 'work'. When the call is received that the victim is to enter the room, Gus is in the toilet and Ben braces himself whilst urging his colleague to preparedness. Gus, surprisingly, is then thrust through the door to face his partner's primed revolver.

These two plays were first performed together in London in a double bill in January 1960. In cautious recognition of the kind of responses his drama had previously elicited, Pinter offered the following in a programme note: 'A character on the stage who can present no convincing argument or information as to his past experience, his present behaviour or his aspirations, nor give a comprehensive analysis of his motives, is as legitimate and as worthy of attention as one who, alarmingly, can do all these things' (VV, p. 15). The word 'alarmingly' is inserted sarcastically and emphatically: one rarely meets a person who immediately offers such comprehensive information about themselves. Why, one can infer from what Pinter says here, should we expect such non-naturalistic behaviour from characters in a play? 'The explicit form which is so often taken in twentieth-century drama is . . . cheating,'[5] Pinter stated in 1960, speaking of the omniscient author, and it is clear that his first plays represented a realignment of the position of an author in relation to the characters he brings into being. To offer characters such as Stanley and Rose, whose pasts are so shrouded in contradiction or mystery as to obfuscate the reason why Goldberg, McCann and Riley might have been sent to confront them, is to abuse an unwritten law of cause and effect in playwriting that had survived centuries.

If, in the theatrical landscape of the fifties, the drawing-room French windows had been replaced by the kitchen sink, the body of work offered by the angry young men and women did not collectively achieve the kind of formalistic revolution that Beckett had tendered with *Waiting for Godot*. Pinter, in his first handful of plays, offered the beginnings of such a formalistic revolution in very British contexts, and this might be considered his contribution to the 'new writing', much of which had been as plainly realistic, as 'well made', as that which it had replaced. What Pinter was experimenting with in *The Room*, *The Dumb Waiter* and *The Birthday Party* was a hybrid form that Bamber Gascoigne was to refer to as 'distilled naturalism'.[6] It certainly looked like naturalism: the action of the plays takes place in recognisable rooms in houses in named British locations. Characters read newspapers, eat breakfast, drink tea, visit the toilet and tend to their domestic and business affairs. They have names, linguistic nuances and behavioural ticks that associate them with specific social groups. The plays sounded like naturalism too, on the whole. Indeed, Pinter was recognised as achieving a hyper-real form of dramatic dialogue, imbuing everyday trivial conversation with charged significance; a Ronald Searle cartoon in *Punch* once represented him as a bespectacled dog, one ear cocked, furtively scribbling down with one paw the babble of two old gentlemen sitting drinking and smoking at a nearby table. There was nothing new either in the overall structural fabric of his plays, as they seemingly drew the shape of many of the types of thrillers that Pinter had spent the previous decade acting in – slowly building to a climactic scene of revelatory crisis: Riley's murder and Rose's traumatic blindness, Gus's confrontation with the wrong end of his friend's revolver and Stanley's irrevocable abduction. But unlike in other naturalistic plays of the time or any conventional thriller, what we learn of these characters is left to be gleaned only from what they have to say about themselves and, just as in meeting people in real life, we can take what they say at face value or distrust the information they give. This is the contract Pinter handed his audiences to negotiate. It caused, and still causes, an uncertainty that may be uncomfortable, but discomfort was certainly one of Pinter's goals. Traditionally, drama is generated in a narrative by the presentation of some conflict that is to be resolved. What Pinter offered instead was plays in which the drama is generated by the very negotiation of the terms of an inferred conflict which slowly and irresistibly rises to a head. We do not know what Stanley did wrong, why Rose must return home or what precise violation Ben is guilty of, but we are left to fill that gap from an accumulation of conflicting and imprecise evidence, red herrings and flippant pronouncements offered by the protagonists and antagonists of those plays. This invites us to invest in these characters quite differently from how we might invest in those who have been presented as tragic victims, hapless losers or malevolent schemers, and our investment can shift pointedly with the turns of the narrative.

In abusing the naturalistic form and the contract it demands of its audience in this way, Pinter was proposing a form of drama that was unprecedented on the British stage. In many ways, what he sought to do was straightforward: he clearly wished to apply a modernist principle to playwriting, one that had become established as commonplace in other arenas of artistic endeavour. The literature of Joyce or Kafka, for example, challenged the notion of there being any reliable and stable perspective upon experience that might be deemed authoritative or 'true'. Instead, multiple and oppositional perspectives might co-exist within representations of reality, and the portrayal of an individual might be coloured by an uncertainty or an insecurity over which elements of behaviour, experience or the mind constitute the 'self'. That which is held to be 'true', then, can only ever be a matter of momentary perspective. This approach makes for the creation of theatre that does not tell an audience what to think, that has no direct agenda, but which is free to operate upon those who receive it on numerous metaphoric levels. What such a play 'means' is no longer a matter of what the author intended it to say, but is more a matter of the consequence the material of the play has to the individuals that constitute an audience.

Whilst a handful of critics and audiences were receptive to

this approach, others readily rejected Pinter and dismissively pigeon-holed him, alongside the other *bêtes noires* of the time, Samuel Beckett and Eugène Ionesco, as a writer of needlessly enigmatic and metaphoric drama, for example decrying Pinter for having 'had the ambition to write an even more exasperating play than *Waiting for Godot* and to couch it in dialogue worthy of Mr Ionesco in its twinkling inconsequence'.[7] A few critics, most notably Harold Hobson, realised that the ambitions of these and other dramatists' work represented yet another new 'movement' and that Pinter was effectively contributing to a redefinition of dramatic purpose. Considering the adverse impact of criticism on emerging talent, and recognising that the new forms demanded new modes of critical appraisal, Hobson appealed for reflective understanding:

> The fall of a sparrow or the murder of a dramatist may have unforeseeable consequences. But it does not concern only Mr Pinter. It concerns the whole future of the British theatre. We are now at a point in the development of the drama comparable to that reached with the coming of Ibsen. The most important writers are moving in a new direction. With Beckett, Adamov, Ionesco, even Simpson – there is arriving a school of drama to which the old criteria of judgement are inapplicable. Why should there be, in an apparently naturalistic play like *The Cherry Orchard*, a sound like that of a breaking string? There is no reasonable answer, but the sound nevertheless touches sensibilities outside the areas of the understanding. It is those sensibilities to which the new drama appeals.[8]

Martin Esslin pursued this perceived resemblance between the dramatists Hobson listed and named this new 'movement' the 'Theatre of the Absurd'. His book of this title, first appearing in 1961, sought to clarify how these authors, when grouped together, had tendered 'a new language, new ideas, new approaches, and a new, vitalized philosophy to transform the modes of thought and feeling of the public'.[9]

Though Pinter's early work was the basis of a chapter in Esslin's book, it could only awkwardly be made to belong to this grouping, his concerns being ultimately more with human interrelationships than the existential crises that Beckett, Adamov and Ionesco explored. Whilst he readily accepted that his love of Beckett must have had some effect on his own writing (when asked directly in 1960 if he'd been influenced by Beckett, he replied: 'Of course I was. You've got to be influenced by someone'),[10] he also recognised that this was a question more of affinity than of direct influence; speaking of his experience of reading Kafka and Beckett for the first time, he realised 'something is going on here which is going on in me too'.[11] As for the more frequent parallels made with the writings of Ionesco, there is little that could corroborate any influence. Though Pinter and Ionesco to some extent both demonstrate how language is used to batter the individual into submission to cultural and social traditions, there is little to compare in their approach to play construction. The two authors might validly be compared, however, by considering the manner in which both defended their methods and ambitions against public and critical assault. When Kenneth Tynan reviewed Ionesco's *The Chairs* and *The Lesson* at the Royal Court in the summer of 1958, he condemned their author as 'a writer ready to declare that all communication between human beings [is] impossible' and cautioned that 'the peril arises when it is held up for general emulation as the gateway to the theatre of the future'. Ionesco swiftly countered that 'to deliver a message to the world, to wish to direct its course, to save it, is the business of the founders of religion, of the moralists or the politicians [. . .]. A playwright simply writes plays, in which he can offer only a testimony, not a didactic message [. . .]. An ideological play can be no more than the vulgarization of an ideology.' He criticised Osborne, Brecht, Miller and Jean-Paul Sartre as 'representatives of a Left Wing conformism which is just as lamentable as the Right Wing sort', and argued that the function of a work of art was not to express objective social reality but to be 'an expression of an incommunicable reality'.[12] In the argument that unfolded in the letters pages of the *Observer* in 1958, the nascent new theatrical landscape of the times was being charted. A debate over the function of theatre and the playwright was establishing two camps: one, taking courage from Brecht and making its angry noises at the kitchen sink, was a theatre that was engaged, committed, certain in the social focus it sought to provide its audiences; the other was the poetic drama, rich in existential metaphor, which sought to offer its audiences not clear narrative but allegorical situation, operating through the kind of poetic inference that Hobson exemplified by reference to guitar strings breaking in Chekhov. Pinter seemed, perhaps, to have had a foot in both camps, for his plays offered a surface reality where objects obeyed the laws of physics (unlike in Ionesco) and characters displayed relative consistency of character (unlike in Beckett) but manipulated space, character and situation to supply metaphorically charged situations. Pinter was concurring with Ionesco when he stated that he distrusted any movement that might demand 'some kind of clear and sensible engagement to be evidently disclosed in contemporary plays'. Writing, he would have it, is not concerned with transferring social truths, but with conveying experience and, in opposition to the repeated call for the 'alive', for 'vitality', 'living', and 'Life' that had become part of the vocabulary of the new movement centred around the Royal Court writers in the late fifties, he countered that he was simply more interested in 'life with a small l, I mean the life we in fact live' (VV, p. 18). In other words, rather than looking outwards at the social dimension of existence, Pinter was curious to examine the individual's response to personal experience. This simple statement, made in a speech to the National Student Drama Festival in 1962, evinces Pinter's conscious separation of his own ambition and achievement from that of Arden, Osborne, Wesker et al.

There is a considerable body of people just now who are asking for some kind of clear and sensible engagement to be evidently disclosed in contemporary plays. They want the playwright to be a prophet [. . .]. If I were to state a moral precept it might be: beware of the writer who puts forward his concern for you to embrace, who leaves you in no doubt of his worthiness, his usefulness, his altruism. (VV, p. 18)

Whilst this is a clear rejection of employing authorship as a means of channelling corrective messages or providing didactic stories, it does not imply, for Pinter, avoiding the representation of disturbing and potentially politically charged situations. Ending *The Room* with the brutal murder of a black character, his head kicked against an iron stove, or the final moments of *The Birthday Party*, where a character with a Jewish surname is led off to whatever fate some intransigent authority will mete out, could hardly be read completely neutrally at a time of increasing racial tension in the UK and within a generation's memory of the Holocaust. Whilst the plays offer no comment on such political realities, it is an audience's awareness of and relationship with these situations that might shape its reading of these early Pinter plays. Functioning almost as parables of the relationship between an individual and any society that makes demands on him or her, *The Room*, *The Dumb Waiter* and *The Birthday Party* present the conflicting tensions between personal space and identity, and invading presences and ideals. In 1960, Pinter clarified that the drama he constructed in his first works is to be found in the uncertainties of the characters over how to interpret and respond to events and circumstances, and offered a clearly political reading of that predicament:

This old woman is living in a room which, she is convinced, is the best in the house, and she refuses to know anything about the basement downstairs. She says it's damp and nasty, and the world outside is cold and icy, and that in her warm and comfortable room her security is complete. But, of course, it isn't; an intruder comes to upset the balance of everything, in other words points to the delusion on which she is basing her life. I think the same thing applies in *The Birthday Party*. Again this man is hidden away in a seaside boarding house . . . then two people arrive out of nowhere, and I don't consider this an unnatural happening. I don't think this it is all that surrealistic and curious because surely this thing, of people arriving at the door, has been happening in Europe in the last twenty years.[13]

Pinter, then, was conscious of having folded specific social and political realities into the fabric of plays he defended as having no direct political message. He wanted clearly to generalise an expression of threat, and to avoid identifying victims and persecutors as categorisable in contemporary or historic groups; and to emphasise this, none of his characters, even figures such as Goldberg and McCann, are seen as immune from the whim of whatever authority maintains control.

The non-present characters of Rose's father, Wilson and Monty in *The Room*, *The Dumb Waiter* and *The Birthday Party* respectively represent a patriarchal hierarchy that would require submission from those, like Rose and Stanley, who have achieved an independence of sorts, or, like Gus, threaten to do so. In *The Hothouse*, which he drafted for radio in 1958 but abandoned until 1980, Pinter locates that patriarchal hierarchy explicitly in the state. The play is set in a sanatorium, but one where the patients, all of whom are 'specially recommended by the Ministry' (P1, p. 197), have their names replaced by numbers, are kept under lock and key and at a distance from their families, and where facilities include sound-proofed 'interview' rooms and electronic torture equipment. This 'care home' might well be the kind of place to which Goldberg and McCann are instructed to deliver Stanley. Prior to their departure with their acquiescent victim in *The Birthday Party*, they promise him that he is to be 're-oriented', 'adjusted', and 'integrated' (P1, pp. 77–8) in a manner that matches the vocabulary used to describe the ambitions of the institution in *The Hothouse*, where the 'patients' are deemed 'people in need of help' and are given 'assistance' to 'regain confidence in themselves, confidence in others, confidence in . . . the world' (P1, p. 197). In both cases, such promises are thinly veiled euphemisms. That which is actually being induced is conformity, and 'having confidence in the world' implies behaving according to imposed expectations in a society where 'common assumptions are shared and common principles observed' (P1, p. 252).

In Roote, the institution's chief of staff, and in the ministry official Lobb, we see only a bumbling incompetence, and Pinter is clearly intending here to extend his representation of the vulnerability of those dispensing the edicts of authority (Roote speaks in passing of his predecessor as having '. . . retired', preceding his choice of word with a telling hesitation). Power is seen as arbitrarily held, as up for negotiation, and shifts according to the wit, wiles and aggression of those holding on to it, and those attempting to gain it. Roote's subordinates, Lush and Gibbs, pick away at his authority with linguistic guile – Gibbs with excessive ingratiating tactics that thinly veil his disdain and Lush with a witty ability to reveal facts and failures from behind the whitewash of Roote's words.

The play's original rejection by its author in 1958 marked the end of his early concern to dramatise the conflicting impulses of individualism and the conformist demands of orthodoxy as represented by family, society, tradition or the state. Some critics recognised these concerns in his first plays. Reviewing the Royal Court double bill of *The Room* and *The Dumb Waiter* in 1960, Tom Milne in *Encore* praised their 'relevance to the problems aroused by our particular society, and our relationship with that society',[14] and, in his essay 'Comedy of Menace', Irving Wardle considered how in *The Birthday Party* Pinter evoked a quality of menace, tempered with comedy, which 'stands for something more substantial: destiny'. He argued for an understanding of the play that appreciated the responsibilities we hold to ourselves and to others: 'Destiny handled in this way – not as an austere exercise in classicism, but as an incurable disease which one forgets about most of the time and whose lethal reminders may take the form of a joke – is an apt dramatic motif for an age of conditioned behaviour in which orthodox man is a willing collaborator in his own destruction.'[15]

While avoiding doctrinal approaches which dictate or enthuse responses to specific social realities (indeed, the plays specifically assault the fabric of doctrine as both fallible and suspect), Pinter's first plays appeal to an individual's own responsibility and promote an awareness of the forces that shape our lives by unpicking the anatomy of authority and representing it as resistible, if wickedly tenacious. They do so by offering allegories of the kinds of power structures that dictate our lives, demonstrating how these are constructed of the discourses of tradition and precedent used to justify the current hierarchy of power. Such discourses come into play most keenly in interrogation scenes, such as when Stanley is reproved for abandoning familial duties (to his wife and mother), shirking religious obligations and betraying some unnamed organisation; or when in, *The Hothouse*, the hapless Lamb is interrogated over his sociability, his ability to function at work, his desire to participate in regulated groups and his relationship to women. In this way, repressive society and tradition are dramatically constructed of complex linguistic scaffoldings supported by brute force, most vividly demonstrated by Roote's punching of 'delegated', 'appointed', 'entrusted' and 'authorised' into his inferior but taxing colleague's stomach (P1, pp. 306–7).

4

An Established Writer

Pinter's rejection of his manuscript of *The Hothouse* as a young dramatist was effectively, though perhaps not consciously, a turning of his back on the political impulses of his first plays. The decision marked the threshold to a new phase of writing in which he began to concentrate on interpersonal issues, on human interaction and the ties between family members and between partners. His first plays had been written with no audiences in mind and no productions expected. The failure of *The Birthday Party* had been a temporary blow to his confidence, not to speak of his bank account, but his talent had been recognised and had earned a fund of respect in numerous quarters. Financially, he was thrown something of a lifeline by the patronage given him by commissioning producers for the BBC Third Programme, for whom he wrote his first radio play, *A Slight Ache*, in 1958. His next venture was to script a collection of revue sketches that were presented at the Lyric Hammersmith and the Apollo theatre in 1959, alongside other pieces by writers such as Peter Cook, and performed by comic actors such as Beryl Reid, Kenneth Williams and Sheila Hancock.[1] In March 1960, his *A Night Out* was broadcast on the BBC Third Programme, followed a month later by a televised version on *Armchair Theatre*. It topped the ratings in its week of broadcast, earning Pinter a national audience of millions and laying the foundation to his becoming a household name.

In July 1960 *The Times* described Pinter's 'meteoric rise from our least understood avant-garde writer to, virtually, our most popular young playwright'.[2] The play that was to seal his reputation was *The Caretaker*. Opening later in the same week as the TV broadcast of *A Night Out*, and starring Donald Pleasence, Alan Bates and Peter Woodthorpe, the play confirmed to critics and audiences that Pinter was a major talent. In stark contrast to *The Birthday Party*'s meagre six-day run, *The Caretaker* clocked up 444 performances following its April 1960 première, and earned an equally enthusiastic reception on Broadway, in New York, the same year.

Written in 1959 in Pinter's rented flat on the Chiswick High Road, with his infant son crawling at his feet, *The Caretaker* examines the failure of a potential friendship between the simple, trusting Aston – a kindly gentleman with a history of mental illness – and the homeless Davies, whom Aston first saves from being roughed up and then puts up in his cramped, junk-cluttered room. We learn that the house belongs to Aston's brother Mick, and infer a strong bond between the two brothers from Mick's entertainment of Aston's ambitions to decorate the house and build a shed in the garden (during the two-week period that the play represents we never see him succeeding even in putting a plug on a toaster, despite his repeated return to that chore). Mick distrusts Davies's motives, and we certainly witness the tramp's intuitive exploitation of Aston's trust and good will. Perhaps not willing to disempower his brother, Mick does not simply kick Davies out but instead plays a strategic game of alternating between threatening and undermining Davies, and encouraging the tramp in developing an allegiance with him and, by implication, against Aston. This is Davies's undoing, for in turning on Aston and believing his association with Mick lends him immunity from reprisal, he brings about the rejection and expulsion that Mick clearly set about to engineer.

The play was widely praised, but within the critical commendations were throwbacks to the baggage of Absurd theatre that had been applied to Pinter previously. Many critics now made a virtue of the lack of traditional narrative ('All that happens is that they talk, fail to communicate with one another, and break into moments of violence')[3] and of the perceived Pinter traits of ambiguity and obscurity, the unanswered questions that arose as the drama unravelled. Kenneth Tynan pointed out that 'where most playwrights devote their technical efforts to making us wonder what will happen next, Mr Pinter focuses our wonder on what is happening *now*. Who are these people? How did they meet, and why?'[4] Now Pinter's mystery had become fashionable, it seemed, and the critics' observation of symbolism ('the grisly comic cryptograms which everyone is afraid to solve')[5] was rife. Pinter's ambition, though, had been something far more straightforward. Shortly after the play had been written, the critic and director Charles Marowitz asked Pinter to explain in simple terms what it was about. The immediate response was: 'Well, it's about love . . . about this house . . . these people . . .'[6]

Whereas in Pinter's early plays the context of power struggles had been between the agents of a homogenising cultural force and those who would resist or escape its strictures, *The Caretaker* returned Pinter's focus to the kinds of struggles for dominance of space and personal advantage that marked his Kullus pieces, but now coloured with the concerns he had articulated in *The Dwarfs* of how bonds and potential bonds between people can be frayed, damaged and broken by the betrayals and shifting allegiances that such struggles engender. Developments in the drafting of *The Caretaker* are indicative of Pinter's shift away from an emphasis on personal threat and towards a subtle concentration of the scaffolds of trust, dependence and expectation that underline social behavioural patterns. Originally, Pinter imagined that Davies would die at the hands of one of the other characters, but, before even committing such an ending to paper, he must have decided that this ran contrary to the nature of the script he was writing. Certainly, such an ending would have deflected from any refined appreciation of the brothers' relationship, turning their anguished, strained communication into sinister conspiracy, or dysfunctional clumsiness at best. Pinter first noted this important reappraisal in a radio interview in 1960. Whilst discussing *The Caretaker* he remarked: 'I feel it's a much simpler play, and it doesn't resort to the cabaret terms which I've been inclined to indulge in the past. There are no sudden blackouts, no blind man's buff, no blind negroes walking about.'[7] In scripting the piece, he had been aware that the play 'is funny up to a point. Beyond that point it ceases to be funny, and it was because of that point that I wrote it.'[8] But by now dismissing the kinds of dramatic devices that had characterised his early plays, by moving away from such symbolism, he was allowing himself to investigate the subtle shifts and re-appraisals that occur in human interaction.

The satisfaction Pinter felt with this piece of writing was compounded by the critical success it earned, and the financial and artistic freedom he could subsequently enjoy as a result. He has, consequently, always held a certain fondness and pride in its achievement, and was easily persuaded, in 1962, that it might be adapted for film. Directed by Clive Donner, the film was released in 1964 and starred Donald Pleasence and Alan Bates in their original roles of Davies and Mick, while Robert Shaw took the part of Aston. The production was originally marred by financial difficulties, and the decision was made to film the script in a real house, as studio rental could not be afforded. Even as filming was to begin, financial backing was not firmly in place. Eventually, sponsors including Richard Burton, Noel Coward, Peter Hall and Peter Sellers came up with the necessary amounts to permit the filming of the piece. Pinter embraced the realism that the real-world location for filming offered, as it visually disallowed any of the dour overtones of mystery that had accumulated around the work in critical commentary. This facet of the film gave opportunities to emphasise character traits and relationships. A street scene where Davies refuses a lift to Sidcup from Mick in his van confirms our suspicions about Davies's delusions or evasions concerning the papers he claims a friend in Sidcup is holding for him: 'They prove who I am! I can't move without those papers' (P2, p. 18), and a scene in the garden of the house between the two brothers by a pile of tarpaulin-covered planks of wood (for

Aston's shed) make the hopelessness of his ambitions – as well as the precariousness of Mick's complex, caring relationship with his brother – all the more explicit.

The Caretaker (released as *The Guest* in the US) had not been Pinter's first screenplay. Michael Anderson had commissioned him in 1961 to produce a screenplay of Robin Maugham's short novel *The Servant*. Anderson, however, had failed to raise the finance for a production and Joseph Losey, who had previously written to Pinter to articulate his admiration for *A Night Out*, approached him to rewrite his screenplay. With *The Servant*, he and Pinter began a collaborative relationship that would develop over three further projects (*Accident* in 1967, *The Go-Between* in 1971 and the unfilmed *Proust Screenplay* of 1972). *The Servant* tells the story of an upper-middle-class layabout, Tony (James Fox), who hires a manservant, Barrett (Dirk Bogarde), to look after his domestic affairs, but who eventually finds himself subject to Barrett's whim within a marriage-like relationship in a transformed house bearing the 'overlay of Barrett everywhere'.[9] Adapting a slight morality tale of a novel into a psychologically revealing screenplay, Pinter removed the narrating character and added a number of scenes that dealt in visual terms with matters of a struggle for dominance between the two protagonists. Notably, a ball game between Tony and Barrett, throwing from either end of a staircase, releases class-ridden reprisals and violent urges between the two men. Pinter's attraction to the story, he admitted, was the capacity it had for articulating in visual terms issues relating to a struggle for dominance. Speaking of it in relation to his own *The Examination*, he said: 'That short story dealt very explicitly with two people in one room having a battle of an unspecified nature, in which the question was one of who was dominant at what point and how they were going to be dominant and what tools they would use to achieve dominance and how they would try to undermine the other person's dominance.'[10]

This interest of Pinter's became a central aspect of the pigeon-holing of his work within terms such as 'Pinteresque', but in

themselves the power struggles in his work are no more than status games played out on stage, and critics, such as Nigel Dennis,
who saw them as key stylistic elements criticised them as such.
Rather than representing the central concern or ambition of any
drama he wrote, though, these power struggles are of interest in
the manner in which they are used to reveal codes of human
social behaviour as a communal language to be honestly or dis-
honestly employed. What Pinter foregrounds is the degree to
which characters are aware of their fluency in this language of
social engagement, and the responsibility that is inherent in the
associated capacity to cause self-harm or damage others.

Three months after the stage première of *The Caretaker*,
Pinter's second piece for TV, *Night School*, was broadcast. This
was the first of three pieces that he was commissioned to write
by Associated Rediffusion Television. The other two, *The
Collection* and *The Lover*, were broadcast in May 1961 and
March 1963 respectively. Later, his *Tea Party* (adapted from his
short story first published in *Playboy*) was broadcast by the
new BBC2 channel in March 1965. By the early sixties, the
one-off television play had become a significant cultural event
and programmers sought out new writers to provide original
dramatic material for the still-young medium. The series
Armchair Theatre (ABC) and the *Wednesday Play* (BBC), for
example, were the weekly outlets for the new, often challenging
TV plays that a wave of new writers were offering. Pinter was
initially wary of the studio- and director-led world of motion
pictures (before meeting Donner, his opinion of the film industry was that it was populated by 'fakes, phonies, charlatans'),[11]
and as the growing British TV drama industry was writer-
dominated, it must have represented a secure alternative platform upon which he might practise his craft.

Night School, *The Collection*, *The Lover* and *Tea Party*,
together with the radio plays *A Slight Ache* (1958) and *The
Dwarfs* (1960), represent Pinter's ongoing experimentation
with the dramatic possibilities inherent in his standpoint that
'the desire for verification is understandable but cannot always

be satisfied' (VV, p. 15). This desire, for example, is what blights Edward in *A Slight Ache* as he queries the motives of a mute vagabond match-seller (a non-verifiable presence in the radio production) who persists daily in standing at his gate, where he is least likely to succeed in his trade. The disturbed Len in *The Dwarfs* tells his friend Mark: 'Occasionally I believe I perceive a little of what you are but that's pure accident [. . .]. It's nothing like an accident, it's deliberate, it's joint pretence. We depend on these accidents, on these contrived accidents, to continue' (P2, p. 100).

Len experiences or contrives images of helper dwarfs to provide him with an equilibrium missing in true experience, where he cannot, as he suggests here, ascertain the difference between genuine human contact in friendship and manoeuvring by those who, wittingly or otherwise, project false representations of themselves. For him, this produces an overwhelming gulf between him and his friends, and his condition – portrayed through images of putrefaction, appetite and alimentary illness – serves to parallel the rot that has set in in the relationships between him, Mark and Pete. In *The Collection*, *Night School* and *Party Time* the desire for verification becomes of a piece with characters' manoeuvres for domination or control, and Pinter deftly merges these interests to create neat intrigues that charmed and disturbed viewers across British suburbia. These TV dramas were the terrain within which Pinter began to explore sexual relationships dramatically. The characters of James, Wally and Disson, respectively in each play, are all obsessed with clarifying the nature and motives of female characters that cause them anguish, and, in their desperation, resort to projecting fantasies or hoped-for truths on to these women to establish control or stability. In *The Lover*, the same fantasy is subscribed to by a husband-and-wife couple, in which Richard leaves for work in the morning, only to return in the role of Sarah's lover, Max. Richard sets out to destroy the sexual game-playing, seeking perhaps more authentic union, by undermining its vocabulary from the outset.

Critics have often focused on Pinter's perceived fascination with femininity in this stage of his writing, and Simon Trussler once commented that 'this sense of the duality of the female psyche has been one of Pinter's least productive preoccupations',[12] but such assessment seems to miss the point that Pinter is not simply sketching female duality (or, indeed, multiple facets) but is in fact exposing the apparatus of the appropriating quality of the male gaze, and drawing women who remain elusively dominant by reflecting and subverting what is projected upon them by men, or whose sexual identities are so robust as to escape male classification. These dramas, focusing as they do on intimate relationships, and the manner in which femininity is defined by men to satisfy their desires or insecurities, were the natural forerunners of *The Homecoming* (1965), which, Ann Hall states, 'exposes the patriarchal process of female objectification'.[13]

The Homecoming stirred controversy upon its release, and remains controversial to this day. Its first performance, by the Royal Shakespeare Company at the Aldwych Theatre in 1965, caused something of a stir. Supported by public money, the RSC had been established in 1960 when Peter Hall transformed and renamed the Stratford Memorial Theatre and then later took over the Aldwych Theatre in London for the production of non-Shakespearean plays. Harold Pinter's affiliation with the RSC at the Aldwych (*The Collection*, *The Home-coming*, *Landscape*, *Silence* and *Old Times* all premièred there) was indicative of the company's dedication to modern writing, to the degree that he and Shakespeare were publicly named 'the two anchors of the company'.[14] With *The Homecoming*, though, he had not received the blessing of the RSC's board. An emphasis on plays that undermined social conventions and challenged the accepted mores of class and morality was, for many, not appropriate behaviour for a state-subsidised theatre. The impresario Emile Littler accused Hall of an obsession with 'dirty plays' following the director's support of the bloody and blasphemous *Marat/Sade* (1964) and of

Roger Vitrac's anti-family, Dada play *Victor* (1964), both products of the RSC's 'Theatre of Cruelty' season of 1963–4.
When *The Home-coming* arrived in their mail, the board
members would have viewed it in the context of this history of
subversive material and the reputation they sought for the still
young company. They disapproved of the play and voiced their
objection at seeing it enter the repertoire at the Aldwych. Hall
listened to their concerns and went ahead regardless. Arguably,
Peter Hall's success in the 'dirty plays' battle of the mid-sixties,
pinnacling with his championing of *The Homecoming* in 1965,
signalled an important shift in British theatre history. A diet of
more confrontational plays was being fed to London audiences. Works such as David Rudkin's *Afore Night Come*
(1962) and Edward Bond's *Saved* (1965), alongside Pinter's
dramas and the other RSC 'dirty plays', contributed to a perceived movement that represented, perhaps, the final triumph
of modernism in theatre repertoires that had upheld a conservative *status quo*. Despite having imported actors and directors
from the Royal Court, the National Theatre, established by
Laurence Olivier in 1962, never truly courted the same contro-
versies until the 1970s, when it became a platform for radical
political plays.

The Homecoming presents a vile and violent family of men
living together in a large, shabby, north-London house. Teddy,
the son who left the family home to become a lecturer in philosophy in America, returns with his wife Ruth. The London
brothers seek Ruth's sexual favours as part of their natural process of ongoing mutual belittling and one-upmanship. Teddy
seems to remain aloof to this behaviour and to his wife's collu-
sion in it, refusing to participate in the vulgar codes of dominance, claiming that he 'won't be lost in it' and that he 'can
operate on things and not in things' (P3, pp. 69–70). In stating
his ability to remain outside the game-playing he condemns
himself to calling his own bluff and thereby reveals himself as
either cowardly or, as the director Peter Hall believed, 'the
biggest bastard in a house full of bastards'.[15] Ruth is offered a

position as prostitute by Lenny, her brother-in-law, to pay her way if she is to stay with the family, and the final tableau sees Teddy's father and two brothers adoringly surrounding her, imploring her for affection, following her agreeing to the proposition upon certain terms.

On the surface, the representation of women in the play is alarming: Max refers to his dead spouse Jessie as 'slutbitch of a wife' (P3, p. 55) and speaks of her in mixed terms of affection and disdain: 'Mind you, she wasn't such a bad woman. Even though it made me sick just to look at her rotten stinking face, she wasn't a bad bitch' (P3, p. 17). Ruth enters this hostile environment, but from her very first words, refusing to conform to Teddy's wishes, she demonstrates an individual spirit. She then neatly fends off Lenny's verbal approaches and dismisses his posturing, and the next day behaves in a manner that manipulates and controls the men around her. As a desired object, she is able to harness the libidinous and domineering impulses of the male characters as tools to wield against them. When Lenny arranges for her to have a flat in Greek Street to use 'for a couple of hours a night' (P3, p. 84), Max tries to warn his sons that Ruth will 'do the dirty on us [. . .] she'll make use of us' (P3, p. 89) but, falling to his knees in the final moments of the play, he too succumbs to his need for the qualities of maternal empathy and sexual gratification that Ruth represents and he craves. The play ends with her in a clear position of power, and, as Pinter argued, 'it is not at all certain she will go off to Greek Street. But even if she did, she would not be a harlot in her own mind.'[16] In other words, Pinter considered Ruth to be capable of adopting any role that would primarily benefit herself. Of course, there is no evidence as the curtain closes on the last act that she *will*, in fact, ever perform the functions of a sex worker. She ends in a position of supremacy, clearly able henceforth to negotiate her terms and conditions in any future arrangement between her and the family.

5

Time Regained

In many ways *The Homecoming* represented a brilliant maturation of a number of artistic concerns that Pinter had been charting in his writing to date. It is unsurprising, then, that, following the intense creative period from 1958 to the play's huge success in London and New York in 1965, Pinter experienced something of a writer's block. Michael Billington points out: 'Pinter did, in fact, go through a low period after the success of *The Homecoming* [. . .]. He found himself jotting odds and ends down on scraps of paper: nothing happened, nothing flowed' (MB, p. 181). 'Why Doesn't He Write More?' was the title given to one interview in 1968, in which he described how his work had become 'constipated',[1] and, that same year, he stated that writing 'becomes more difficult the older you get, at least it does for me [. . .] I'm thirty-seven now. I feel as if I'm eighty' (MB, p. 195). In an acceptance speech for the German Shakespeare Prize in 1970, he admitted: 'At the moment I am writing nothing and can write nothing. I don't know why. It's a very bad feeling, I know that, but I must say I want more than anything else to fill up a blank page again' (P3, p. 12).

Recognised by 1968 as a playwright of international significance, Harold Pinter had nevertheless yet to transcend upheld views of his output. His reputation was firmly established as a writer of challenging and sometimes controversial dramas involving enigmatic narratives constructed around the activities of collections of mysterious invaders, manipulative schemers and hapless victims who collide and collude for control or dominance. The first full-length studies of his dramatic work were being published at this time and the appropriation of Pinter's dramatic texts by academic studies had the effect, through quantifying and appraising his achievements, of prematurely historicising them and lending them the canonical authority and stature that such serious study inescapably confers.[2] For an artist intent on development and growth, the flattery afforded by such attention must have been countered by some discomfort at being so eagerly and readily categorised. In a letter to the National Theatre bookshop a decade later he requested that two of the first studies of his work be removed from the shelves, referring to them as 'parasitical crap'. Evidently, whilst he was content that academics should appraise his work, some of the results of their ruminations rubbed him up the wrong way. 'Harold Pinter sits on my damn back,' the author complained in 1971. 'He's not me. He's someone else's creation' (MG, p. 25). At a time of a difficult creative respite, the undeviating expectancies that critical definition can occasion may just have exacerbated his concerns at re-evaluating his practice and considering future writing projects.

Added to this, Pinter also risked becoming marginalised by current trends in the theatre. The influence of Antonin Artaud, whose *The Theatre and its Double* had been published in English in 1958, had crept over from the European stage, and a growing focus upon the theatre director as *auteur*, and away from playwrights, began to manifest itself in the sixties in certain quarters. Jerzy Growtowski's 'poor theatre' work at the Laboratory Theatre in Krakow, Poland, and movements such as the Living Theater in New York were exemplary of this spirit. In Britain, the first signs of such experimentation in the mainstream theatre had sprouted in the autumn of 1963 when Peter Brook and Charles Marowitz formed an experimental group affiliated to the Royal Shakespeare Company, with the intention of exploring certain problems of acting and stagecraft in laboratory conditions, without the commercial pressures of performance. Peter Brook applied some of what he discovered during these sessions to his much lauded *Marat/Sade* (1964), the anti-war *US* (1966) and *A Midsummer Night's Dream* (1970). In 1968 the Arts Council of Great Britain recognised the shifting climate and began to provide funds to alternative and fringe theatre, effectively pump-priming the experimental and avant-garde in a manner it had never done previously. Pinter found himself 'out of synch' with the kinds of new rehearsal techniques that were proliferating and made plain his distrust and dislike of experiments in non-scripted, *auteur*-driven theatre: 'I am not interested in theatre used simply as a means of self-expression on the part of the people engaged in it. I find in so much group theatre, under the sweat and assault and noise, nothing but valueless generalizations, naive and quite unfruitful' (P3, p. 12).

During his stay in New York while *The Homecoming* was produced there in 1967, Pinter witnessed the experimental work that was fashionable, and hugely influential off-Broadway fare. His experience of being approached by an actor encouraging audience members to feel his flexed bicep during a performance of Sam Shepard's *La Turista* made him furious, and he gave the actor 'a look of utter detestation'.[3] For Pinter, such displays of audience-egging egocentrism are wholly contrary to his experience of theatre as a space for the negotiation of emotion. In stark contrast to experimentation such as the Brook/Marowitz 'Theatre of Cruelty' season at the RSC, and all that had followed in its wake, Pinter was and remained an essentially traditional playwright, born of the repertory system he had endured as a young actor and its idiom of proscenium arches and powerful lines upon which the curtain might descend. Suspicious of theorising and non-textual exploration, he lives by the discipline of those traditions ('A rehearsal period which consists of philosophical discourse or political treatise does not get the curtain up at eight o'clock,' he once said [P3, p. 9]) and maintains a focus on the text. Typical of this attitude, is this small anecdote he related in 1997:

> I remember when I was auditioning an actress, years and years ago, and she said, 'Can I improvise first?' and I said, 'What?' and she said, 'Well I like, before I read your play,

your speech from your play, I'd like to improvise,' and I said, 'Okay, you improvise and I'll come back in ten minutes,' which I did. So I left her and she had a great time improvising. It's not my cup of tea really, in other words.[4]

Clearly, if Pinter was experiencing a form of writer's block in the late sixties, he was not going to turn to the new experimental forms for inspiration. Instead, it was to be engaging with other artists that seemingly provided a spur to original creativity. Discussing the depressing feeling of perhaps being unable ever to write another play after *The Homecoming*, Pinter said his response was to immerse himself in the relative satisfaction of other types of work: 'Films, I suppose. It's not quite the same thing as something coming out from the bottom of your spine' (MG, p. 45). Certainly, the five years that followed the première of *The Homecoming* in 1965 saw a more active involvement in screenplay writing, and the processes of filming, than any other time in his career before or since. He had previously produced two critically lauded screenplays in *The Servant* and *The Pumpkin Eater* (both 1963),[5] and went on to script four further screen adaptations of novels in five years: *The Quiller Memorandum* (1965), *Accident* (1967), *The Go-Between* (1969) and *Langrishe, Go Down* (1970). He also participated in the filming of *The Birthday Party* (1967), *The Basement* (1967) and *The Homecoming* (1969), though work on these screenplays might have felt more like consolidatory than regenerative enterprises.[6] One response, then, to a perceived creative lull was to engage fully in the creative challenge of adapting the work of other writers for the screen, and in the satisfaction provided by the rigorous disciplines associated with the transfer from a literary medium to a primarily visual one. The adaptation of novels to film is an act of communion with and support for another creative mind, but also one that promotes the creativity of the adapter. Pinter evidently opted to integrate such experience into his everyday working activities, as further attested by his decision to direct the work of other writers in the theatre. In 1967 he formed Glasshouse Productions, together with Robert Shaw and Donald Pleasence, a vehicle for the staging of Shaw's play *The Man in the Glass Booth* at the St Martin's Theatre that year. This represented Pinter's first directing credit not attached to one of his own plays. In 1970 he announced the launch of a more substantial undertaking in the shape of Shield Productions, a new West End management partnership he set up alongside David Mercer, Christopher Morahan, Jimmy Wax and Terence Baker. The group aimed 'to offer a fresh approach to theatrical management [and] to achieve a situation in which dramatists and directors would have collaboration in all aspects of theatrical production'. 'We believe the author should be totally involved in all levels of production,' Pinter stated,[7] announcing his evaluation of the role of the author in the implied objective of solidarity amongst and support for writers.

Pinter took the helm for Shield Production's presentation of James Joyce's much maligned play *Exiles*. Integrating the role of director more firmly into his artistic career was perhaps an affirming manoeuvre, and one he was quickly to consolidate by establishing his director/author partnership with Simon Gray in 1971 (when he directed Alan Bates in Gray's *Butley*) and by subsequently accepting the post of associate director of the National Theatre in 1973. Effecting alliances with other writers as a part of his professional existence in these ways (screenplays, production, directing), Pinter could be seen to be reconsidering and examining the nature of authorship via the intermediation of other artists' accomplishments.

Though he recognised the second half of the decade as fallow relative to the first half, Pinter did produce two short one-act plays in the late sixties. *Landscape* (1967) and *Silence* (1968) offered the first signs of a purgation of a style that was recognisably 'Pinter', through experimentation with lyrical forms of expression and dramatic representation. These Pinter considered 'a hell of a release' (MG, p. 21), but, in themselves, the pair of short plays offered no distinct sense of progression.

Though they certainly cannot be dismissed as mere distractions from an artistic cause (*Landscape* in particular is often lauded as one of Pinter's most compelling lyrical, emotional pieces), they seem the results of an author's exercises in theatrical style and are uncharacteristic of most of his output before or since in the manner in which the form of disconnected dialogue acts as a scaffold to the plays' themes (rather than dialogic negotiations between characters). What is more, they certainly did not come easily to their author; Pinter explained to Mel Gussow that *Silence* took him the longest to write of all his plays (MG, p. 47). *Old Times* (1971), by contrast, came relatively swiftly, and a first draft was penned in three days. This play, alongside the threshold exercises of *Landscape*, *Silence* and *Night* (1969), signalled a new phase in Pinter's creativity, one that was to be informed by a strengthening in his interest in the experience of how the past invades and informs the present moment, and a concentration on the nature of intimate emotional relationships.

In *Landscape*, a husband and wife pair, Beth and Duff (the play was written while Pinter's wife was playing Lady Macbeth at Stratford, inspiring these diminutive names) engage in tangential monologues, their words only loosely intersecting to form a conversation. Duff, who speaks in coarse, provocative language, tries to engage his wife directly, but Beth seems lost in her remembrances and does not appear to hear his voice. She speaks of a time of romantic love, reminiscing fondly about the attentions of a lover with whom she might have had children. Perhaps the remembered lover is a younger, less uncouth Duff, or perhaps it is their former employer, Mr Sykes – the facts of the matter are unclear and unnecessary to appreciation of the drama. What the play projects for an audience is a contrast between a sterile present domestic relationship and an idealised past bond constructed from memories. *Landscape*, though conceived for the stage, was first performed on BBC Radio in 1968. It had been censured by the Lord Chamberlain for the inclusion of profanities that Pinter refused to edit or adjust. He had to wait a year for the Theatres Act (1968) to be passed by Parliament, ending centuries of censorship of the British stage. *Landscape* was then finally performed in a double bill with *Silence* at the Aldwych Theatre, in 1969.

Silence approached the relationship between past and present, memory and lived experience, from a different angle. 'For the first time the characters aren't in a room,' Pinter stated in 1968. 'I don't know where they are or where they're going.'[8] Ellen, Bates and Rumsey each occupy a chair in what is only described as 'three areas' and use both present and past tenses as they remember a time when they were engaged together in a love triangle. Ellen once loved Rumsey, an older man who recommended that she find someone younger, and we learn how she settled for the not so young Bates. The characters evoke a past which dates back to Ellen's childhood. As they speak in the present tense of older existences, a temporal shift is visually dramatised between present age and the physical presence of actors cast as the character ages of the remembered past. With the exception of Rumsey, the characters move between each others' spaces to create miniature 'flashback' vignettes – a symptom perhaps of Pinter's absorbing techniques from the cinema he was engaged in writing for. The flashbacks provide a structure of narrative that gives the audience anchors for contemplating the characters' past and their present lonely state. Whereas *Landscape* examines the seductive pull of a remembered past of potential and fulfilment, *Silence* theatrically demonstrates the manner in which characters recall and apply their memories in a process of explaining themselves, or of rewriting themselves. There is little talk of love in this love story, which instead is a sorry tale of attempted self-affirmation by three isolated beings who threw away opportunities for enriching connection.

Landscape and *Silence* proved to Pinter there was a rich seam to be mined in how characters relate to the past, and in the relationship with remembered and actual experience. Of particular fascination for him as an author was the phenomenon of how memory, by its very nature, is an act of the present, and cannot therefore be a verifiable record of the past. This interest in how 'the past is not the past' and how one's 'previous parts are alive and present' (MG, p. 38) was the premise to his next full length-play, *Old Times* (1971). The character of Anna articulates the principle as part of her tactical manoeuvring: 'There are some things one remembers even though they may never have happened. There are things I remember which may never have happened but as I recall them so they take place' (P3, pp. 269–70).

Anna is a figure from Kate's past, and as such represents a threat to Kate's husband Deeley. By depositing such doubt as a tool, Anna applies it in her subtle claim to possession of Kate through her discussion of their shared past. She retells details that Deeley has recounted, writing him out of his own memories by, for example, 'remembering' a time when Kate and she went to the cinema together. She then writes Deeley into Kate and her shared bedsit life, painting an unflattering picture of a man crying, failing in his sexual advances to both and resting his sorry head on Kate's lap. Deeley, in turn, attempts to undermine Anna's perceived invasion into his marriage by constructing a memory of the past when, at a party, Anna permitted him to look up her skirt, creating a rift between the two women which Anna swiftly restores by claiming she would borrow and wear Kate's underwear. Kate, a submissive force in the play thus far, takes control of the narrative that has been spun around her and metaphorically kills the past Anna off with a remembered ritual bed-top burial. She then applies the same game to Deeley, having introduced their relationship as being subsequent to her acquaintance with Anna. The narrative concluded, Deeley bursts into tears, and, drying his eyes, approaches both women in turn. Rejected by both he makes to leave but turns instead to rest his head on Kate's lap, effectively enacting the memory Anna had told, or invented, of him.

With *Old Times*, Pinter demonstrated how the past and memory are exploitable as tools for gaining advantage, and

added them to the arsenal of verbal equipment that his catalogue of characters had at their disposal when confronting one
another. The past is presented as possessing fluid, amorphous
qualities that ultimately belie any attempt to construct present
certainty from them. Like Beth's description of drawing in the
sand in *Landscape* and how the 'sand kept on slipping, mixing
the contours' (P3, p. 178), or like Kate's description of how,
looking out to sea, 'you can't see where it begins or ends' (P3,
p. 297), memory is elusive and uncapturable. As such it not
only serves as a rich source of content for an artist, but also has
powerful metaphoric qualities when paralleled with an individual's confrontation with what constitutes their own identity.
Pinter explored these qualities in his plays, and also in his
screenplays of the period, including *Accident*, *The Go-Between*
and *Langrishe, Go Down*. Most notably, though, was his year-
long labour of love spent working on writing a screenplay
adaptation of Marcel Proust's epic novel of evoked past, recap-
tured in literature, *A la Recherche du temps perdu*. In his own
writing, Pinter had clearly been manifesting an interest in the
dramatic potential of the experience of how, in Proust's words,
'what we call reality is a certain connection between these
immediate sensations and the memories which envelop us
simultaneously within them'.[9] Working on condensing the
3,200-page novel to a credible-length screenplay, Pinter faced
one of the greatest challenges of his artistic life. It was one he
enjoyed immensely, taking most of 1972 to complete the task.
He was particularly interested in how, for the character of
Marcel, 'memory of the experience [of childhood], is more real,
more acute than the experience itself',[10] and managed to con-
jure by cinematic means the manner in which Proust's involun-
tary memories are engendered. The screenplay, commissioned
by Joseph Losey, was unfortunately never to see the screen,
though it was finally adapted into a successful stage play by Di
Trevis in 2000 and premièred at the National Theatre.

Pinter's next full-length play, *No Man's Land* (1975), turned
a reliance on the past as a site of self-definition into a burden

for the key character of Hirst, a formerly renowned poet. Having met an eloquent but broke writer, Spooner, and spent an evening in the pub with him, Hirst invites his new companion home. Spooner tries gently to ingratiate himself into Hirst's employ but is rebuffed and kept verbally in his place by the menservants Foster and Briggs (all four characters are named after Victorian cricketers). The past is invoked as part of the game-playing, and captured in an atrophied state in the photograph album that Hirst yields. His inability to make, or fear of making, new connections with his creativity or with society leave him locked in a stalemate of old age captured in the play's title. Hirst's static, icy no man's land is the stagnant limbo between a need for creative recognition and the comfortable grip of his established but stultifying routines. The play charts the human failure to connect, and the betrayals and compromises that are inherent in human bonds.

6

Fraternity and Betrayal

In the winter of 1970 Pinter directed James Joyce's only play, *Exiles*. It was a production he was immensely proud of and it remains to this day one of his fondest theatrical memories. Irving Wardle considered Pinter's directorial contribution was to have offered 'the kind of insight which only one creative artist can perform in the service of another [. . .] and reveals an extraordinary affinity between Joyce and Pinter'.[1] *Exiles* is not typical of Joyce's writing, in that it is short and written in straightforward dialogue. In form it resembles Ibsen, Hauptmann or Wilde's social commentaries. It has failed to achieve any production history of substance and its early rejection would certainly have been due in part to its bold disregard of conventional Edwardian morality. The play tells a story of friendship, betrayal and infidelity. The writer Richard Rowan and his common-law wife Bertha have returned to Dublin from their 'exile' in Italy with their young child, Archie. Robert Hand, a journalist and old friend of Richard's but also a former suitor of Bertha's, makes advances towards Bertha in the first act and invites her to spend the evening alone with him. Richard puts his liberal-minded money where his mouth is, and recommends that Bertha follow her own desires, causing her to doubt the longevity of his affection. He suffers from jealousy at the implications of the liaison between his wife and friend and turns up in the second act at Robert's country cottage ahead of Bertha, only to meet her there and repeat his suggestion that she follow her own will. In the third act, Richard is tormented by not knowing what has gone on between his friend and wife, and faces this doubt as a form of creative inspiration. Following a series of confrontations, Robert leaves for England, and Bertha is hopeful of having regained her husband. In relating Pinter to Joyce, Katherine Worth discusses how 'knowing and wanting to know lead into "not knowing" in *Exiles*, as in all Pinter's plays',[2] and it is of course clear that Pinter had made common dramatic currency of the 'wound of doubt' throughout his career before *Exiles*, *The Collection* being the clearest example. This uncertainty that a character might experience with regard to another they wish to possess or control is also seen at work in *Old Times*, *Betrayal* and *Ashes to Ashes*. The elusiveness and malleability of the truth, diluted by violable memory, plays no small part in these later works.

Pinter had previously represented forms of male communion that involved a catalytic female character, most notably in the novel of *The Dwarfs*, in which the characters of Pete and Mark 'share an intellectual and social intimacy which is later reinforced by the fact that they both sleep with Virginia' (MB, p. 138). The theme was further extrapolated in *The Basement*, *The Collection*, *The Servant* screenplay and, of course, *The Homecoming*. With *Landscape* and *Silence*, though, Pinter had introduced a quality of sorrow at the inability of the two sexes to commune successfully in and through the needs and desires they manifested for one another within established or fledgling relationships. *Landscape*, *Silence*, *Night* and *Old Times* each document this form of paralysis in different ways. When Pinter returned, after *Exiles*, to this earlier interest in male interaction through the intermediary of a woman, it was to illustrate the dangers inherent in that behaviour, and the betrayals to self and to others that it might bring about. *Monologue* (1973) recalls the situation of the end of the novel *The Dwarfs*, and the dissolution of the friendship of two men following their sexual liaisons with the same woman:

> Now you're going to say you loved her soul and I loved her body. You're going to trot that one out. I know you were much more beautiful than me, much more *aquiline*, I know *that*, that I'll give you, more *ethereal*, more thoughtful,

slyer, while I had both feet firmly planted on the deck. But I'll tell you one thing you don't know. She loved my soul. It was my soul she loved [. . .] I loved her body. Not that, between ourselves, it's one way or another of any importance. My spasms could have been your spasms. (P4, p. 123)

In activating a 'body and soul' binary in this way, the unnamed character of Man reveals his need for the implied potential for a successful union that it offers – not just a sexual union, but also a strong bond with his estranged friend, and the fantasy of both things being available simultaneously. The imagined mixed-colour children that he states he would have loved represent the fruits of the carnal/spiritual resolution that he craves but so visibly lacks. This state of loss would become emphasised in Pinter's writing in the 1970s, as his observations moved away from the dystopian representation of stagnation and infestation that we have at the end of *The Dwarfs*, or of the stalemate and compromised negotiation that *The Homecoming* offered. The results of failed or compromised attempts to achieve emotional independence or union through intimacy are defined powerfully by Pinter in *Monologue* as sterility and isolation, and plays such as *Old Times*, *No Man's Land* and *Betrayal* present warnings against behaviour that might lead to emotional or social paralysis.

Betrayal (1978) concerns, at face value, a very traditional theme for drama: a love triangle involving an affair between a publisher's wife and his best friend, a literary agent. The story is told in reverse, opening after the end of the affair and closing on the passionate declaration of love that instigated the liaison. This backwards structure stops its audience concentrating on cause and effect, and making the associated moral judgements that this might ordinarily induce. Instead, it is difficult to isolate a villain of the piece, and each of the characters elicits our disdain and admiration in different measures at different stages. Pinter allows his audience to consider the framework of self-deception that is activated by acts of betrayal, and how this is a common function of everyday interaction – a symptom rather than a disease. Structured around the failure to maintain a bond and profit on admiration and friendship, as first demonstrated in *Monologue*, the mutual desire for a single woman in *Betrayal* is, however, not the psychological location of a struggle for dominance, as it was in *The Homecoming*, for example. Instead, a sexual bond between men through the intermediary of a shared woman is accentuated as characteristic of an emotional immaturity, and there is a compensatory emphasis on the will and need of the woman in the equation. This places in strong relief the inefficiencies of the male manifestation and articulation of need. Whilst Emma in *Betrayal* moves away from emotional paralysis to competent independence, effectively moving towards creativity (from publisher, to literary agent, to writer, to managing her own art gallery), the men, betraying their literary ideals to market forces, move backwards and away from one another and her. In this way, Pinter chooses to represent, and warn against, failure and paralysis.

Following *Betrayal*, Pinter seemed creatively to concentrate on the dissolution of the potentially protective family unit in three plays that were to be performed together under the collective title of *Other Places*: *Victoria Station*, *Family Voices* and *A Kind of Alaska* (all 1982). In *Victoria Station*, the controller of a fleet of London taxis seeks desperately to get a cab to a businessman arriving at the eponymous station. He fails to connect with any drivers over his radio system with the exception of driver 274, who evades the controller's questions and refuses the instruction to take this fare. In a hilarious exchange, the driver comes across as being in a carefree, almost hallucinogenic state. This causes the stressed controller to respond first with irritation and eventually with threats of physical violence. The driver bizarrely claims to park outside the Crystal Palace – which burned down in 1936 – and to have asleep on his back seat a young girl with whom he has fallen in love. A short, enigmatic piece, the play seems to articulate a desired retreat from the world of occupation and obligation, and a yearning for the order and peace of a comfortable, idealised domestic arrangement. The controller's final claim that he is closing his office to track down driver 274 may be in empathy with the driver's opt-out, or may be representative of a more sinister threat to such individualism. *Family Voices* more overtly expresses the tensions between belonging to one family (or social) group and pursuing an individual agenda towards a personal definition of family. Originally a play for radio, the drama is constructed of three voices, a son addressing his mother, as though in a letter, and a mother and father, addressing that son. The voices, though, remain unheard by their intended targets and the evidently failed communication, or enforced separation, emphasises the loss that this unit is experiencing. The words of Voice 1 (the son) place him in between two families – his biological family and the Winters, with whom he now lodges. He speaks of having found his family whilst innocently and dispassionately detailing various incidents of exposure to sexually charged or threatening behaviour on the part of his housemates. Voice 2 (his mother) contrasts this with her lonely existence, reproaching her son for abandoning her while imploring him to return. In this way Pinter activates the regressive impulse towards established emotional bonds that offer restriction but stable affection and contrasts that with the progressive impulse towards discovering and manufacturing fresh bonds that offer the promise of emotional fulfilment but carry the risk of compromise or failure. The two voices' yearning for satisfied connection is never satisfied and the third voice, that of the father, interjects as the play winds down. He plaintively offers an admonition from beyond the grave warning against isolation that might result from any failure to create and maintain bonds.

A Kind of Alaska is also set within a family structure, but this time one that is fractured as a result of the illness *ncephalitis lethargica*. In the opening scene Deborah is rought back to consciousness, after years in a coma-like state, by a drug administered by her carer Hornby. She slowly has to come to terms with the fact that she is no longer a teenager, but instead inhabits a middle-aged woman's body. Hornby and his wife, Deborah's sister Pauline, help her with her predicament by feeding her a mixture of truth and lies about her condition and the health of her parents. The illness eventually regains its grip on Deborah and as the play closes she is once again physically restricted. As she loses volition, she states, of what she has been told, that she has 'the matter in proportion' (P4, p. 190), though she has clearly opted to absorb the bits of information she is most comfortable with. The stagnation of her enforced existence has seemingly infected her extended family, or at least seems to serve as a metaphor for death and sterility in the family group: Pauline claims to have been widowed by her husband's attention to Deborah's care, the other sister, Estelle, is unmarried and tends to the blind father, and the mother is dead. Deborah's brief awakening seems to be a small flickering flame of hope in this history, but one that is quickly extinguished and, again, the effect of this play is one of a warning against isolation, and against the failure to connect.

Family structures in these plays demonstrate the contradictory human impulses to either remain comfortably in a known situation or move on to new, self-enriching discoveries, and this contradiction is played out within desired or regretfully fragmented family structures. The comfort of family is in the protection afforded by the bonds of mutual affection and understanding, but this is undermined by the natural inclination to establish new bonds and form new families (either in social groupings or literally, by having children). Whereas previously Pinter had equated the family with repression or social manipulation (*The Birthday Party*, *A Night Out* and *The Homecoming*, for example), in this group of short plays he seems to have wanted to examine the notion of family as the site of stable emotional being. Pinter was to return to examining that site, the threats to the stability it might offer and the regrets that failure to connect can bring about, in his last full length play, *Moonlight* (1993), which stages the emotional gaps between members of a nuclear family, and the various manners in which the individual members of the family cope with those gaps. The elderly, terminally ill Andy lies in his bed, being rude to his wife Bel, bemoaning his condition and the fact that his two sons have shown no interest in his fate. The unforgiving portrait of a crude and brutal patriarch that Pinter paints contrasts directly with the description first tendered by Bel and Andy's daughter Bridget in the play's prologue, suggesting a more harmonious family past, and hinting at a fund of expired emotional security. Bridget, who opens and closes the play and shares a flashback scene with her brothers Jake and Fred, is an odd presence, and one that does not integrate into the rest of the drama. She is physically separated from her family on stage, set apart in a pool of light up stage, whilst the family is separated into two factions on either side of the stage: Andy and Bel on one side, and Jake and Fred on the other. The meeting of Andy and Bridget in the kitchen in the night would indicate that she is dead, now an apparition, making sense of her theatrical presence and of the family's emotional reticence. Suppressed emotional need is hidden behind vicious or sarcastic language in the play, and this is wielded brutally by Andy, Jake and Fred in an almost wilful attempt to ignore the value and potential of a family that Bridget reveals as having once existed and which she now embodies. The characters of Maria and Ralph take on a conciliatory role and even the memories they evoke of the past infidelities they have enjoyed with both Andy and Bel serve to fold the theme of successful union into the play.

Family Voices represents a fulcrum in the shift of Pinter's representation of family, where the family becomes a unit offering hope of resistant shelter from homogenising ideological forces (rather than simply serving as a metaphor for such forces, as in *The Birthday Party* or *The Homecoming*), and this becomes most painfully evident in the treatment of a family, and the wilful elimination of such hope, in *One for the Road* (1984).

Indeed, all of Pinter's 'political' plays represent repression, in part if not wholly, by way of fragmented families – the husband-and-wife and mother-and-son couples in *Mountain Language* (1988), or Dusty's concern for her brother, whose tortured mind articulates its terrors in the closing moments, in *Party Time* (1991). It was in part by evoking the disturbance to familial quietude that Pinter was to sketch the horror of torture and oppression in the next stage of his writing for the stage.

7

The Dead

In 1980 Peter Hall reviewed the schedule of proposed plays that the National Theatre was to run, and asked Harold Pinter if he was interested in directing a Cottesloe production of Thomas Otway's *Venice Preserv'd*. Pinter turned down the suggestion, and other proposals that he direct Brian Friel's *Translations* and Wesker's *Caritas*, in order to work on an old text of his own. At home he had recently come across the script of *The Hothouse*, abandoned twenty years previously, and, having sat down to read it, found himself chuckling at his younger self's witty satire. With a few adjustments to the script, he decided, it was worth putting on. Directed in 1980 by the author with 'an odd mixture of laughter and chill',[1] *The Hothouse* was recognised as a shift in Pinter's temperament. One critic noticed the grim representation of an institution of repression, 'permeated with strange groans and screams, lights flickering on and off down dismal civil service corridors, patrolled by shadowy security officers'.[2] Given the recent revelation that the USSR had upheld a policy of incarcerating outspoken opponents in mental health hospitals, the rediscovered play had a contemporary political charge. 'It was fantasy when I wrote it,' Pinter stated, 'but now it has become, I think, far more relevant. Reality has overtaken it.'[3] In this way, his production of *The Hothouse* inaugurated a period in his writing when he was to turn his attention onto the clash between institutional dogma and individual freedoms.

In 1983 Pinter offered a sketch, entitled 'Precisely', for a revue evening called *The Big One* at the Apollo Theatre in December of that year. A satire, the sketch demonstrates the rage of two politician types accusing the nuclear disarmament groups of distorting the numbers of potential dead from a nuclear attack from a factual, they would have it, twenty million to upwards of thirty million. Their indignant behaviour exposes an all-too-easy dismissal of human life, and the satire cuts into the motivations of government or its apologists in the press that would seek to undermine opposing voices. In fact, the following month, Pinter wrote to *The Times* to complain at how a 'responsible newspaper' should claim in an editorial that 'many in the "peace movement" [. . .] agree substantially with the principles of communist theory', a 'classic smear technique', he noted.[4] The unthinking, dismissive equating of intellectual or liberal attitudes to the Cold War threat of communism had been noted in 'Precisely', when Stephen angrily declares, of the peace campaigners: 'I want to see the colour of their entrails,' and Roger darkly retorts: 'Same colour as the Red Flag, old boy' (P4, p. 218). Pinter came up against the same attitude at a dinner party in 1984 when he engaged in a conversation with some Turkish guests and attempted to discuss their views on the reported use of torture in their country's jails. He was shocked by their reply: 'Oh, well it was probably deserved [. . .] they were probably communists.'[5] He returned home that evening and wrote *One for the Road*, the only play he claims to have written in anger.

The play contains four scenes, in which the confident, jocular official Nicolas interrogates Victor, his wife Gila and their son Nicky. We do not hear what infraction the family is considered guilty of, but witness and hear of the punishment that is being meted out. Victor is badly bruised, as is Gila, who is forced to discuss the multiple rapes she has been subjected to by Nicolas's henchmen. Nicky's future is dismissed as of no consequence, and the suggestion at the end of the play is that he has been, or is to be, killed. Like Roote in *The Hothouse*, Nicolas thrives on the belief that he is working for the greater good, and we learn that the torture he dispenses is authorised by the head of state. Nicolas informs Victor: 'You have no other obligation' but to be honest (P4, p. 230). 'Honesty' here is an undisguised euphemism for not opposing the government. In the play's final scene Victor returns smartly dressed and with his tongue cut, ready for his orderly re-integration into the society he previously criticised. As such, his final appearance very closely resembles that of the mute, besuited Stanley in the final scene of *The Birthday Party*. This time there is no metaphor, and the focus is consequently sharply attuned to the political abuse of rhetoric and power. One critic expressed how the play 'floods the mind with despair, the eyes with tears, the stomach with sickness, the heart with dread'.[6]

In March 1985, Pinter visited Turkey with Arthur Miller to represent International PEN, an organisation that voices solidarity with imprisoned writers around the world. Turkey had experienced a military coup in 1980 and by 1985 the country had an estimated two thousand political prisoners locked up under martial law. At a dinner arranged by the US ambassador there, Pinter responded to the ambassador's statement that there could be varied opinions about the state of affairs in the country with: 'Not if you've got an electric wire hooked to your genitals,' referring to the incidences of torture he had learned of during his stay.[7] This outspokenness was to prove characteristic of his new persona as a politically active artist. Pinter was happy to acknowledge that he had made a conscious decision to voice his concerns publicly and was now assuredly 'making a bit of a nuisance of [him]self'.[8] What had changed for him, perhaps, was a conception of himself as a citizen and artist within a democratic country whose elected representatives took or endorsed action that substantially impacted on others' lives:

I remember years ago I regarded myself as an artist in an ivory tower – really when it comes down to it a rather nineteenth-century idea. I've now totally rejected that and I find that the things that are actually happening are not only of the greatest importance but [have] the most crucial bearing on our lives, including this matter of censorship of people and writers' imprisonment, torture, and the whole question of how we are dealt with by governments who are in power.[9]

Much has been made about Harold Pinter's 'sudden' decision to explore political issues in his drama of the 1980s. There is, however, very little that was sudden about this perceived shift in his concerns. As has been discussed, his first plays were flavoured with a distinctive resistant spirit, and he was keen to point this out when asked, in 1984, if his attitude to his work had changed. Speaking of *The Dumb Waiter* he reminded his interviewer that the 'political metaphor was very clear to the actors and director of the first production in 1960', that *The Birthday Party* 'has a central figure who is squeezed by certain authoritarian forces' and that *The Hothouse* 'is essentially about the abuse of authority'.[10] Some critics have gone further and isolated essentially political dynamics in many of the plays that Pinter himself would concede have no direct political ambition of expression. In regarding the models of human interaction that Pinter documented in the sixties and seventies, many commentators point out that an inferred commentary on behaviour is acutely tuned towards modes of resistance. For instance, in speaking of *The Collection*, *The Homecoming* and *Old Times*, Marc Silverstein states:

> We can only fully grasp the political resonance of the power struggles in these plays if we see the question of who will occupy the dominant position within the marriage as inseparable from the larger question of whether the family will serve as a stable site for the articulation of patriarchal power or as the vanishing point that works to undermine that power and the cultural order it supports.[11]

Other critics, such as D. Keith Peacock, fairly point out that to say that all human interaction is inherently political is to dilute the field of what constitutes political writing to meaningless extremes. But if Pinter's writing has often dealt with behavioural strategies adopted in the face of oppressive cultural forces, then it has to be recognised that his ambition has been more sophisticated than simply to represent that human interaction. In any case, to trace Pinter's interest in political issues solely by trawling his own plays is a myopic approach which will glean results that cannot speak for Pinter's stance as a citizen. Casting the net wider, and looking at some of his other activities, reveals that a certain anger over oppression and the ideological clouding of issues of justice has never been far from his mind. His screenplay of *The Quiller Memorandum* (1965), for example, or his decision to direct Robert Shaw's play *The Man in the Glass Booth* in 1967, both in different ways dealing with the aftermath of the Second World War, are clearly informed by a focused political stance.

Though it would be true to say that in the early eighties Pinter must have come to a decision to become more vocally engaged and harness his celebrity to make his concerns public, it is clearly not the case that he only became politicised in the early eighties. The evidence for his supposed lack of interest in political issues prior to his political drama stems from his early statements regarding his position on the responsibility of the writer (see pp. 29–32). These, of course, were given against a background of writers such as Arden and Wesker, who sought to politicise plays and audiences, but the notion of Pinter's being apolitical was seemingly confirmed by a statement he made when asked in 1962 by *Encounter* about the burning issue of the day, Britain's relationship with the Common Market, the forerunner of the European Union: 'I have no interest in the matter and do not care what happens. I don't think I have any kind of social function that's of any value.'[12] As it turned out, he was not altogether indifferent to the issue of the UK's subscription to the Common Market, and once was signatory to a letter to *The Times* from artists disagreeing with the premise that the Treaty of Rome would offer greater pan-European artistic relationships than already existed.[13] Nevertheless, when he was asked, in 1967, whether that original statement summed up his 'feeling about politics, or current affairs', he quickly retorted, 'Not really. Though that's exactly what I feel about the Common Market. But it isn't quite true to say that I'm in any way indifferent to current affairs' and went on to clarify: 'I'll tell you what I really think about politicians. The other night I watched some politicians on television talking about Vietnam. I wanted very much to burst through the screen with a flame-thrower and burn their eyes out and their balls off and then inquire from them how they would assess this action from a political point of view.'[14]

These are not the words of a man uninterested in politics, and are consistent with his present-day evaluation of politicians: 'Do not let us listen to what people say but what they actually do.'[15] They are also acutely revealing about the irritation he seeks to articulate over the manner in which the discourses of professional politics often involve a purposeful verbal obfuscation of the material facts of suffering. Speaking of a line in his 1991 sketch 'The New World Order', he reveals how this is an attitude which has remained consistent from his teenage years:

> There's a little exchange in which one of the two men who are about to torture a prisoner says to the other: 'I don't know, I feel so pure.' And the other one replies: 'You're right to feel pure, you know why, because you're keeping the world clean for democracy.' I used that line with Henry Woolf and my other friends in the late 1940s. We used to use it, it was one of our phrases. 'That's what they're doing, they're dropping the Atom Bomb to keep the world clean for democracy.'[16]

Pinter, prior to his supposed political phase, was never, in fact, averse to making statements concerning political matters ('I'm categorically against the Americans in Vietnam. And, I feel strongly in favour of Israel,'[17] he stated in 1968. 'I'm quite horrified by South Africa' [MG, p. 40], he said in 1971.) What is more, he has never simply been a man of words: his 1949

stand as a conscientious objector, refusing 'to join an organisation whose main purpose is mass murder',[18] is often cited as an
example of his willingness to be politically proactive and, to
offer a further example from after the period of his rise to
fame, in 1972 he joined with a group of other artists to send a
letter to *The Times* decrying the miscarriage of justice that saw
Vladimir Bukovsky jailed in the USSR for protesting about the
certification of dissenters as lunatics, and was prepared to
stand vigil outside the Russian Embassy as the Soviet Court of
Appeal heard the case.[19]

Similarly, his distrust of US foreign policy did not arise fully
formed in the 1980s, when he began to publish material critical of Ronald Reagan's administration. His unease at the
manoeuvres of the American superpower dates from his awareness, in the 1950s, of some of the more questionable aspects of
US domestic policy. With regard to the McCarthy trials, he
remembers: 'I think my detestation of the manifestations of
American power probably began or was solidified then.'[20] This
consciousness became more fully mobilised in Pinter following the American-supported coup of 11 September 1973 in
Chile, when General Pinochet deposed the democratically
elected government of Salvador Allende to replace it with a
military dictatorship: 'I suddenly woke up. With the support of
the United States they were killing people.'[21] This awakening
led to a persistent distrust of and repeated outcry against successive US governments, and he is often keen to relate this
antagonism he feels specifically to the manner in which policy
is represented:

> It's to do with my fascination with our separation between
> reality and our interpretation of it. Our human experience
> can be totally dislocated by these facts and it happens every
> day of the week. But it's not dislocated for people having
> drinks at a cocktail party. It's exactly the same as when peo-
> ple talk about nuclear war. The words have simply become
> abstractions – people can't face them . . . This play [*One for*

the Road] comes out of my life and of my understanding of life. What we are encouraged to think in the West is that we have a moral advantage, that we inhabit a superior moral position. But the United States brought down the Chilean regime and they're doing the same in Nicaragua. They are supporting the most fiendishly appalling system in El Salvador. If you shake hands with murderers you have no moral position.[22]

His anger at US intervention in the domestic affairs of numerous Latin American countries is well documented in a series of articles and interviews published in *Various Voices* (1998).

Perhaps another reason for the critical shift in focus (either of derision or admiration) for Pinter's political voice was that previously he did not fit the description of a committed writer – either of the kitchen-sink dramatists or of the generation of playwrights that, in the late sixties and seventies following the angry young men of Pinter's cohort, took on social issues and forged new forms to express their concerns. Marxist-radical works on the National Theatre and RSC stages saw the rise of 'State of the Nation' plays such as David Edgar's *Destiny* (1976), David Hare's *Plenty* (1978) and Howard Brenton's *The Romans in Britain* (1980). Such works came to be exemplary of British political theatre in the 1970s, the yardstick by which political theatre became commonly measured. Against this backdrop, with works such as *No Man's Land* and *Betrayal*, Pinter seemed in the 1970s to be receding further away from social concerns and concentrating on the personal and the domestic. As an associate director (from 1973) at the National Theatre he manifested no interest in such work, and once, for example, rejected a Brenton script that crossed his desk. His choice of the productions he directed there in the seventies (such as Noel Coward's *Blithe Spirit* or Simon Gray's *Otherwise Engaged*) was indicative of his persistent lack of interest in drama that contained 'warnings, sermons, admonitions, ideological exhortations, moral judgements, defined problems with built-in solutions' (VV, p. 18). Importantly, just as he has remained consistent as regards his contempt for freedom-cramping ideologies, such statements concerning the role of the artist remained true when applied to his so-called political plays. *One for the Road*, for example, contained no 'defined problems with built-in solutions', nor could it even be said overtly to be a warning or a sermon. The same holds true of *Mountain Language* (1988) and *Party Time* (1991). Along with *One for the Road*, these plays simply sought to document the reality of human-rights abuses and to place in high relief the discourses that circulated around such incidences of abuse. The plays did not point the finger of blame directly, and this is the chief ingredient that makes them so potent. Faced with such images and scenarios of torture, an audience is left with a gap where those responsible might be named and held morally accountable.

Mountain Language is a short play of four scenes set in a prison camp. The first scene is set in the cold outside, where women have been made to wait for eight hours, taunted and bitten by guard dogs, hoping to visit their imprisoned relatives. We learn that the men's crimes are related to a martial law that has forbidden the use of their ethnic language. One woman's protests reveal that her husband is among the wrong grouping of prisoners. His crime, it would seem, is being an intellectual. She reappears in scene three to witness her incapacitated, hooded husband being beaten. Scenes two and four are shared by an elderly woman and her imprisoned son and involve the dire consequences of her being unable to understand the language of the guard, who demands that she no longer speak her own tongue. *Party Time* illustrates another side to the oppressors' world, and is set at a dinner party where the elite gather to wine and dine, whilst roadblocks and a curfew deal with the general population outside. A luxurious, exclusive lifestyle is equated with moral rigour through repeated references to standards at a health club of which most party guests are members. An elderly Margaret Thatcher figure, Dame Melissa, seals this metaphor into a truism, claiming: 'Our club – is a club which is activated, which is inspired by a moral sense, a moral awareness, a set of moral values which is – I have to say – unshakeable, rigorous, fundamental, constant' (P4, p. 311). Against this logic, which essentially equates morality with power, Pinter contrasts the grim reality of the oppression that perpetuates power. One guest, Dusty, disturbs the moral sheen by repeatedly asking after her disappeared brother Jimmy, only to be warned by her husband Terry that 'nobody is discussing this' (P4, p. 284). Her dignified insistence on getting an answer cannot be silenced and she is taken to one side and threatened in a manner that clarifies the state's true 'moral' objective: 'You're all going to die together, you and all your lot' (P4, p. 302). Dusty's brother Jimmy appears on stage in a brief epilogue to offer a stuttered account of his existence in a torturous solitary confinement where he sits 'sucking the darkness' (P4, p. 314).

When *Mountain Language* was first published in the *Times Literary Supplement*, an advert announcing this the previous week had stated that the play 'was inspired by his trip to Turkey with Arthur Miller and is a parable about torture and the fate of the Kurdish people'. This caused Pinter to write a letter to point out that, though it was true it had been inspired by his experiences in Turkey, 'The play is not . . . "about the fate of the Kurdish people" and, above all, it is not intended as "a parable".'[23] He was keen to dismiss any notion of his recent plays functioning metaphorically, as now he was dealing in the documented reality of torture and abuse. Perhaps to make his point clearer, when he directed the play at the National Theatre, he dressed the soldiers in recognisably British Army uniforms. Effectively, this was a dramatisation of his belief, stated above, that 'if you shake hands with murderers you have no moral position'. If *One for the Road*, *Mountain Language* or *Party Time* had been clearly set in Iraq, China or North Korea, where human rights violations were widely acknowledged, then all Pinter would have achieved with such plays would have been to contribute to the climate of threat and fear propagated by home-grown ideologies, a climate that permitted the turning of blind eyes to human-rights violations and UN-resolution-flouting by US and NATO allies such as Turkey and Israel, whilst condemning the very same action elsewhere. Instead of wishing to preach to the converted, he sought to dismantle the vocabulary of the preaching and ask how we had been converted to accept the injustices carried out in our names. At a meeting of PEN on 2 August 1988 Pinter read and answered questions on *Mountain Language*:

> Asked whether he was talking about Britain, he replied 'Yes'. Our 'Mountain people' whose language is being suppressed are the homosexuals. 'Who knows where these measures may end?' He also spoke about those who, under interrogation by the British in Northern Ireland, managed to keep their spirits from being broken by replying in Gaelic. Torture, he emphasised, is not 'out there'. He said that when Mrs Thatcher visited Turkey last April, her sole concern was to gain the contract for a third bridge over the Bosporus, and that when she had been asked about torture at her final press conference she replied that all that had been sorted out.[24]

Pinter is referring initially to the infamous Clause 28 of the 1988 Local Government Act, which sought to limit the teaching of literature that might promote homosexuality. He was concerned about such reductions of civil liberties under the Conservative government of the 1980s and 1990s and, for example, opposed the strengthening of the Official Secrets Act and, later, the citizen's loss of the right to silence in 1992 and the 1996 Prevention of Terrorism (Additional Powers) Act, which was strengthened further still by the Labour government under the auspices of the 'War on Terror'. Such legislation, he believed, had nothing 'to do with democratic aspirations' but instead 'with the intensification and consolidation of state power' (VV, p. 174). The ambiguity of the location of his political plays, then, serves to remind an audience about the responsibilities we have towards our own freedoms, and the care we should take when recognising political double-speak.

The 1996 play *Ashes to Ashes* brought genocide explicitly to British shores in the questionable remembrances of Rebecca, who talks of having seen refugees herded out off the beach and into the sea in Dorset. Whilst this account serves to undermine the authenticity of some of her memories, the painfully genuine attribution she has made of Holocaust atrocities to her own present childless state is emotionally potent (she repeatedly recalls having her baby taken away from her at a train station, in a scenario reminiscent of William Styron's novel *Sophie's Choice*). Within an extended dialogue between a domineering bully of a husband and a clearly disturbed wife, Pinter neatly intertwines personal responsibility for political manoeuvring with a domestic arrangement.

Pinter had initiated a renewed interest in the Holocaust and an attachment to Holocaust literature in 1990 with the preparations of his screenplay of Fred Ulhman's *Reunion*, following on from his screenplay for Margaret Atwood's vision of a future totalitarian Western state, *The Handmaid's Tale* (1987). In 1993 he was reported to be working on an adaptation of *An Interrupted Life: the diaries of Etty Hillesum 1941–1943*.[25] Hillesum kept a diary of her life in Amsterdam under Nazi occupation and sent correspondence whilst on her way to Auschwitz, which she did not survive. Pinter's interest in the politics of the aftermath of the Second World War was also revisited in his direction of Ronald Harwood's *Taking Sides* in 1995, a play that, like *The Man in the Glass Booth*, which he had directed in 1967, examined the zeal of the Allies to seek Nazi convictions whilst shoving under the carpet evidence of their own moral double standards. Such concerns are embedded in his own work, and are focused within the use of language by those in positions of power. As *Party Time* demonstrates, the appropriation of a moral position is made possible by structuring discourses of virtue around governmental behaviour in ways that undermine straightforward rejection and encourage unthinking obedience.

In his 1991 sketch 'The New World Order' Pinter presents two thugs about to inflict violence upon a blindfolded lecturer and articulating the purity of their actions as sanctioned by the protection of freedom and democracy. In *Celebration* (2000) such thinking is articulated by the crudely spoken characters of Matt and Lambert who, as 'strategy consultants', are involved worldwide in 'keeping the peace' (p. 60), and have clearly made a good deal of money out of it. Pinter's concern is clearly to lift the veil off sanctimonious language to reveal the profitable thuggery beneath it. The facts of suffering should not, according to Pinter, be smokescreened by language:

> You have to know what happened and face it and I think
> everybody has to do that. Memory can so easily be sup-
> pressed if it's uncomfortable and painful – and it's not in
> the interests of the various powers-that-be to have that
> memory still with us. I think our actual memories are very
> easily manipulated, distorted and changed, so that we don't
> remember. There's so much that happens in the media, or
> rather that doesn't happen through the media and through
> the structures of the way we live, that half of the time we
> don't know what we're actually being subjected to.[26]

Over the past two decades, Pinter has become more and more vocal in matters of international human rights violations, and attempts specifically to undermine the language that is applied by politicians to sanitise or justify actions that have resulted in the deaths of thousands of civilians. The US-led Gulf War of 1991 and its more devastating sequel, the ten years of sanctions against Iraq and the NATO bombing of Belgrade in 1999 have in particular enraged him, given the death counts brought about by such 'peace-keeping' policies. His most recent piece of writing for the stage, the 2002 *Press Conference*, represents a summation of his indignation at the language of politicians. The sketch has a Minister for Culture fielding questions from the press with startling honesty: as former head of Secret Police he has had children abducted or killed, women raped and dissenters beaten up. This, he argues, is in keeping with his current post in that the state adopts 'a muscular and tender understanding of our cultural heritage and our cultural obligations' (p. 7). Prefaced by the admissions of brutal state control, these otherwise innocent words have sinister overtones that plainly demonstrate Pinter's contempt for those politicians who speak of exporting democracy, or bringing about freedom, or liberating peoples, whilst employing devastating military means to do so.

On 2 November 2004, the date of the US Presidential election that saw George W. Bush re-elected to a second term in office, Harold Pinter took part in a 'Naming the Dead' ceremony in Trafalgar Square, London. He lent his deep, serious baritone to the slow public reading of the names, one by one, of the thousands of civilians, soldiers and aid workers who had been killed as a result of the US invasion and occupation of Iraq. His investment in such events is demonstrative of his strongly held conviction that we, as citizens of democratic countries, ought to be concerned about the killing that is done in our name, to protect our security and economic concerns. In a speech accepting an honorary degree awarded to him by the University of Turin in 2002, Pinter questioned why, for the US, the three thousand deaths caused by the atrocious terrorist attack in New York on 11 September 2001 'are the only deaths that count' and emphasised that 'the three thousand deaths in Afghanistan [and] the hundreds of thousands of Iraqi children dead [. . .] are never referred to'. His war poetry, published in 2003 in *War*, collectively contrasts his desire to rehumanise this depersonalisation of individual death –

> Who was the father or daughter or brother
> Or uncle or sister or mother or son
> Of the dead and abandoned body?[27]

– with an impulse to malign the glorification of military victory:

Here they go again
The Yanks in their armoured parade
Chanting their ballads of joy
As they gallop across the big world
Praising America's God.
The gutters are clogged with the dead.[28]

In August 2004, *War* was awarded the Wilfred Owen Prize
for war poetry by the Wilfred Owen Association for its pithy
articulation of the moral concerns behind the killing. In
essence, the questions Pinter raises are the same as have fascinated him throughout his artistic career, and concern the
threats or dangers of slipping into the gap between lived experience and representation within language:

Does reality essentially remain outside language, separate,
obdurate, alien, not susceptible to description? Is an accurate and vital correspondence between what *is* and our perception of it impossible? Or is it that we are obliged to use
language only in order to obscure and distort reality – to
distort what *is*, to distort what *happens* – because we fear
it? We are encouraged to be cowards. We can't face the
dead. But we must face the dead because they die in our
name. We must pay attention to what is being done in our
name. (VV, p. 182)

8

Pinter Views: Pinter on Pinter

A commonly held misconception about Harold Pinter is that he rarely gives interviews. Whilst it is true that he closed his doors to a good deal of the British press for a period of years following the insensitive media treatment he and Antonia Fraser received at the onset of their relationship and eventual marriage, it is remarkable that, over the past decade or so, numerous published interviews are still prefaced with phrases such as 'in a rare interview'. In fact, since his first published interview in 1959, there have been seventy or so dialogues with the author which have been printed, in excess of forty radio and television discussions granted and innumerable live talks given in theatres and meeting rooms. Given these figures, Harold Pinter must, after all, be one of the most interviewed artists of the last fifty years. He has always been happy to discuss all aspects of his life and work as writer, actor, director, screenplay writer and political activist. This section is given over to the writer's own words, and documents his own thoughts and responses to his life, his work and the manner in which it has been received. The first interview here was conducted on 16 September 2004 for inclusion in this book. In it, Pinter discusses much of his career and some of his political views.

MB: *As a young boy and young man you were predominantly interested in literature and poetry. You never went to the theatre a great deal, you were never interested in drama, apart from some of the stuff you were introduced to at school. What was the reason that led you to choose to go into acting?*
HP: It was the only job I could possibly do or wanted to do. It

was just a question of earning a living. I had no real ambitions. I was quite a competent actor, and I hope quite an intelligent actor at that time. It seemed to be the way to go. I was writing a lot of poetry at the time, but you couldn't possibly live on poetry.

Did you ever have any ambitions to become a playwright?
No, no, not at all, absolutely not. As I say, I wrote a great deal of poetry and I wrote one novel. It didn't occur to me that I was going to write plays. The only interest I really had in the theatre was Shakespeare. Of course I read Webster . . . I mean the Jacobeans. But I didn't know very much about modern dramatic literature at the time.

Were your first plays written with any expectation of their being performed? The Birthday Party, *for example?*
No, I didn't expect it to be performed. I had seen *The Room* performed, of course, but I didn't quite see who was going to do *The Birthday Party*. By then I had an agent, and Michael Codron, in fact, phoned and asked to read whatever I'd written and by that time I had written *The Birthday Party*. He put it on and much to his dismay it was totally dismissed, as you know. *The Room* and *The Dumb Waiter* were eventually done in 1960 at what was then called the Hampstead Theatre Club, and then things moved along: 1960 was a very active year.

It was the year, of course, of The Caretaker, *which was very, very successful – in ways that perhaps you hadn't expected, given the reception thus far to your work. It just ran and ran . . .*
. . . It ran for about a year and then it was done all over the world.

It must have been a great relief to you, as a writer, to have that success with a piece of writing that you were also very satisfied with artistically.
Yes. I must say it was rather dizzying in one way. I didn't know

what had hit me or why it had hit me. It also allowed me to be very practical about my parents. Because my father – he was only about fifty-nine but he was on his last legs, he was a tailor and he was working twelve hours a day in an appalling factory. He was really going to snuff it, you know. Because of *The Caretaker* I was able to tell him to stop working and move them down to Brighton, because for the first time in my life I was actually earning money. It was really rather a shock, but it allowed me to do that and he lived for another forty years. He died when he was ninety-six.

Between the successes of The Caretaker *and* The Homecoming, *in 1965, you wrote a good deal for television. Why the switch in media at that point?*
I was asked to write one TV play, *A Night Out*, for *Armchair Theatre*. That was in 1960 also. That was done and went very well. Then my agent told me that this chap Peter Willes, Head of Drama at Associated Rediffusion, wanted to see me. He said, 'He's seen a few sketches and wants to have a word. I sent him *The Birthday Party*, I have no idea if he's read it or not but anyway he wants to see you.' Anyway I went along. This was before *The Caretaker* was produced.

So you were still in some state of uncertainty about the future of your writing?
Absolutely. I was also absolutely broke. Not quite as broke as I had been, but pretty broke. I went up and was ushered into this man's office and he was standing at the window looking out of the window. He didn't turn at all. So his secretary took me in and I stood there for a moment and he suddenly wheeled round and looked at me and said – she said, 'This is Harold Pinter' – and he wheeled round and looked at me and said, 'How dare you!' And I said, 'What?' He said, 'How dare you write such a play.' He said, 'I haven't had a wink of sleep for three bloody nights! Oh well I suppose we'd better do it. Who do you want to direct it?' It was the most extraordinary thing, then he –

sometime before 1961 or the beginning or end of 1960 – he commissioned me to write three television plays. So I wrote *The Lover*, *The Collection* and another one called *Night School*. It was just three plays and I wrote them, and I was feeling pretty . . . the writing was really coming out.

I'd like to ask about your writing process. You have consistently stated over the years that you write from a given impulse, as though you're unwrapping some kernel of inspiration that has come to you, but without really knowing where it's going. When this happens what form does it take? Is it anger, is it excitement . . . what kind of inspiration is it that usually causes you to pick up a pen?

Yes, some kind of excitement . . . not anger. I have written one play out of anger, as I think you might know – *One For The Road*. That was really written out of anger. I didn't know what I was going to write, but I remember coming back to this place and being very, very angry after a conversation that I'd had with some women. There are so many ingredients in writing something and you can't define and analyse glibly how it happens or why it is happening or what is happening. When I wrote that sketch of mine called 'The New World Order', for example, I wrote it not out of anger but out of hatred for these people and for the authorities which they represented, and for the procedures that were authorised. Incidentally, the same thing applies to *The Hothouse*, going back many, many years – that was actually the impulse for that, also. Although I think, coming back to *The Hothouse*, although Roote is one of the funniest parts I have ever written – I have played it myself – I still think he's one of the most ghastly characters I have ever written, the most appalling, disgusting, but he represents I think a number of things that we're actually faced with in authoritarian systems.

I want to ask you about some of your other work: screenplay writing and directing. I was reading the other day an interview you gave in the early seventies, in which you were talking about directing Simon Gray's Butley *and you said what attracted you to the play was the fact that this character of Butley had this intellectual attraction to the company of men, which wasn't homosexual. We can certainly see a similar fascination in your own work from* The Dwarfs *to* Betrayal *and onwards. I then wondered if working on Joyce, working on Proust and working with all sorts of adaptations of other people's material – latterly working on Shakespeare, the* King Lear *screenplay – whether that for you is some form of communing with these artists, that you hold an intellectual attraction to?*

Yes. I certainly had a wonderful relationship with James Joyce. Unfortunately it was never embodied, for obvious reasons. But I always thought that I would love to have had a drink with him. I would have loved him to have seen my production of *Exiles*. Because remember, Ezra Pound said it was unstageable and I have to say that I proved quite categorically that it was not unstageable and I would have like Pound to have seen it also.

Considering how people have responded to your work, you've had to live with – suffer, you might even say – the eyes of academia since the early sixties. I think the first books on your plays came out in '64, '65.

You've seen the shelves downstairs?

Yes. You've got a couple of shelves dedicated to things people have written about you. Is all that a burden? Do you or did you ever feel that being defined by people is an anchor to your creativity in some way, or just something that you could brush off easily? Or do you simply find it flattering?

I think it would be disingenuous of me to say that I don't get a certain kind of pleasure having these books, not that I read them. I can't say I don't dip into them either, because I do. I couldn't possibly finish any of them.

Is any of the analysis in these books irritating to you, or do you find any of them enlightening in any odd way?

I don't find them terribly enlightening. It's a very mixed thing here because I do, as I say, derive a certain amount of pleasure in the fact that they exist and that they are bothering to write about my work, all these people. At the same time it tends to be rather suffocating. You know Ionesco's play *The New Tenant*? He walks into the room and the furniture-remover follows him, bringing in chairs and tables and stuff, and finally he's buried underneath. Well I tend towards that occasionally. At the same time I'm not going to throw them all into the bin, because I respect such people who care to do this. I've also even met a few of them and they turn out to be perfectly reasonable human beings.

You've said consistently throughout your career that you're not interested in the audience necessarily, you don't care what they think. In the rehearsal room you say to the actors not to worry about them and not to be concerned about the audience. This seems to indicate to me that you are not particularly interested in whether anyone loves your work or not, you don't particularly care what the response is . . .

No. I think that is the point; I don't want people to love me, that is one thing I can say without fear or favour. But I tend to exaggerate sometimes. When I made this motif for the actors saying the one thing to remember is 'Fuck the audience', well what I am really saying by that is not really 'Fuck the audience' but 'Do what you choose to do, what we have decided to do, and not what they want.' I think that's the essential thing here. So don't go out on the stage and give them what they want, because giving them what they want is going to do serious damage to the work. To a certain extent this stems back to when I was acting myself in Ireland in rep. You know, I really thought there was a contest between the actors and the audience and someone had to win. And it couldn't be the audience!

You have often returned to your own plays as a director or actor. May I ask if there is ever any conscious decision on your part whether you choose to direct a play that you have written once you've completed it, or whether you hand it over to another director. Is it possible to say that there's a relationship that you are still having with some plays which you want to continue and see through in the rehearsal room?

I suppose that might be the case. I am quite even-handed about the plays of mine which I direct and the plays that I am very happy for other directors to direct. For example, did you see *Old Times* recently? I was very happy about that. I loved the whole thing. I also like the work of David Leveaux very much and lots of other people going back to Peter Hall. But occasionally something tells me that I'd like to do this myself – like *Celebration* for example, I just wanted to do it.

Is that something to do with 'unfinished business'? Is it as though you were still finishing the play off, in some way, on the rehearsal room floor?

Well it might be, you know I've never analysed it, rationalised it, I don't know, it might be.

When I've talked to actors who've worked with you, they tell me you come to your plays with a sense of not knowing where they've really come from, that they are as fresh to you as they are to them, which clearly cannot quite be the case. And yet that attitude indicates that you're still genuinely discovering something.

Well certainly. When I did *No Man's Land* at the National three years ago with Corin Redgrave and John Wood, I really did discover the play anew. Don't forget that when I did *The Room*, which I did with *Celebration*, *The Room* had been written over forty years ago, but I wanted to direct it – I never had done – and to discover it, to rediscover it, if you like. And I certainly did and I found it a very interesting activity. Working with actors I was able to unearth things which I didn't really know were there until I was working on it with them and I found these aspects, elements and shades and I realised that the kind of discipline that had to be exerted . . . You know there's a line in my novel *The Dwarfs*, Pete talks about if you crack a nut with a nutcracker the cracker cracks the nut but the nutcracker gives out an energy or heat which is incidental to the particular idea. This is Pete talking, but the fact is that I am aware in directing my own work and perhaps generally speaking other people's work too that there has to be a point finally where – you can stand on your head and do double somersaults, do anything – but finally you have to find a very rigorous and precise definition of any given moment and hold on to it.

Let's talk a little bit about your politics. You grew up part of a Jewish community in the East End at a time when it was infected by fascists and fascist meetings, and you stumbled across more than one of those and were involved in one or two uncomfortable incidents, I think. This was shortly after the war and the details of the Holocaust were coming out and it must have also been very clear at that time that we had only escaped Nazi occupation by the skin of our teeth . . .
That's right.

So – I can't possibly imagine – but that must have given you some relationship with the Holocaust that's difficult to quantify, with what happened in Germany and Eastern Europe.
Yes.

And I wonder to what degree the shadow of the Holocaust inhabits a lot of your work? It's certainly quite explicit in Ashes to Ashes, *but you can see it as early as* The Birthday Party *with someone knocking on the door and grabbing someone and taking them away.*
Well I agree.

I wonder how conscious you are of that, how deliberate it is, or whether it's just something that subtly informs what you do.

Well by the time I got to *Ashes for Ashes* I was certainly conscious of it, it would be stupid to say I wasn't. But *The Birthday Party* – I think it was much more . . . unconscious. The interesting thing about *The Birthday Party* as far as I'm concerned is Goldberg. This authoritarian figure, this bloke who says, you know, you do what you're told, is Jewish without any question. But the idea of two men coming into a room and subjecting a third man to what they subject him to I'm sure was affected by my knowledge of the Holocaust, as well as my knowledge of rigid religious and nationalistic – well mostly religious, let's call it religious forces. I mean, McCann doesn't exactly express a religious idea, nor in fact does Goldberg, but nevertheless they do represent pretty rigid forces and one's Jewish the other's Irish. You know, work it out!

You point out that the important thing is that Goldberg is Jewish, perhaps indicating that the concept of moral superiority is not as simplistic as written history would allow us to make out, and that seems to me something that you've pursued in a lot of what you've worked on. Engaging with that, certainly in pieces such as Taking Sides, *you also have this fascination, it seems to me, with the notion that the moral victors, so to speak, can be guilty through a kind of complicity with atrocity: that we can't be comfortably complacent about our position as the moral victors, historically.*

We certainly can't be complacent; we can't be complacent at all. The one thing I find utterly detestable – and a lot of my recent poetry, as you know, has been devoted to this – is that moral position that 'we' take – 'we' in inverted commas. Particularly Tony Blair and George Bush, I mean, take a moral position and think they have moral authority and believe that what they are doing is morally correct, whereas that is all absolute crap! They have no such moral authority and they are actually gangsters. That's the way I see it. The whole damn lot of them really!

They would say their moral responsibility or their moral imperative is rooted in their Christian beliefs . . .
Oh yes, absolutely! God's right behind both of them, isn't he . . .? I think Bush has actually said that God asked him to do this job.

Kofi Annan recently stated that the invasion of Iraq was illegal, that it was contrary to the United Nations charter . . .
Bit late in the day for that . . . nevertheless . . .

Does that not make war criminals of Blair and Bush, in your view?
The answer to that is yes. But I didn't need Kofi Annan to tell me that, I've believed that from the word go actually. I believe that Bush and Blair should be arraigned before an International Criminal Court of Justice. In fact, Blair could be, because we've signed up to that, the creation of that court, whereas Bush cunningly and wisely has kept out of it. He won't sign up for it but he still doesn't mind it for everyone else. He wouldn't have Americans, including himself, or other Americans, for example Kissinger, tried in that way.

But he claims to speak and act in the name of international justice. What defines this international justice? Is it, in your view, similar to this notion of God, an abstraction that is used to justify action?
Well exactly. It's meaningless. His use of the term 'international justice' is, as I say, a posture, it is a piece of rhetoric which means absolutely nothing. Do not let us listen to what people say but what they actually do, and I think his actions and Blair's actions absolutely deny their moral claims. I mean the fact is, Mark, that there are getting on for 14,000 Iraqi civilians that have been killed. And they're never mentioned. They're not even counted. I've got a thing here called 'Iraq Body Count', which is a non-government organisation which does its very, very best to document exactly how many Iraqi civilians

have been killed and they make it thirteen to fourteen thousand. They're very responsible. But to Bush and Blair these people don't exist and indeed they don't exist on two counts: one, they don't exist because they're dead, and two, they don't exist because they never existed, they're irrelevant. So I think their 'moral position' is an insult to all of us.

You bring this indignation into a lot of what you write, and what you manage to do is certainly, I think, to say that we are not separate from these responsibilities. You said once in a more recent interview that the dead are watching us because they have been killed in our name.
That is right.

Within what you write creatively, it seems to me, you are attempting to suggest that we too have a responsibility, that we have a responsibility toward those atrocities that are carried out in our name.
Yes.

And yet do you not feel that your message is quite pessimistic, given that in a lot of your plays you suggest that this atrocious force, this power committing these atrocities, cannot be resisted, that we can do little against it. Stanley and Victor are both led out mute and broken. There is no way we can fight back against these forces.
Well I think, in those plays that you refer to, I'm just trying to look at things as they are, as they can be, and I've never been able to see a way in which you have a happy ending in those particular plays and a number of others. No, the forces – these kind of forces – are also powerful and so ruthless that they win, but in my own life as I've said before as a citizen I won't accept that. Fuck 'em! That's what I say . . .

Do you hope to incite indignation, the kind of indignation that you feel . . .?

I hope to incite an understanding of what is actually going on, and for that to be addressed. But personally, as I have said in the past one way or the other, I feel I have an absolute responsibility to resist.

Both Bush and Blair are facing forthcoming elections, they may be replaced . . .
I doubt it.

. . . but even if they were to be replaced, looking at the global economics that drive political motives, are we in a situation now where they are simply local manifestations of a prevailing ideology that we are going to have to live with for a long time? You mean market forces and multinationals, the whole damn thing, neo-liberalism? Well, I think you're right. It's appalling. One of the manifestations of that is what happens to so many people who come into – who are elected, like the extraordinary election in Brazil, this fellow Lula, whose party is called the Workers' Party, or something to that effect, and he was really a left-wing bloke and he was elected after many years but he is now, I gather, under such pressure from the forces you've just referred to that he's not doing what he said had to be done. In other words, the whole question of education, health and so on, public services. No, it's privatisation and on we go again – that's very, very depressing. It is indeed a stranglehold that is being exerted throughout the whole world.

You must feel like you're shouting in the wind sometimes . . . it's a labour of Sisyphus to rail against these forces. Do you not feel like giving up sometimes or just retiring, as it were, putting your feet up and let them get on with it . . .
No. I know exactly what you mean! Sometimes I can't pretend that I don't have moments of depression and exhaustion because it is . . . you are quite right it is a bit like shouting into the wind, but not entirely. You see there is always that chink. I was part of that great march in February 2003, you know, and

actually addressed in Hyde Park the public, a million people, which was quite astonishing.[1] It was amazing and what impressed me so much was I really thought there were going to be a lot of rattles waving and great disarray and hysteria, but these million people in Hyde Park and another million walking towards Hyde Park who couldn't get in were totally focused. Not just on me, I'm not just talking about me, but the whole damn thing – what it was about. They were still an extraordinary manifestation of public will and so that was a great kick.

You called on Tony Blair to resign, I remember, at the end of your speech.
I did.

Is it any comfort to you to know that he was having doubts at that time, that he was considering backing down? Or do we believe the fact that –
Oh I don't know what to believe about that man, I think he's a deluded idiot, that's what I think.

The last time we met, I remember, you opened the door and, when I asked how you were, you informed me that you had cancer. I've wondered since then what effect having to face something as final as that might have had. You once said that Petey's line 'Don't let them tell you what to do' sums up your life, but cancer was something that you couldn't fight against on your own, it was telling you what to do and you didn't have much choice in the matter . . .
That's right.

. . . until a surgeon came and released you from it. I know it's a cliché to ask this, but has that changed your perspective? Have you relaxed in terms of your political engagement or has it made you consider your artistic output in any different way? Or do you just simply go on as before now that you're free from it?
You know the only thing that I can say to that is that having

escaped death, by the skin of my teeth by the way, I'm much, much more aware of what mortality is and I know I didn't think about death before I had cancer. I mean, I thought about death but not from right in the pit of my stomach, you know, and now I realise that having escaped once I am not going to escape twice. All I'm saying is, all I can say is, that I'm more aware of death since the operation than I was ever before, and I sometimes look back on the operation, which was a grisly experience, the whole damn thing, and wonder in heaven's name how I survived it really. Quite apart from the surgeon's brilliance, the whole experience was so . . . it was like a nightmare really. So I've really been through the valley of the shadow, that's what it is. I am seventy-four next month and now I look ahead and realise in ten years I'll be eighty-four, if I'm going to make that, and you know that's the way it is. I have a very happy personal life and that means everything.

The Artist as a Young Man

From *The Pinter Review*

This abridged interview with B. S. Johnson, from 1968, concerns some of Pinter's first memories, as a child evacuated from London to escape the German bombing raids of the capital. It was first published in 1994 in The Pinter Review: Collected Essays 1993–1994, *pages 8–13. This interview differs slightly from the original published version. Where this occurs, here or in subsequent interviews, it is to ensure clarity in places where passages have been omitted, or to correct factual ambiguities, and has been done in consultation with Harold Pinter. Where small additions are made, the words are those of Harold Pinter.*

HP: I was evacuated to Cornwall very shortly after the war broke out to a place right on the coast about five miles from Mevagissey.

BJ: *Was this with your school?*
Yes, my elementary school in Hackney, which was a big school, but only twenty-four of us, not all from my class, of different ages, went to this castle. It was quite a castle, really; I don't know that it was all that old but it had great grounds and a lake and it was only a couple of hundred yards from the sea and it had a private beach. [...]

Did the break from your parents seem very painful at the time?
Not so much painful: I think I was completely bewildered by the whole thing. I was very lonely and very uncomfortable. I was nine at the time, and I didn't know why I was there and what it was all about. [...]

Did the experience make you more self-dependent, independent?
Not at all, only more cunning in being able to operate, having to cope with all those . . . monsters one didn't know, the other boys. They became monsters because of the qualities one didn't know of. The boys you knew at school were very different when you had to live with them as well, and cunning had to be used in every way in order to survive. [...]

Did you know anything of the theatre at this time?
No, I'd never even heard of it, didn't know it was there to visit. I don't think I was doing any writing then at all. No I didn't think of myself as a writer, or as anything at all, for that matter. It's as if the whole thing, then and now, is a kind of very resonant echo in which one moved: an echo chamber, the walls almost being of rubber. One rebounded in echoes all the time, echoes of the sea, echoes of London, the past, echoes of . . . colours, if you like, echoes of just *things* happening, like your tea and your dinner, whatever it was, and going to school.

Defining yourself in relation to these things?

Yes, but I say echo, rebound, because there was no fixed sense of being . . . of *being* . . . at all. [. . .]

Have you ever been back to any of the places to which you were evacuated?
I went down there eleven or twelve years after the war had finished. The castle still looked the same; the lake looked exactly the same; it was the same, a very beautiful, large lake. I didn't go into the castle; it looked as though no one was there. And, one or two of the villages around had the same quality of silence and waiting, and not a soul to be seen. And on this occasion, of course, I went into the nearest pub and opened the door and there was still no one there. It's that kind of silence I think that I grew to know, which meant something to me when I was a child there, and which still means something to me now. I think I can best describe it as a slightly sullen silence, a sullen quietude about the place. I'm talking about twenty-seven years ago, now. This is how I think I felt it then, how I gathered it then, how I would say it now. I may be quite wrong. I think it is important to bear in mind that one's memories are completely wrong, completely inaccurate, about everything, and this is particularly true of talking about an experience like evacuation. Certain images are selected and remain, but are those the most important ones because they come to the forefront of one's mind, are they the most significant or the most interesting? I was there about a year in this particular place, Cornwall, and my mind and body lived a year's life, and who knows what happened, what took place, in that time and in relation to those people and that environment? What does one remember in the best of circumstances, if any circumstances can be described as best, about one's childhood? Some people probably remember more than others. I don't remember very much, and what I do remember is quite painful, and there are probably many more painful recollections which I refuse to remember.

From the *New Yorker magazine*

The following is Pinter's reflection on his youth and his memories of the Second World War, given in discussion with a journalist from the New Yorker *magazine (25 February 1967).*

I lived in a brick house on Thistlethwaite Road, near Clapton Pond, which had a few ducks in it. It was a working-class area – some big, run-down Victorian houses, and soap factories with a terrible smell and a lot of railway yards. And shops. It had a lot of shops. But down the road a bit from our house there was a river, the Lea River, which is a tributary of the Thames, and if you go up the river two miles you find yourself in a marsh. And near a filthy canal as well. There is a terrible factory of some kind, with an enormous dirty chimney, that shoves things down to this canal. [. . .]. My father worked terribly hard. He worked a twelve-hour day, making clothes in his shop, but eventually lost his business and went to work for someone else. In the war, he was an air-raid warden. I was evacuated twice to the country. [. . .] On the second occasion, on my return to London, in 1944, I saw the first flying bomb. I was in the street, and I saw it come over. It looked like a tiny airplane. It was an innocent-looking thing. It just chugged along. And then I saw it come down. There were times when I would open our back door and find our garden in flames. Our house never burned, but we had to evacuate several times. Every time we evacuated, I took my cricket bat with me.

From the *Jewish Quarterly*

In an interview in 1991 with Barry Davis, a journalist with the Jewish Quarterly *(no. 144, Winter 91/92), Pinter recollected his youth in Hackney, and discussed his relationship with Judaism.*

HP: I was born into a very large extended family, though I was an only child. On both sides there were lots of aunts and uncles, cousins, grandmothers, not many grandfathers by that time. We had a marvellous standard of living, given that my father worked for it [. . .] twelve hours a day. My mother was a *baleboosta*, a great cook; she looked after us wonderfully.

BD: *You've written quite a lot about family. Anything to do with your own experience?*
The only real play, as far as I can remember, that I've written about the family is *The Homecoming*. It would be silly to deny that there are certain *seeds* within it that are very well known to Jewish people. I am talking about the stranger bringing back into the family a wife whom they've never met before; it's bound to be trouble, to put it mildly. I don't find it limited in any way to Jews. *The Homecoming*, as far as I am concerned, is not about Jewish family life, because I took it away from that. It's from my imagination. I've never known a situation like that in my own experience. It's not realism.

But the situation, the relationships are very real, particularly in Jewish families. You can recognise something in the characters' speech patterns, the attitudes and types.
Yes, but many people will understand the play who are not Jews; they also find it recognisable. Oddly enough, the main feature of my family as I experienced it over some years, from childhood to late teens, was actually affection. There was a lot of aggravation and the usual stuff that goes on in families, in any family, but there was a considerable body of shared affection and care about other people. There was always – and this isn't to do with being Jewish, but to do with certain class conventions – a great deal of criticism of the one who wasn't like everyone else, who didn't go along the normal path. For example, my cousin Sue, who was a pianist, was regarded as a bit fast; she married out of the religion very early on, and that was frowned upon. And it's certainly true that when I did – I married out of the religion – I was almost bound to do so, because I was a very unreligious person. I just wanted to marry that particular person at that time. I was quite an independent

young man and always had been and I was always aware of the prohibitions. I'm talking about the early 1950s, and I knew of certain friends of mine at the time, two boys from school, who were absolutely banned from their houses. In that classic phrase, they were regarded 'as dead'.

You didn't want to be burdened by the legacy? Was it just that you wanted to live your own life, or did you feel that there was something of the restrictive ghetto about Jewish life?
I felt that this kind of attitude was not fruitful; it wasn't positive because it was embattled, defensive and protective. I understood it, but it seemed to me that very little fruit could grow on that tree in terms of the world we actually lived in, and I still think that. [. . .]

Did you go to Talmud Torah?
Oh, sure I did. I did my bar mitzvah at Lea Bridge Road *shul*. I did that because I knew I had to do it and I had very little control over it. But after the age of thirteen, that was it.

There is also a very modern sense of how positive it is to be Jewish, to proclaim your ethnicity. You weren't really interested in self-proclamation for self-proclamation's sake?
That's right, but perhaps I can refer to the question in this way, with a true story. I think it's quite pertinent. I didn't go around proclaiming that I was a Jew, although I always was a Jew and remain so. I was in Sloane Square tube station about 1957. Or 1958. I popped into the bar there whilst waiting for a train, and there was a man, very well dressed in a suit, standing at the bar, talking to another man, who clearly wasn't with him. I heard him say something like: 'Hitler didn't go far enough. That's the big problem.' The other man didn't really answer and he just carried on. He wasn't drunk. He was very clear and insistent on giving this view and he went on talking about: the Jews. I was buying myself my half-pint and I said to myself, 'What am I going to do here, just what am I going to do? Am I

going to stand here, listening to, this, or am I going to take some kind of action?' Before I had a chance to come to any kind of conclusion, the other man, to whom he was talking, said: 'Well, that's a load of rubbish.' So I said, spontaneously, 'Yes, it's a load of balls.' I remember these words very, very clearly. I remember everything that happened. These images of the 1950s, in that bar in Sloane Square tube station have never left me. And this man turned to me and he said: 'I suppose you're a filthy Yid yourself.' So I said: 'You know, you really mustn't say that kind of thing to me or to anybody else. You've got to stop saying it.' He said: 'No, answer the question.' I said: 'Say that again.' He said: 'You want me to say that again?' He said it again: 'You're a filthy Yid.' Whereupon I hit him. I remember there was a moment when he went absolutely white. He just went back against the bar and then there was blood spurting out of his cheek. Whereupon, I turned away and he hit me. I suddenly went for him and it was really very ugly. I was actually pulled off him in the end. Then the police came and we all went to the station master's office where the man said that he had been assaulted. The other man said that I had been insulted. The police officer told the first man to go home: 'You go around saying things like that, you're bound to run into trouble.' Then the man came up to me and said, 'Are you a Jew?' and I said, 'Yes' and he said: 'Well, I can understand why you hit me, but why did you hit me so hard?'

But the answer to your question and why I am telling you this story – and why I hit him so hard – is because he wasn't just insulting me, he was insulting lots of other people. He was insulting people who were dead, people who had suffered. I hadn't expected this to happen when I walked into that bar, but it did happen and my fury with him came from some part of my being which I didn't consciously analyse or think about.

A reaction against what you see as the oppressing personality who wants to deny other people's suffering?
Absolutely.

In the final analysis you feel a Jew when you feel beleaguered?
It is to identify with Jewish suffering.

That's when the emotional side comes out, but the connection, if it's not in religion, is it in culture?
I think so, particularly in relation to the Holocaust. I find that the poetry, the art that has come out of the Holocaust, is very strong and leaves a very strong impression.

You've read quite a lot?
Paul Célan, Nelly Sachs, Primo Levi, Wiesel. The whole thing, and going back to the pogroms of the nineteenth century.

Is the literary response to oppression (and suffering) something you can relate to?
I certainly can relate to it. But there is another side to the question. We were talking about intermarriage earlier. When I was at Hackney Downs Grammar School, in the late 1940s, there were a lot of Jews and there were a lot of Gentiles. There was a tremendous cross-current of people. I cannot remember any problem arising at the school. Other problems arose in those days, when the fascist groups were around. Very few people remember that. We clashed with them after the war. They were rampant. But within the school it was different. There was a group of five of us, two non-Jews and three Jews. We used to hang around together and talk about this, that and the other, and the question didn't arise.

Really, then, the experience of Hackney Downs has informed your view of society. Had you gone to a school where there had been a greater degree of anti-Semitism, you might have become more aware of it and it might have had a more decisive influence on your sensibility.
I think that's very likely.

From *Theatre at Work*

Whilst Pinter's experience at school was of a tolerant micro-society, the East End after the war was not the most politically stable of environments, and he remembers the threat to Jews that was present in certain areas of his neighbourhood. Here, in an excerpt from a 1966 interview with Lawrence M. Bensky (Charles Marowitz and Simon Trussler (eds.), Theatre at Work, London: Methuen, 1967, pp. 96–109), he recalls the verbal manoeuvres he might employ to escape serious incident, and the tale is reminiscent of the evasive and tactical use of language in many of his works.

Everyone encounters violence in some way or other. It so happens I did encounter it in quite an extreme form after the war in the East End, when the Fascists were coming back to life in England. I got into quite a few fights down there. If you looked remotely like a Jew you might be in trouble. Also, I went to a Jewish club, by an old railway arch, and there were quite a lot of people often waiting with broken milk bottles in a particular alley we used to walk through. There were one or two ways of getting out of it – one was a purely physical way, of course, but you couldn't do anything about the milk bottles – *we* didn't have any milk bottles. The best way was to talk to them, you know, sort of 'Are you all right?' 'Yes, I'm all right.' 'Well, that's all right then, isn't it?' And all the time keep walking towards the lights of the main road.

Another thing: we were often taken for Communists. If you went by, or happened to be passing, a Fascists' street meeting and looked in any way antagonistic – this was in Ridley Road market, near Dalston Junction – they'd interpret your very being, especially if you had books under your arms, as evidence of your being a Communist. There was a good deal of violence there, in those days.

Early Writing and Becoming a Playwright

In 1990 Pinter's first and only novel, The Dwarfs, *was published by Faber and Faber. The work had been written originally in the early 1950s, before his first plays. To coincide with its publication, Pinter spoke to David Blow in an interview for Waterstone's winter 'new books' catalogue.*

Waterstone's

I wrote a great deal of poetry, and short prose pieces, from the age of, I should think, twelve, and then throughout my teens. I think I started writing *The Dwarfs* in 1952, when I was twenty-two. I suppose the novel is, in many respects, autobiographical, as young men's novels notoriously are. Mine is no exception. The novel is based on a story I felt I had to tell myself, in prose. I had to write about friendships and about various kinds of betrayals. [. . .] I didn't plan anything for myself. I had no idea at that time that I was going to be, in any sense, a professional writer. I was an actor who wrote in his spare time. The main bulk of my writing had been poetry, which I had published in poetry magazines of the time – and you'd get about five bob a poem at the outside – so it never occurred to me that there was any kind of profession in this act of writing. I didn't look ahead and see myself as a professional writer. And it didn't occur to me that anyone would want to publish it. I couldn't conceive it in those terms.

From *Theatre at Work* and the *Sunday Times*

The Birthday Party *was Pinter's first play to appear on a London stage. It was met harshly by the critics and, failing to draw audiences, was taken off after six days. Speaking to Lawrence Bensky in 1966 (see above, p. 100), Pinter recalled the disappointment. Later, he confided to Kate Saunders (*Sunday Times, *9 July 1995) that he might have chosen not to persevere.*

LB: *What was the effect of this adversity on you? How was it different from unfavourable criticism of your acting, which surely you'd had before?*

HP: It was a great shock, and I was very depressed for about forty-eight hours. It was my wife, actually, who said just that to me, 'You've had bad notices before,' etc. There's no question but that her common sense and practical help got me over that depression, and I've never felt anything like that again.

(*to Kate Saunders*) I nearly gave up the whole thing. I was thinking of forgetting the stage altogether. There was quite a collision between me and the critics. I would hardly say 'and the audience', because there wasn't an audience – in London anyway. It is sometimes forgotten that before London, it went to Oxford and Cambridge, and got totally different reactions – pretty enthusiastic. Perhaps because the audience was younger.

From *The Times*

In 1959 Pinter saw a collection of his revue sketches performed in two London revue shows. This event occasioned his first ever interview ('Avant-Garde Playwright and Intimate Revue', The Times, 16 November 1959). Speaking here about the circumstances of writing for revue, he reveals more about how his writing was very much based upon real-life situations and dilemmas, and gives a further example of how the avoidance of communication fascinated him as a writer.

Disley Jones, of the Lyric, Hammersmith, had worked with me before on *The Birthday Party*, and when he became involved with planning a new revue for the theatre he asked me if I would care to contribute. I'd never done anything like that before, but I thought about it, and then wrote 'The Black and White', which, along with 'The Last to Go', is my favourite among my sketches. Actually, I had had the two old tramp-women in the all-night café in my mind for years, ever since I used to live in the East End and spend quite a lot of time wandering round the deserted town at night waiting for the all-night buses back home. In those cafés you find these curious night-wanderers who don't seem to be going anywhere or doing anything, though obviously they must have some interest in the future, even if it only keeps them going from moment to moment – till the next bus goes by, or the last paper is sold. They seemed to me extraordinarily solitary, unable to communicate with each other or anyone else, and often not even wanting to: the whole point of 'The Last to Go', as far as it has a point in the obvious sense, is that the newspaperman and the stallkeeper talk to each other but they never communicate at all, a situation which is both funny and tragic, like any misunderstanding. I had never done anything with the tramp-women because they fitted naturally into a complete play which just happened to be four minutes long: it couldn't be expanded or worked into a more general framework, but on the other hand what can you do with a one-act play which is only four minutes? The only thing, of course, though I would never have considered it a possibility unprompted, is to put into a revue as a sketch. [. . .] I regard myself very much as an amateur revue-writer, a dramatist some of whose work just happens to fit into the framework of a revue. As far as I am concerned there is no real difference between my sketches and my plays. In both I am interested primarily in people: I want to present living people to the audience, worthy of their interest basically because they are, they exist, not because of any moral the author may draw from them. In many recent British plays I find myself put off by the spectre of the author looming above his characters, telling the audience at every stage just what they are to think about them. I want as far as possible to leave comment to the audience; let them decide whether the characters and situations are funny or sad. Take the woman in 'Request Stop'. We've all met them, the people who talk to themselves in crowds, enlarging upon a slight or imagined grievance, making fragmentary attempts to communicate and slipping back into muttered protest. Is the reaction of other people to them, as they edge uneasily away, funny or tragic? Obviously it can be both, but I think my job as a dramatist is simply to present the situation, shaped in dramatic terms, and let the audience decide for themselves.

BBC Radio

Speaking to the influential critic Kenneth Tynan on the BBC's Home Service on 28 October 1960, Pinter offered the first survey of his then three-year career as a playwright.

KT: *Were you writing plays for your own amusement or with an idea of having them staged, and if so what kind of plays did you start out attempting to write? Had you any models in mind, or did you just write off the top of your head?*
HP: It never occurred to me that the plays I was writing would be staged. It was just simply a matter that had no relevance to my writing of them. Obviously one writes to be performed, but at that time when I started to write plays I wrote purely, as you say, for my own amusement or my own interest, and my own excitement. Explorations of words and characters. It was absolutely out of the question that they should be performed. I didn't know how people did get plays performed. I wasn't considering that aspect of it.

How did you get yours performed?
Well the first play I wrote was called *The Room*, which I happened to give a pal of mine at Bristol University, which was the only drama department in the country, and he wrote to me. I told him the idea actually and he wrote and said, 'Well what about this idea?' And I said . . . I wrote back and said, 'Impossible, I haven't written it, haven't even thought about it and it would take me at least six months to write.' And he said,

'If we are going to get this done at the university, we'll have to
have it very, very shortly.' And in fact in a week. So I wrote
back and told him to forget about the whole thing. And then I
sat down and wrote it in four days. I don't quite know how
that happened, but it did. And I sent it to him and he did it
there, and things began to proceed from there.

After that what happened? What was the next play?
Well, when this play was done I went down to see it at Bristol
at the university and it seemed to get a very definite positive
response from the audience – university audience, though. And
I started thinking in terms of drama. As I say, I had been writing for a long time before that, not drama, and I started to
write *The Birthday Party*. I nearly gave it up very early on
because I felt the characters were so horrible. But I didn't and I
finished it. And then I wrote another one. I wrote *The Dumb
Waiter*. This was all in 1957. By that time I was enjoying writing plays very much.

And acting or not at this stage? Had you given up acting?
I was acting all the time. I was rehearsing in the morning and
playing at night. This was in weekly rep in Torquay and
Bournemouth.

How could you write? I don't understand.
I just did. I happened – I don't quite know how it happened – I
just happened to have, I think, a sense of balance. I was able to
separate my life. I was able to act and smile at everyone in the
morning and carry on rehearsing, and act in the evening and
get down with considerable enjoyment in the afternoon to
write. This wasn't every afternoon. It wasn't a ritual, it wasn't
a regular thing at all. [. . .]

*Now you've become what's rather unpleasantly known as a
fashionable playwright, and critics are beginning to talk about
something called a Pinter play, a Pinter-type play. Now how do*

you react to that sort of criticism?
I react very strongly. I think it's very misguided and most unfortunate, and also has the most depressing effect on the playwright concerned. When I began to write these, three years ago in 1957, life was very simple. I enjoyed writing and acting. Walking about. Nobody knew me, except the regular patrons of the theatre in Torquay let us say, and I wrote, I think I can say, completely naturally. It didn't occur to me that there was anything uncommon or out of the norm in what I was writing.

An Established Writer

Pinter's plays had met with a good deal of critical attention following the success of The Caretaker, *and his work for radio, television, revue and stage had made him a significant name on the London stage by 1960. There is nothing disingenuous about his claim, above, that it hadn't occurred to him 'that there was anything uncommon or out of the norm' in what he was writing, and in numerous contemporaneous interviews he seems genuinely baffled by the critical reaction to the 'mystery' of his works. This led to a certain defensiveness in interview, and an insistence on the 'everydayness' of his language, as exemplified by his words to Philip Purser (News Chronicle, 28 July 1960).*

From the *News Chronicle*

My situations and characters aren't always explicit. Well, I don't see life as being very explicit. Our personalities are too complex to be cut and dried and labelled. Then the dialogue – I don't see myself doing anything uncommon. It's not Pinter. It's people. I don't mine it, like gold. It's there all the time. You only need to listen to people, listen to *yourself*. I catch my wife saying to me at breakfast, 'Do you like the cornflakes? Are they nice this morning ?' and I say, 'Yes, they're very nice. How's the tea? Is that nice?' – because I've made the tea – and she says

'Yes, the tea's very nice,' and on we go. Critics talk a lot about the problem of non-communication amongst my characters, as if they can't understand each other. It's not really that. I'm interested in people who have *chosen* not to communicate, not to understand each other. Incidentally, there's nothing symbolic about anything I write. If a character doesn't immediately declare himself, some people always want to put him on a shelf as a symbol.

BBC Radio

Returning to the BBC Home Service interview with Kenneth Tynan (see above, p. 104), Pinter adds to his defence against writing about the failure of communication.

I feel rather than an inability to communicate – there is a deliberate evasion of communication. Communication itself between people is so frightening that rather than do that there is a continual cross-talk between people, a continual talking about other things, rather than what is at the root of their relationship. What is on the table between them. I think that one particular case I might quote is a one-act play of mine called *The Dumb Waiter*, and it's quite clear there, in which two men, two killers, are waiting in a room at the behest of their boss, they are waiting for a man to appear who is to be their victim. And certain strange things begin to happen. An envelope containing matches comes under the door. They are frightened of the . . . of what is upstairs. They are not quite certain of their boss, what is happening, of what they are required to do. And they launch into quite a vigorous, a very vigorous argument about whether one lights the kettle or one lights the gas. [. . .] But they deliberately go into this argument as an evasion of the issue. The issue being that they are both in fact frightened of their condition, of their situation, of their state.

From *The Times*

Pinter was often compared to Beckett and Ionesco by critics who sought to categorise the dramatic world he was offering his audiences. In the Times *interview quoted above (see p. 102) he was happy to address this.*

Speaking for myself, I have been deeply impressed by Beckett's work, presumably because his qualities happen to be those I most admire in drama. He seems to me a much more solid and serious writer than Ionesco, and I don't really see any close similarity between Ionesco's plays and my own (or, for that matter, Simpson's and Mortimer's). In any case, when I wrote *The Birthday Party* I had only seen one of his plays: *The New Tenant*.

From *New Theatre* magazine

*Comparing his output with other contemporary writers would also often involve contrasting his ambition with the more socially engaged writers of the Royal Court scene. Pinter engaged with this type of categorisation frequently, as in this example, speaking to Harry Thompson (*New Theatre *magazine, vol. 2, no. 2, January 1961).*

HT: *Have you ever consciously looked to any other playwright for the sources of your work?*
HP: No, I certainly have not, but there is no question that Beckett is a writer whom I admire very much and have admired for a number of years. If Beckett's influence shows in my work that's all right with me. You don't write in a vacuum; you're bound to absorb and digest other writing; and I admire Beckett's work so much that something of its texture might appear in my own. I myself have no idea whether this is so, but if it is, then I am grateful for it. However, I do think that I have succeeded in expressing something of myself.

*One accepts that you reflect certain aspects of the time more
closely than any other playwright, especially the hidden fears
that seem to affect so many of us today. Are you yourself aware
of such fears? Did you begin to write out of a sense of contemporary strains and tensions, or does your style come to you
objectively, by observation?*

The last thing I would attempt to do is to disassociate myself
from my work, to suggest that I am merely making a study of
observable reality, from a distance. I am objective in my selection
and arrangement, but, as far as I'm concerned, my characters
and I inhabit the same world. The only difference between them
and me is that they don't arrange and select. I do the donkey
work. But they carry the can. I think we're all in the same boat.

*Among playwrights, Arnold Wesker has made the problem of
political conscience very much his own. Do politics interest
you?*

I find most political thinking and terminology suspect, defi-
cient. It seems to me a dramatist is entitled to portray the political confusion in a play if his characters naturally act in a
political context, that is, if the political influences operating on
them are more significant than any other consideration. But I
object to the stage being used as a substitute for the soap box,
where the author desires to make a direct statement at all costs,
and forces his characters into fixed and artificial postures in
order to achieve this. This is hardly fair on the characters. I
don't care for the didactic or moralistic theatre. In England I
find this theatre, on the whole, sentimental and unconvincing.

*Would you like to say anything about Arnold Wesker's
approach to the unions?*

To me, this seems to be happening on the other side of the
moon. I mean, I can't fix the matter as having any grave or significant import for me. I suppose it's a laudable attitude from
certain points of view, but these points of view simply do not
interest me.

You say that your plays spring essentially out of a situation. Would you say your creative imagination was more visual than verbal? Have you any idea of the mental process that goes on when you are writing?

I see things pretty clearly, certainly, but I am continually surprised by what I see and by what suddenly happens in the play while I am writing it. I do not know, however, that the visual is more important to me than the verbal, because I am pretty well obsessed with words when they get going. It is a matter of tying the words to the image of the character standing on the stage. The two things go very closely together.

There is this question of formula. When success comes to a writer in the theatre, he tends towards making a formula to which he works. Do you think that you are conscious of a formula or of aiming at a formula?

No. I am aware that I was expected in some quarters to elaborate on my own formula. I did not see it as such, however, until I was told it was becoming one. Later I realised that in one short television play of mine there were characteristics that implied I was slipping into a formula. It so happened this was the worst thing I've written. The words and ideas had become automatic, redundant. That was the red light for me and I don't feel I shall fall into that pit again. I trust that when I next fail it will be for different reasons. My basic approach to my work, anyway, is strongly opposed to such mechanism.

In the above interview, Pinter is talking of his television play Night School, *which he once considered omitting from his published collected works. His consciousness, as articulated above, of the danger of slipping into a comfortable style rather than progressing as an artist must have been exacerbated by the efforts of critics to define his achievement. In one of his numerous interviews with New York critic Mel Gussow he once stated: 'I also tend to get quite exhausted about being this Harold Pinter fellow. This is quite apart from being me. Harold Pinter sits on my damn back' (MG, pp. 24–5). Whilst, of course, spoken with some irony, there is more than a hint of genuine frustration in such remarks. The summation of his style and achievement in the word 'Pinteresque', which entered the* Oxford English Dictionary *in the 1960s, caused not a little irritation, as evinced by his words in the following paragraph here to Kate Saunders, followed by a final return to the Kenneth Tynan interview (see above, pp. 101 and 104).*

From the *Sunday Times* and BBC Radio

(*to Saunders*): Oh this dread word Pinteresque. It makes people reach for their guns. Or behave as if they were going to church. It's highly regrettable. But when the audience is actually there, I am always gratified when I hear laughter. There is a great deal of humour in my plays.

KT: *If you hear somebody say now, 'Oh that's a very Harold Pinter kind of situation,' what do you think they mean?*
HP: It puts me in a very false position. I think I can say that. For witness, there was an article a few weeks ago in a Sunday paper in which somebody said a particular speech of mine in *The Caretaker* did not belong in a Pinter play. Well, I find that a gross statement to make. What it comes down to, doesn't it, is that this particular gentleman – I don't think he is alone – is telling me what kind of plays to write. He's saying that I should conform to their idea of what a Pinter play is. Which means that I am not, apparently, allowed to develop, to explore other angles, other ways of writing. One can't be expected to stay where you are, where you have been, you know, all the time.

But you've been described as having invented a new sort of comedy, the 'comedy of menace' or the 'comedy of dread'. Now do you agree with that?
Well I don't know where . . . this question of invention I think is . . . must be wrong. I don't think one really . . . I don't think

any of us is new. Anything one writes can't be new. You've just got to find your own individual way of saying it, what has been said and must have been said for centuries. There is comedy in life and there is menace in life, and I think the two things certainly go together. To a certain extent, but there comes a point where things cease to be funny.

Pinter was not averse to engaging with his audiences directly. Two letters he wrote in response to enquiries are particularly revealing. The second exchange here, concerning The Caretaker, *was published on the letters pages of the* Sunday Times *(14 August 1960) and in it Pinter responds seriously to his use of comedy in the play, as hinted at in the final words of the interview above. In the first exchange here he is more flippant, but beneath the flippancy he is emphasising his fundamental interest as a writer in how 'a character on the stage who can present no convincing argument or information as to his past experience, his present behaviour or his aspirations, nor give a comprehensive analysis of his motives is as legitimate and worthy of attention as one who, alarmingly, can do all these things' (VV, p. 15). Written following the US première of* The Birthday Party, *this exchange was reported in the* Daily Mail *(28 November 1967) under the title 'Pinter unperturbed'.*

From the *Daily Mail*

Dear Sir,
    I would be obliged if you would kindly explain the meaning to me of your play *The Birthday Party*. These are the points that I do not understand: 1. Who are the two men? 2. Where did Stanley come from? 3. Were they all supposed to be normal? You will appreciate that without the answers to my questions I cannot fully understand your play.

Dear Madam,
    I would be obliged if you would kindly explain to me the

meaning of your letter. These are the points I do not understand: 1. Who are you? 2. Where do you come from? 3. Are
you supposed to be normal? You will appreciate that without the answers to my questions I cannot fully understand
your letter.

From the *Sunday Times*

Dear Mr Pinter,

Those of us who are apt to lag in the dusty rear of new
movements in the arts, and in consequence missed seeing
The Birthday Party, *The Room* and *The Dumb Waiter*, now
have the opportunity, as you are aware, of acquiring a book
containing these three plays. It is just what a lot of us old
slowcoaches need to help us make up our minds about your
work.

Of course, we haven't been caught napping with *The
Caretaker*. I for one set off doggedly for the Duchess
Theatre last week, and I will go so far as to admit that I
found it a strangely menacing and disturbing evening. It
was also a highly puzzling evening; and here I refer not to
the play but to the behaviour of the audience.

On the evening I was present a large majority had no
doubt at all that your special contribution to the theatre is
to take a heart-breaking theme and treat it farcically. Gales
of happy, persistent, and, it seemed to me, totally indiscriminate laughter greeted a play which I take to be, for all its
funny moments, a tragic reading of life.

May I ask this question – are you yourself happy with
this atmosphere of rollicking good fun?
Leonard Russell

Dear Mr Russell,

Your question is an easy one to answer.

Certainly I laughed myself while writing *The Caretaker*,
but not all the time, not 'indiscriminately'. An element of

the absurd is, I think, one of the features of the play, but at the same time I did not intend it to be merely a laughable farce. If there hadn't been other issues at stake the play would not have been written.

Audience reaction can't be regulated, and no one would want it to be, nor is it easy to analyse. But where the comic and the tragic (for want of a better word) are closely interwoven, certain members of an audience will always give emphasis to the comic as opposed to the other, for by doing so they rationalise the other out of existence.

On most evenings at the Duchess there is a sensible balance of laughter and silence. Where, though, this indiscriminate mirth is found, I feel it represents a cheerful patronage of the characters on the part of the merrymakers, and thus participation is avoided. This laughter is in fact a smokescreen, a refusal to accept what is happening as recognisable (which I think it is) and instead to view the actors (a) as actors always and not as characters and (b) as chimpanzees.

From this kind of uneasy jollification I must, of course, disassociate myself, though I do think you were unfortunate in your choice of evening. As far as I'm concerned *The Caretaker* is funny, up to a point. Beyond that point it ceases to be funny, and it was because of that point that I wrote it.

With Patrick Marber

Pinter was happy to reminisce about the first production of The Caretaker *to Patrick Marber in September 2000. Their conversation, which is presented in abridged form here, was published in the programme for Marber's fortieth-anniversary revival of the play at London's Comedy Theatre in the winter of 2000–1*

PM: *Am I right in thinking you wrote the play in the autumn of 1959?*
HP: Yes. It took about three months to write, I think it was

about that . . . September, October, November. [. . .]

Did you have a room that you could go away and write in?
No.

So you were writing with family around you at the time?
We lived in two rooms in Chiswick High Road . . . a flat . . .
two rooms, a kitchen and a bathroom. A kitchen/bathroom
rather – the bath was in the kitchen. [. . .] My son was born in
January '58 so he was then about eighteen months . . . and he
was crawling about under my feet at the time . . . I was writing
on a card table on an old Olympia portable.

*Were you writing in the day or trying to get some peace at night
to write?*
Oh I think I wrote both day and night.

Who was the first person to read the play, apart from yourself?
My wife read it and she was very upset by it because it was
inspired by the man who lived in the house . . . in a way . . . and
by a visitor or guest who he'd invited in for a few weeks . . . so
there was a concrete, if you like, stimulus there. The man who
lived in the house was a very retiring, reticent man and he did
tell me once that he'd been in a mental hospital when he was
young and he was badly treated . . . that it was an injustice, you
know . . . and then he invited this old man into the house, it
was a homeless old man whom I bumped into on the stairs a
few times. The actual inspiration though for me to write the
play was an image when I looked into the room in which they
both lived, they both inhabited one room.

Above you?
No below . . . on the landing, just off the landing . . . and I once
passed the room and looked in, the door was open, half-open
and I saw the landlord as I call him looking out of the window,
just standing looking out of the window onto his garden and

the old man was rooting about in a bag and there was silence
. . . there was nothing . . . they were totally separate . . . the only
sound was the rooting about in this bag . . . he just carried on
rooting . . . I don't know what he was looking for and I never
found out . . . but the point about my wife was that she thought
it was wrong of me to write about this man . . . to write in any
way about this man. But of course I wasn't literally writing
about the man, I knew very little about him when it came down
to it and the same thing applies to the tramp. The play is a
work of fiction.

But the image and the people triggered the play.
It triggered the play, yes. [. . .]

*So, at what point did it occur to you that Donald Pleasence
seemed like a good idea?*
Well he came up and he seemed to be right on the ball . . . on
the first day of rehearsal, I'm jumping the gun here a bit, but let
me just say that Peter Woodthorpe was Estragon in Peter Hall's
production of *Godot* and Donald McWhinnie was extremely
keen on him for Aston and I also liked his Estragon very much,
he was very good, and then Alan Bates was a really up-and-
coming chap so he just walked into it really. [. . .] The week
we opened at the Arts was really interesting, because we
opened the same week as a production of *Rhinoceros* by
Ionesco at the Royal Court.

With Olivier?
With Olivier in it and directed by Orson Welles and all the
money was on that, naturally, it was an extraordinarily glam-
orous set-up altogether. [. . .]

*Was there a fear within the production at the time 'Oh we're
going to get lost as all the reviews are going to be about the
Ionesco and we're just going to be some little . . .'*
Absolutely.

. . . but in fact the original reviews were good . . .
They were terrific.

Was it a good first night?
Yes it was great.

They did the play well?
They were all very, very nervous . . . and they did it very, very
fast . . . I'm not saying, I don't think Aston did it . . . It's the
other two I'm talking about . . . Aston had to take a bit of time,
but Davies and Mick went like a bomb . . . and it certainly was
a great night . . .

Where were you sitting? Were you in the stalls?
I was in the Dress Circle [. . .] I don't want to be trapped in the
stalls – I much prefer a gangway seat . . . the funny thing about
the whole thing was that the next day – I mean I was still living
in Chiswick and the next evening I got on the tube at Chiswick
High Road to go up to Leicester Square to see everybody . . .
and I was standing – it was a crowded train and a woman
turned to her chap and said, 'Did you read that review this
morning of this play at the Arts?' and he said, 'Yes I did, I did
read it – I think we should see it, don't you?' and she said, 'Yes
I'm really interested to see it,' and I said to them – I was standing right by them – and I said, 'I wrote it,' and they said, 'You
didn't, did you?' and I said, 'Well I did, yes,' and they said,
'Well that's terrific and we're coming to see it etc. etc. etc. . . .'
of course I remind you that I was then twenty-nine – which I
regard as quite young . . .

It is, I regard it as young.
I haven't ever said anything like that to anyone on a tube train
since.

Well, no, I didn't think it was your style in general.
No.

But it indicates the level of excitement you felt at the time.
Yes you're absolutely right.

So the play transferred from the Arts to the Duchess and then you, I believe, played Mick for four weeks . . . Was that an enjoyable thing to do?
Alan Bates wanted to do a film – *Whistle Down the Wind* – so I took over for four weeks and the critics came [. . .]. They had no idea, to put it baldly, that I was actually an actor, but I felt perfectly all right [. . .] I knew the lines . . . and I enjoyed playing Mick . . . it's not a bad part! [. . .] I was aware that the critics, and possibly a great deal of the audience, thought that I was going to fall on my arse – that I was an impostor, that I was just the bloody author, indulging myself . . .

And how were the reviews of your performance?
Quite good . . . But I was aware that it was a contest . . . as you might know, I always think it's a bit of a contest, in other words between plays and the audience and critics, the whole thing . . . a bit of a battleground really, one way or the other . . .

Have you seen any shocking foreign productions over the years?
Well the first one I ever saw was . . . no wait a minute, the first one – I saw a marvellous production in Holland, in Amsterdam . . . about a year after this one – which was bloody good – a fellow call Gus Hermus played the Caretaker and actually oddly enough he looks a bit like Michael Gambon – he was the only other big Caretaker that I've ever come across . . . he was great, but then I went to see the German première in Düsseldorf, that was this notorious occasion – I don't know if you know about it – well it was a very odd production, very formal and heavy and on the first night – there was an actor playing the Caretaker who just stood in the centre of the stage throughout the whole evening. He was a bulky thickset man, I can't remember his name, but there he was declaring the Caretaker

in very guttural terms and at the end of the evening – which was pretty lugubrious I have to say – I had to go onto the stage – you know it's the continental fashion.

You have to take the bow, don't you?
And immediately I stepped on with the actors the boos started and they continued, but the actors and director and so on were extremely obstinate and insisted on going back and back for more bows after more bows to more boos after more boos and finally I had to take my single call in which the boos were magnified slightly, but this time I was feeling quite chirpy about the whole thing and I smiled and said 'Thank you, thank you, thank you' . . . and we actually took thirty-four curtain calls to boos. [. . .]

It's odd bowing when you feel that your work's been – how shall I put it? – 'murdered'.
Well in this case, you can imagine how bizarre it was for me as I thought it was a really lousy production, but I then saw a very good production in Paris with Roger Blin – he directed it and played Davies – that didn't go very well either. That was the first time I met Beckett – he saw it – he was a great friend of Roger Blin. [. . .]

And how do you feel about the play now? It's an old pal, I should imagine?
Well it still makes me laugh.

From the *Saturday Review*

Pinter spent several months in New York in 1967 during preparations for the Broadway production of The Homecoming. *In something of a throwback to the kinds of questioning he had endured in the UK at the onset of the decade, the American critics saw symbolism and abstraction as his key writing strategies, and in this interview about the play (*Saturday Review, *8 April*

1967) he negotiates that line of enquiry patiently.

SR: *What is* The Homecoming *about?*
HP: It's about love and lack of love. The people are harsh and cruel, to be sure. Still, they aren't acting arbitrarily but for very deep seated-reasons. [. . .]

Do the members of the family stand for or represent universal forces in modern society and are they therefore distorted from reality?
I was only concerned with this particular family. I didn't relate them to any other possible or concrete family. I certainly didn't distort them in any way from any other kind of reality. I was only concerned with their reality. The whole play happens on a quite realistic level from my point of view. [. . .]

Does this family represent a disintegration into pure evil?
There's no question that the family does behave very calculatedly and pretty horribly to each other and to the returning son. But they do it out of the texture of their lives and for other reasons which are not evil, but slightly desperate. [. . .]

Is it realistic for a husband to stand by while his wife rolls on the couch with another man?
Look! What would happen if he interfered? He would have had a messy fight on his hands, wouldn't he? And this particular man would avoid that. As for rolling on the couch, there are thousands of women in this very country who at this very moment are rolling off couches with their brothers, or cousins, or their next-door neighbours. The most respectable women do this. It's a splendid activity. It's a little curious, certainly, when your husband is looking on, but it doesn't mean you're a harlot.

Is it credible that the wife stay behind and become a prostitute?
If this had been a happy marriage it wouldn't have happened. But she didn't want to go back to America with her husband,

so what the hell's she going to do? She's misinterpreted deliberately and used by this family. But eventually she comes back at
them with a whip. She says, 'If you want to play this game I can
play it as well as you.' She does not become a harlot. At the end
of the play she's in possession of a certain kind of freedom. She
can do what she wants and it is not at all certain she will go off
to Greek Street. But even if she did, she would not be a harlot
in her own mind.

*Is there, then, a danger in accepting everything the characters
say and do as what the playwright intends and means?*
Finding the characters and letting them speak for themselves is
the great excitement of writing. I would never distort the consistency of a character by a kind of hoarding in which I say, 'By
the way, these characters are doing this because of such and
such.' I find out what they are doing, allow them to do it, and
keep out of it. Then it is up to the audience to decide how much
is truth and how much is lies.

Writing for the Stage

*The above interview closed with Pinter speaking of a kind of
distance between him and his imagined characters. He has consistently maintained that his plays are written from unconscious impulses, often inspired by real-world events or images
that he has witnessed, but that, in writing, he is not always sure
where the plays might end once he has begun to compile them.
The most interesting thoughts he has offered on this process
are in pieces such as 'Writing for the Theatre' and 'On the
Birthday Party II' and in an interview with Mireia Aragay (all
available in* Various Voices*). In the first paragraph below, to Sue
Summers of the* Independent *(18 October 1988) he clarifies his
approach to writing. This is followed by a final excerpt from
the Bensky interview (see above, p. 100) which offers interesting reflection on his relationship with his plays in writing and
staging them.*

From the *Independent*

The great thing about writing plays is you don't think. I'm putting it quite badly, but the fact is in order to write what's called imaginative literature, you have to let something go, you have to release the imagination. If you think too much you simply are not going to do that, you are going to inhibit the imagination. There is a tension between being creative – i.e. not thinking – and living your life as a citizen in which you are obliged to think. It can sometimes be exhausting.

From *Theatre at Work*

LB: *Do you get impatient with the limitations of writing for the theatre?*
HP: No. It's quite different; the theatre's much the most difficult kind of writing for me, the most naked kind, you're so entirely restricted. I've done some film work, but for some reason or other I haven't found it very easy to satisfy myself on an original idea for a film. *Tea Party*, which I did for television, is actually a film, cinematic, I wrote it like that. Television and films are simpler than the theatre – if you get tired of a scene you just drop it and go on to another one. (I'm exaggerating, of course.) What *is* so different about the stage is that you're just *there*, stuck – there are your characters stuck on the stage, you've got to live with them and deal with them. I'm not a very inventive writer in the sense of using the technical devices other playwrights do – look at Brecht! I can't use the stage the way he does, I just haven't got that kind of imagination, so I find myself stuck with these characters who are either sitting or standing, and they've either got to walk out of a door, or come in through a door, and that's about all they can do.

And talk.
Or keep silent. [. . .]

Since you are an actor, do actors in your plays ever approach

you and ask you to change lines or aspects of their roles?
Sometimes, quite rarely, lines are changed when we're working together. I don't at all believe in the anarchic theatre of so-called 'creative' actors – the actors can do that in someone else's plays. Which wouldn't, however, at all affect their ability to play in mine. [. . .]

Is there more than one way to direct your plays successfully?
Oh, yes, but always around the same central truth of the play – if that's distorted, then it's bad. The main difference in interpretation comes from the actors. The director can certainly be responsible for a disaster, too – the first performance of *The Caretaker* in Germany was heavy and posturised. There's no blueprint for any play, and several have been done entirely successfully without me helping in the production at all.

When you are working on one, what is the key to a good writer-director relationship?
What is absolutely essential is avoiding all defensiveness between author and director. It's a matter of mutual trust and openness. If that isn't there, it's just a waste of time.

Peter Hall, who has directed many of your plays, says that they rely on precise verbal form and rhythm, and when you write 'pause' it means something other than 'silence', and three dots are different from a full stop. Is his sensitivity to this kind of writing responsible for your working well together?
Yes, it is, very much so. I do pay great attention to those points you just mentioned. Hall once held a 'dot and pause' rehearsal for the actors in *The Homecoming*. Although it sounds bloody pretentious it was apparently very valuable.

Do you outline plays before you start to write them?
Not at all. I don't know what kind of characters my plays will have until they . . . well, until they *are*. Until they indicate to me what they are. I don't conceptualise in any way. Once I've got

the clues I follow them – that's my job, really, to follow the clues.

What do you mean by clues? Can you remember how one of your plays developed in your mind – or was it a line-by-line progression?
Of course I can't remember exactly how a given play developed in my mind. I think what happens is that I write in a very high state of excitement and frustration. I follow what I see on the paper in front of me – one sentence after another. That doesn't mean I don't have a dim, possible overall idea – the image that starts off doesn't just engender what happens – immediately, it engenders the possibility of an overall happening, which carries me through. I've got an idea of what *might* happen – sometimes I'm absolutely right, but on many occasions I've been proved wrong by what does actually happen. Sometimes I'm going along and I find myself writing 'C. comes in' when I didn't know that he was going to come in; he *had* to come in at that point, that's all.

In The Homecoming, *Sam, a character who hasn't been very active for a while, suddenly cries out and collapses several minutes from the end of the play. Is this an example of what you mean? It seems abrupt.*
It suddenly seemed to me right. It just came. I knew he'd have to say something at one time in this section and this is what happened, that's what he said.

Might characters therefore develop beyond your control of them, changing your idea – even if it's a vague idea – of what the play's about?
I'm ultimately holding the ropes, so they never get too far away.

Do you sense when you should bring down the curtain, or do you work the text consciously towards a moment you've already determined?

124

It's pure instinct. The curtain comes down when the rhythm seems right – when the action calls for a finish. I'm very fond of curtain lines, of doing them properly.

Do you feel your plays are therefore structurally successful? That you're able to communicate this instinct for rhythm to the play?
No, not really, and that's my main concern, to get the structure right. I always write three drafts, but you have to leave it eventually. There comes a point when you say that's it, I can't do anything more. The only play which gets remotely near to a structural entity which satisfies me is *The Homecoming. The Birthday Party* and *The Caretaker* have too much writing . . . I want to iron it down, eliminate things. Too many words irritate me sometimes, but I can't help them, they just seem to come out – out of the fellow's mouth. I don't really examine my works too much, but I'm aware that quite often in what I write, some fellow at some point says an awful lot.

Screenplays and Film Work

Harold Pinter had been a keen cinema-goer since his youth, and has, of course, contributed significantly to the cinema over the past forty years with his screenplays for, amongst others, The Servant, Accident, The Go-Between, The French Lieutenant's Woman, Reunion *and* The Trial. *Sixteen of his screenplays are published by Faber and Faber in the three-volume* Collected Screenplays. *A conversation between Pinter and his biographer Michael Billington published in the* Various Voices *collection (pp. 50–57) provides an excellent survey of his interest and activity in film, and is recommended complementary reading to the following collection of interviews. Pinter's first experience of dramatic material was at the cinema, through his local film club. He discussed his early attraction to cinema with Irish journalist Ciaran Carty of* Tribune *magazine (23 March 1997).*

From *Tribune*

I was really brought up on English war films, some of which were pretty good – *The Way Ahead* and the documentary *Fires Were Started*. Also American black-and-white B-thrillers. One of the greatest films I've ever seen anywhere was *The Grapes of Wrath*. I must have seen it when I was thirteen. It has always remained with me. And other films too, like *The Ox-bow Incident*. And then later, I was very fortunate. I stumbled upon a film society when I was fifteen or sixteen. I managed to get ten bob together and joined. I don't know how I got in but I did get in [. . .]. I saw all the French cinema right through to Carné. The Russians too, Eisenstein and all that crowd. It was extraordinary for a boy of that age. It was like opening a door into a totally new world. I was actually seeing Buñuel's *L'Age d'Or* and *Un chien Andalou*. That woke me up all right. One of the great jump cuts I've ever seen is in *Un chien Andalou*. You remember the scene with the woman and the man who is trying to get her? He's prevented by a grand piano and two dead cows and two live priests lying on the piano. He's roped to this piano. They're three storeys up in the middle of Paris. And you can see the traffic, down below. The man has almost got hold of her. And she escapes. She opens the door, walks out – and in the next shot she walks straight onto the beach. Now that was breathtaking. And that's the freedom and mystery of cinema. [. . .] I was brought up on cinema, really. I was right into films years before I went to the theatre, but I never dreamed at that time that I would be working in cinema.

From the *New York Herald Tribune Magazine*

Pinter's first experiences of filming were to be on the sets of The Caretaker *and* The Servant. *From the following brief extract, he was clearly highly motivated by these experiences, and unembarrassed to admit his initial lack of knowledge of the business of making films. The excerpt is taken from an article on* The Servant *('From* Caretaker *to* Servant*', Lee Langley,*

New York Herald Tribune Magazine, *1 March 1964, p. 24).*

The cinema was tattooed into me from a very early age, it never occurred to me that I would do anything for it. *Other* people wrote films. *Other* people made films. But I've taken to it like a duck to water: I find – it's a cliché to say one finds a thing exciting – but I do gain an enormous excitement from it. For instance, the other day I went into the cutting room for the first time, and saw exactly how it's done. How it's all put together. I wanted to try and cut some dialogue, and I asked the director if we could cut a line in one place and make it a pause. He twiddled a few things, and the line was gone – had become a pause. You can delete dialogue, alter rhythm. This is marvellous. [. . .] Another thing, film directors have got to be very careful not to get a glib and facile effect. The use of music, the ready tears. Cliché comes more swiftly in films than in any other medium, if one isn't careful. All the component parts, including dialogue, however spare or prolix, have to be treated with considerable discipline and lack of indulgence. Making a film demands clearsightedness and respect. It is not a question of the differences between stage and film work. Rather, I would say, one identical discipline: economy. On the stage, if thirty words are needed and you write thirty-one, it is an indulgence. On the screen if eight words are needed and you make them nine, *that* is indulgence.

From *Behind the Scenes*

Harold Pinter and Clive Donner, the director of the film of The Caretaker, *were interviewed on the release of the film (Joseph McCrindle (ed.),* Behind the Scenes, *London: Pitman, 1971). Whilst providing an interesting document of Pinter's exposure to filming techniques, it also offers fascinating further insight into the play itself.*

JM: *Had you been approached to make adaptations of your own work before?*
HP: Yes, but I'd never agreed to anything.

Why?
The circumstances didn't seem right. I thought there were all sorts of things needed for film production which I wasn't prepared to deal with. And I was extremely reluctant to make a film of *The Caretaker* because I thought I couldn't possibly get anything fresh from the subject. I'd been associated with the play, you see, through various productions in London and New York for a couple of years.

What persuaded you this time?
It might have been something about . . . I don't know, the general common sense and relaxation of the people I met. I put up a lot of defence mechanisms about it, and said I couldn't possibly even write the draft of a screenplay, couldn't do anything at all, and then someone said, 'You don't have to do anything' (though it turned out I did) . . . and I let myself be won over. I was behaving rather like a child about it.
CD: I think it's slightly unfair to say that you've been behaving like a child. I think you were expecting a more conventional approach to the adaptation of the work

How did you get over this feeling of having worked through it?
HP: Well, I suppose it was because no one said to me, 'This is a film with a capital F.' That would have frightened me off, I think. They simply said, 'This is the idea, this is the work, these are the characters – how can it all be transposed into a film in keeping with what we have, what must be there?' We had long discussions about it and I worked out a kind of draft. [. . .] We saw it as a film, and we worked on it as a film. We weren't thinking about something that was set in any kind of pattern. There was an obvious overall pattern to the work, but we had to see it and work on it in terms of movement from one thing to another.

CD: And you see there's a sort of compulsion in film-makers to 'open out' (whatever that means) subjects that they set out to film. I decided from the beginning that this approach was a blind alley. It seemed to me that within the situation, and within the relationships that developed between the characters, there was enough action, enough excitement seen through the eye of a film camera, without imposing conventional film action treatment.

HP: It seemed to me that when you have two people standing on the stairs and one asks the other if he would like to be caretaker in this house, and the other bloke, you know, who is work-shy, doesn't want in fact to say no, he doesn't want the job, but at the same time he wants to edge it around . . . Now it seems to me there's an enormous amount of internal conflict within one of the characters and external conflict between them – and it's exciting cinema. [. . .] You can say the play has been 'opened out' in the sense that things I'd yearned to do, without knowing it, in writing for the stage, crystallised when I came to think about it as a film. Until then I didn't know that I wanted to do them because I'd accepted the limitations of the stage. For instance, there's a scene in the garden of the house, which is very silent; two silent figures with a third looking on. I think in the film one has been able to hit the relationship of the brothers more clearly than in the play. [. . .] I think the actors on the stage are under the delusion that they have to project in a particular way. There's a scene in the film, also in the play, when the elder brother asks the other if he'd like to be caretaker in the place. On film it's played in terms of great intimacy and I think it's extraordinarily successful. They speak quite normally, it's a quiet scene, and it works. But on stage it didn't ever work like that. The actors get a certain kind of comfort, I think, in the fact that they're so close to the camera. [. . .]

Did you ever think you might do it in a studio?
CD: No, never!
HP: I wish the actors were here to ask, but I'm sure that for

them it was tremendous – I'm sorry to say this, it sounds rather strange, almost as if I'm asking for realism, which I'm not – but I think it did an awful lot for the actors to go up real stairs, open real doors in a house which existed, with a dirty garden and a back wall. [. . .] What I'm very pleased about myself is that in the film, as opposed to the play, we see a real house and real snow outside, dirty snow, and the streets. We don't see them very often but they're there, the backs of houses and windows, attics in the distance. There is actually sky as well, a dirty one, and these characters move in the context of a real world – as I believe they do. In the play, when people were confronted with just a set, a room and a door, they often assumed it was all taking place in limbo, in a vacuum, and the world outside hardly existed, or had existed at some point but was only half-remembered. Now one thing which I think is triumphantly expressed in the film is Clive's concentration on the characters when they are outside the room, outside the house. Not that there aren't others. There are others. There are streets, there is traffic, shadows, shapes about, but he is for me concentrating on the characters as they walk, and while we go into the world outside it is almost as if only these characters exist.

From *Sight and Sound*

Following their successful collaboration on The Servant *in 1963, Harold Pinter and Joseph Losey worked together again in 1967 on an adaptation of Nicholas Mosley's novel* Accident. *Pinter discussed that project on set with John Russell Taylor (*Sight and Sound, *Autumn 1966, vol. 35, no. 4, pp. 179–84) and discussed the process of adapting for the screen.*

It was Losey who first sent me the book. He wanted to do it, and when I read it I wanted to do it. I think we wanted to do it for the same reasons. We thought a lot about how it should be done, to find a direct film equivalent to the free-association, stream-of-consciousness style of the novel. I tried a draft that way, but it just wouldn't work – anyway, I couldn't do it. You see, suppose a character is walking down a lane, this lane, as we are now. You could easily note down a stream of thought which might be perfectly accurate and believable, and then translate it into a series of images: road, field, hedge, grass, corn, wheat, ear, her ear on the pillow, tumbled hair, love, love years ago . . . But when one's mind wanders and associates things in this way it's perfectly unselfconscious. Do exactly the same thing on film and the result is precious, self-conscious, over-elaborate – you're using absurdly complex means to convey something very simple. Instead, you should be able to convey the same sort of apprehension not by opening out, proliferating, but by closing in, looking closer and closer, harder and harder at things that are there before you.

For example, it seems to me that *Marienbad* works very well in its own terms, on the level of fantasy. But there is another way of doing it, and one I would personally find more interesting to explore. In a real, recognisable Paris an ordinary, reasonably attractive woman sits at a café table wearing what she would be wearing, eating and drinking what she would be eating and drinking. An equally ordinary, everyday sort of man comes up to her. 'Excuse me, but don't you remember, we met last year at Marienbad?' 'Marienbad? Impossible – I was never in Marienbad last year . . .' and she gets up, walks out to an ordinary, believable street and gets into a real taxi . . . And so on. Wouldn't that be just as strange and mysterious and frightening as the way the film does it? Perhaps more so, because of the very ordinariness of the surroundings and apparent normality of the characters.

It's something of that sort of feeling we're trying to get here. In the book, for example, there is a scene in which Stephen, coming home, sees a car outside his house and Charlie (Stanley Baker) standing by it. To convey what effect this has on him the novel needs a couple of pages of free association. But in the film, it seems to me, all that can be conveyed just by the shot of what he sees, photographed in a certain way, held on the screen for a certain length of time, with the two characters in the sort of relationship to each other that we know to exist already. It's just the same as the way that a novelist may need five or six pages to introduce a character, to tell us what we need to know about his appearance, age, bearing, education, social background and so on. In a film the actor just walks into a room and it's done, it's all there – or should be. So in this film everything is buried, it is implicit. There is really very little dialogue, and that is mostly trivial, meaningless. The drama goes on inside the characters, and by looking hard at the smooth surface we come to see something of what is going on underneath. [. . .]

JT: *I have always thought that there is a lot to be said for drama which uses, as it were, only the most elementary syntax of a child's story-telling: 'and then . . . and then . . . and then . . .' Without all the becauses and therefores and notwithstandings of psychological drama.*
HP: What you are saying is biblical, it's holy writ for a dramatist – well, for me anyway. I do so hate the becauses of drama. Who are we to say that this happens because that happened, that one thing is the consequence of another? How do we know? What reason have we to suppose that life is so neat and tidy? The most we know for sure is that the things which have happened have happened in a certain order: any connections we think we see, or choose to make, are pure guesswork. Life is much more mysterious than plays make it out to be. And it is this mystery which fascinates me: what happens between the words, what happens when no words are spoken . . . In this film everything happens, nothing is explained. It has been pared down and down, all unnecessary words and actions are eliminated. If it is interesting to see a man cross a room, then we see him do it; if not, then we leave out the insignificant stages of the action. I think you'll be surprised at the directness, the simplicity with which Losey is directing this film: no elaborations, no odd angles, no darting about. Just a level, intense

look at people, at things. As though if you look at them hard enough they will give up their secrets. Not that they will, for however much you see and guess at there is always that something more . . .

From *Village Voice*

Pinter and Losey's final collaboration was to be the unfilmed screenplay of Proust's A la recherche du temps perdu. *Pinter discussed this project with Stephen Menick for* Village Voice *(12 December 1977, pp. 45–7).*

HP: I read Proust for three solid months. For those three months I would do nothing else but read Proust all day, and I emerged, to say the least, dizzy. I say this in my introduction – which really killed me to write actually. Very difficult – to be precise. That's why it's so short, by the way. And then I was totally imbedded in the thing for nine months after that. But it *was* the best working year of my life. I really felt alive throughout one year, and normally, as Monsieur Proust himself says, one doesn't.

The actual reading was in fact an inspiration. I have to use that word. It was a profound – a very large experience. And yet I wasn't left with the feeling that I was dealing with a blockbuster, if you will. I mean, you can't miss a word out in Proust, can you? You've got to read every damn word because it *is* so precise and so considered and so felt. I was left with how significant, of course, everything in there really is. I was left with the power and significance of the most delicate sort of experience.

I remember my first conversation with Joe Losey just after I'd finished the reading. I went to him and said, 'Well, what the hell do I do?' We hadn't made any decisions whatsoever at that point. Nobody knew what was going to go or be sacrificed, or what form the thing could possibly take. Eventually, one day when I was in more than my usual despair, Joe said, 'There's only one thing to do. Go home – tomorrow morning – and start. Just start.'

So what I was immediately plunged into was the question of what caught me – well, *everything* caught me, I was totally consumed – but what I was aware of in terms of film. I'm pretty sure that I suddenly went straight into images. I actually threw a lot of images down on paper and found myself left with them. And that's how I got started. [. . .] I was always rather surprised that I was asked to do it in the first place. I was surprised, quite honestly, that French writers have not attempted it. [. . .]

It may have been that their silence before Proust has had something to do with awe.
They couldn't have been more awed than I was.

But you went ahead nevertheless.
Because it was the greatest excitement to do so. What you see here, whatever this is worth, it's something based on absolute devotion. [. . .]

There's nothing about the Madeleine – the famous Madeleine, so dear to those readers of Proust who have tired after the first sixty pages [. . .].
That's absolutely correct. Because apart from any other consideration – and there were other considerations, which you've put your finger on – it could only work on paper, as you say. Look, here's your fellow with his Madeleine. Now, what can you see? The fellow looking up and saying, 'Jesus! Something's hit me!' and when you come down to it, I don't find it as interesting an emblem as the others, which, for me, really resound.

You must know that the one that had the deepest effect on me personally was the bell – the garden gate bell of his childhood. He actually hears it again at the matinee. And he says something to the effect, 'I then realized that *this bell had been in me all my life!*' I must say that when I read that I was quite

... excruciatingly moved. [. . .] He sways backwards and forward, then he's still. Nothing happens. He sways back again, desperately trying to get the damn thing, to recapture the damn thing. And you notice that he remains still, concentrating. And then, what I think is good, the chauffeurs. The world of the chauffeurs. In the direction of the film you'd have him aware of them earlier, but then all of a sudden he's oblivious to them. Blue glow. [. . .]

Joe Losey has a real feeling for space, for very precise detail within space. He has a wonderful ability – a disposition – to concentrate on an object. I have a great respect for Joe, and I think somehow or other he can pull it off [. . .]. Joe and I did a hell of a lot of homework, over there, by the way. We had the locations. We found a wonderful place for the Guermantes house in Paris. And for Balbec – we went to the very place. Cabourg. We actually spent the night at the Grand-Hôtel. The terrible thing was that the place was about to be torn down, and the mayor of Cabourg kept it for us to do the shoot! I think it's going to fall down any minute, I'm afraid.

The big problem, of course, has been with financiers. It was very close, apparently, to solution, here and there, but it remained insuperable. And I think for the simple reason that it's a long film. I read the screenplay with my son, once, and acted the whole thing out – conducted it, as it were. With all those silences. And it came out to three hours and thirty-five minutes. [. . .] and I should point out to you that the length, the three and a half hours, was an artistic decision, purely. I mean, if it was going to be an eight-hour film then it was going to be an eight-hour film, as far as I was concerned. In fact the whole structure of the film is the structure that was found, not predetermined in any way, not from any other point of view or consideration. [. . .] I must say that this conversation, after this length of time, has quickened my desire to see the thing up on the screen.

From the *New York Times Magazine*

Perhaps the most commercially successful and popular film for which Pinter produced the screenplay was Karel Reisz's The French Lieutenant's Woman *(1981). Here, Pinter talks about the problems of adapting John Fowles's novel to Leslie Garis. This interview is from the* New York Times Magazine *of 5 October 1981, pp. 24–69.*

LG: *Did you write many drafts?*
HP: I wrote one draft. The script suffered considerable sea changes, particularly in structure, but it was all based on my one draft. [. . .] I remain very, very interested as to whether a given audience will find the presence of the modern scenes undermining to the Victorian tale. But I'm not a theoretician. I work mainly by instinct and sense of smell as it were. [. . .]

Why do you write only adaptations?
Any original ideas I may have . . . I don't have very many of them . . . always seem to go immediately into the theatre.

Do you derive particular pleasure from working on someone else's material?
Oh, yes. Very much indeed. What is it? Well . . . of course, the technical demands are, to use a cliché, a great challenge to solve. But it's entering into another man's mind, which is very interesting . . . to try to find the true mind.

Do you enjoy the constrictions, or do you feel there's a lot of freedom in adaptation?
Well, there are both. I'm not sure that the word 'constrictions' is quite right. I would say there are boundaries, proper limitations, that you have to adhere to, otherwise you are distorting, playing about, and having your own good time, which is not the idea. But there remains within that the freedom of the medium. And that is the whole point. So I don't really feel . . .

any kind of constrictions. I always work – and certainly in the case of *The French Lieutenant's Woman* – from a substantial respect of the work itself. The excitement exists in finding out how to keep faith with Fowles's complexity without being tortuous in film terms. [. . .]

Is collaboration part of the enjoyment of working in film?
Well, it's great when you're working with a man like Karel, yes. I mean, you have a fervour. It's two minds. Quite apart from the mind of the author.

When you were on set, did you make line changes?
Certainly not.

I gather the movie follows your screenplay precisely.
Yes. Well, you don't take a damn year to write the damn thing and have the actors change the lines [. . .]. In my contracts, I have something very explicit, precise and concrete: the screenplay is decided before we shoot. Done, that's it. I mean, certainly Karel would ring me during shooting and say, 'Look, can we say . . .?' And then it's up to me to write the new line, or whatever it is. It never came to a speech. It was always a matter of phrases.

Do you have a greater artistic stake in the theatre or in films?
I take both things very seriously. I just do both. That's all.

What would you say is the difference between writing for films and for the stage?
It's to do with certain images that you get in film you can't possibly get on the stage. A single image of Meryl Streep, for example, silent, expresses a whole volume of things . . . immediately. Now you can, of course, achieve the same kind of thing on the stage. But you have to dictate the focus by other means.

By purely verbal means?

No. Not at all. I don't work in purely verbal terms on the stage, by any means. I feel that the way an actor is sitting or standing is much to the point. But if there are other people on stage, you have to focus in quite a subtle way, actually. The discipline is very different. In film, you select the image. [. . .]

Have you found through the years that it has become more or less difficult to write?
Oh, more difficult, without any question. One's judgement is much more critical . . . of one's self. There was a kind of wild freedom once. I wrote a lot of poetry, which was doubtless incomprehensible. But the freedom . . . of words . . . was marvellous. [. . .] Plays I start mainly when I'm drunk. And very impulsively. Write down a few lines.

Politics and Political Writing

Harold Pinter's reputation, as currently defined by the British press, is for being a grumpy old man of letters, his doors locked to the world, active only in obsessively ranting in knee-jerk indignation against the British and US governments. This notion of a reclusive, permanently outraged figure is, as Pinter himself recognises, 'one that's been cultivated by the Press. That's the Harold Pinter they choose to create.'[2] Pinter responded eloquently to this media construction of a 'Pinter of Discontent'[3] and the attacks upon him in this interview published in the Independent *(20 September 1993) and presents some of the reasoning for his anger at US foreign policy in the years after the first Gulf War.*

From the *Independent*

The attacks represent a well-established tradition of mockery of the artist in this country. I was going to say 'intellectual', but I'm not that, I'm just a working writer; but any writer who pops his head over the trenches and dares to speak in this country is really placed outside the pale. I suppose it stems from the fact that a writer is supposed to be some kind of entertainer, it's true in the United States too. But this has never been the case in Europe or Latin America.

All that I can say is that if they have contempt for me it is as nothing to the contempt I have for them, and I really *mean* that. Not because they are insulting me, but because they are insulting standards of truth and seriousness which I believe should obtain in any civilised society. There was a time when I was attacked by everyone in sight and I've survived that. So there's no way I can go under. I did a programme on Channel 4, *Opinions*, on American foreign policy and I was accused of 'ranting', of being a 'ranting emotional playwright', the usual accusation the press deliver to someone they wish to discredit. But I got a record number of letters from people who said, 'We feel the same way as you do, but we can't say it as a bus conductor or a factory worker because if we do we'll be ostracised or even sacked.' But I can't be sacked, you see, because I haven't got a job. Therefore, I'll continue to say whatever I like. [. . .]

I believe the United States is a truly monstrous force in the world, now off the leash for obvious reasons. Take the US missile attack on Baghdad, ostensibly a retort to the assassination attempt on Bush, but actually telling the American people that Clinton could really kick ass.[4] One person who was killed over there happens to be a friend of someone I know; she was a celebrated artist in her own right, the curator of a museum. And she's dead, and so is her husband, and plenty of other people too. And the morning after, Clinton was walking out of church saying he felt good about this and so would the American people, and what he's talking about is murder, which he feels good about. The fact of death and Clinton's attitude towards that death are miles apart.

Nicaragua was on course to being a truly democratic society, a very rare thing indeed. The US organised an economic blockade, a terrorist group that killed 30,000 people and the people overwhelmed by death and hunger voted the Sandinistas out of power. So a society which was humane, dignified and vital now has a situation where infant mortality has risen by seventy per cent, where there is over sixty per cent unemployment, and education and health services are in ruins. A triumph for President Clinton and the World Bank!

We have been educated by the Western press since the last war to believe in the good and the bad – we are good, the others are bad. We contribute to those lies because everything we do is supposed to be in the name of freedom and democracy . . . I do think we have an obligation to see through the crap that we're fed.

With One for the Road, Mountain Language *and* Party Time, *Pinter was seen to have turned to writing political theatre. Speaking to Sue Summers (*Independent, *18 October 1988), he spoke of the dangers of writing politically. Appended to this, in an interview with French journalist Marion Thébaud (*Figaro, *19 March 1998 – translated by Mark Batty), he discussed his views on political theatre.*

From the *Independent*

(*to Sue Summers*) The problem is that you know where you are before you start. A play is essentially a voyage of discovery, and so if you get it all worked out before you start, the danger is that the play is redundant. When I started becoming involved in politics, I found I wasn't able to construct a framework in terms of a full-length play which would satisfy me and be of interest to anyone else.

From *Figaro*

MT: *What is political theatre?*
HP: I don't see many examples of political theatre today, except the plays of Heiner Müller and Thomas Bernhard, which I love. It is a theatre that reflects the world in which we live, the world

as it is, stripped of the double-speak used by the powers that be. A theatre that implicates the outside world. [. . .] I direct, I act and I write plays, but, at the same time and with the same energy, I apply myself to political engagement. I write articles in the press, I speak on television, and on radio. I'm as much an activist as I am a writer and it has become more and more important in my life. All the tissues of lies that are peddled by the government, by the media – especially the American media – must be denounced. I apply myself to this in my life as much as I do in my writing. Because, little by little, freedom of thought is being suffocated. The media in the hands of governments offer programmes which encourage people not to think. And, at the same time, these governments speak about nothing but freedom, democracy and justice. Who can believe them any more?

What, for you, are the great political plays?
Coriolanus, by Shakespeare, Brecht's *Mother Courage* and the most beautiful of all, perhaps, *The Cherry Orchard*. Chekhov, without any propagandist agenda, explains the end of a world, the disappearance of a society. It is very beautiful, subtle and profound.

One for the Road *was the first angry play to flow from Pinter's pen, and the first that sought to engage an audience with issues of moral responsibility within clearly political contexts. In an interview (from which the following extracts are drawn) printed with the first published edition of that play (London: Methuen, 1985, pp. 5–24) he discussed his motivations in writing the play, and his new political persona.*

'A Play and its Politics: a conversation between Harold Pinter and Nicholas Hern'

NH: *Was there anything particular that prompted you to write* One for the Road?
HP: Yes, there was. I've been concerned, for a number of years

now, more and more with two things. One is the fact of torture, of official torture, subscribed to by so many governments. And the other is the whole nuclear situation. I've been a member of CND for some years now and have been quite active in one way or the other. In Turkey, in the last year, members of the Turkish Peace Association – the equivalent of CND if you like – were imprisoned for eight years' hard labour for being members of the Turkish Peace Association. They're all extremely respectable and in some cases distinguished people. I got to know about this, and went into it. In investigating the Turkish situation I found something that I was slightly aware of but had no idea of the depths of . . . that the Turkish prisons, in which there are thousands of political prisoners, really are among the worst in the world. After arrest, a political prisoner is held incommunicado for forty-five days, under martial law.[5] Torture is systematic. People are crippled every day. This is documented by the Helsinki Watch Committee, Amnesty, International PEN and so on, and hardly denied by the Turkish authorities, who don't give a fuck because they know they're on safe ground since they have American subscription and American weapons. They're on the frontier of Russia and it's very important to America that Turkey is one of 'us'. However, I found out a good deal more about the Turkish prisons and I've been in touch with Turkish people here. I then found myself at a party, where I came across two Turkish girls, extremely attractive and intelligent young women, and I asked them what they thought about this trial which had recently taken place, the sentences . . . and they said, 'Oh, well it was probably deserved.' 'What do you mean by that, why was it probably deserved?' They said, 'Well, they were probably communists. We have to protect ourselves against communism.' I said, 'When you say "probably", what kind of facts do you have?' They of course had no facts at all at their fingertips. They were ignorant, in fact. I then asked them whether they knew what Turkish military prisons were like and about torture in Turkey, and they shrugged and said, 'Well, communists are communists, you know.' 'But what do you have to say about torture?' I asked. They looked at me and one of them said, 'Oh, you're a man of such imagination'. I said, 'Do you mean it's worse for me than for the victims?' They gave yet another shrug and said, 'Yes, possibly.' Whereupon instead of strangling them, I came back immediately, sat down and, it's true, out of rage started to write *One for the Road*. It was a very immediate thing, yes. But, it wasn't only that that caused me to write the play. The subject was on my mind.

It does seem to me that to a lot of people who've looked at your work over the years this play did come as something very, very fresh. Did you hope to shock the audiences, to inform them, to say, 'This is going on now, do you realise this, you people?'
I feel very strongly that people should know what's going on in this world, on all levels. But at the time, when I came back from that drinks party, and sat down in the chair and took out a piece of paper, I had an image in my mind of a man with a victim, an interrogator with a victim. And I was simply investigating what might take place. Given a certain state of affairs, what would the attitude of the interrogator to his victims be? So I was simply writing the play. I wasn't thinking then of my audience. Having started on the play, letting the images and the action develop, I did go the whole way, to the hilt, as far as I could. The end result being that the play is pretty remorseless. And the hilt, in this case, is the fact that the child is killed, murdered. I don't believe that anything in the play is an exaggeration, by any means. One thing I tried to do, however, when I named the characters – which was later, as I always write A, B, and C initially; I never think of names at the time of writing – was to make the names non-specific . . .

Multi-national names, in a sense . . .
Yes. Whether this was right or wrong is another matter. I remember that Michael Billington had a reservation as far as I recall which was to do with the fact that the play wasn't specific.

And their offence was never named.

That's right, their offence was never named. Well, I must say that I think that's bloody ridiculous, because these people, generally speaking – in any country, whether it's Czechoslovakia or whether it's Chile – ninety per cent of them have committed no offence. There's no such thing as an offence, apart from the fact that everything is – their very life is an offence, as far as the authorities go. Their very existence is an offence, since that existence in some way or another poses critical questions or is understood to do so. [. . .]

Given the passionate nature of your beliefs, I wonder whether you've felt like standing up and using the fact that you can command a certain amount of attention by virtue of the work you've done? Are you experiencing a dilemma as to whether you carry on writing, or whether you do something more direct?

That question is very acute, I must say. I can't go on writing plays about torture. I wrote one sketch about the nuclear bureaucracy, because I believe there is an enormous conspiracy to hide the truth in this country. But still, I can't go on writing that kind of play either. They're very difficult to write. You can only write them if you can make it real, make it an authentic thing. But you can't do that at the drop of a hat. I don't see much of a future for me as a writer in this respect. It also makes it very difficult to write anything, however. I don't know what my future is as a writer . . .

But as a political animal and a member of society, you feel the need for some more direct action? Not necessarily through the pen? Or if through the pen, then in a more direct way?

Well, yes, the answer is yes, I do. But at the same time . . . it's a bit difficult to take an objective view of myself. But I'm aware that I do possess two things. One is that I'm quite violent, myself I have violent feelings and . . . I feel quite strongly about things. On the other hand, however, I'm quite reticent. You have to look very carefully at your motives if you become a public figure. The danger is that you become an exhibitionist, self-important, pompous. [. . .] You know I do believe that what old Sam Beckett says at the end of *The Unnameable* is right on the ball. 'You must go on, I can't go on, I'll go on.' Now in this particular reference, if he'll forgive me using his language in this context, there's no point, it's hopeless. That's my view. I believe that there's no chance of the world coming to other than a very grisly end in twenty-five years at the outside. Unless God, as it were, finally speaks. Because reason is not going to do anything. Me writing *One for the Road*, documentaries, articles, lucid analyses, Averell Harriman writing in the *New York Times*, voices raised here and there, people walking down the road and demonstrating. Finally it's hopeless. There's nothing one can achieve. Because the modes of thinking of those in power are worn out, threadbare, atrophied. Their minds are a brick wall. But still one can't stop attempting to try to think and see things as clearly as possible.

All we're talking about, finally, is what is real. What is real. There's only one reality, you know. You can interpret reality in various ways. But there's only one. And if that reality is thousands of people being tortured to death at this very moment and hundreds of thousands of megatons of nuclear bombs standing there waiting to go off at this very moment, then that's it and that's that. It has to be faced.

I'll tell you this little story. Great Hampden was a new fixture for our cricket club. We didn't know where it was. We finally found it. It turned out to be in the Chilterns, outside High Wycombe, exquisite place. It was everything that one romanticises about but, nevertheless, is true in rural England. The little village, the cricket pitch, trees, etc. And we had a lovely game of cricket.

Now, let me quote from the *Guardian*, 22 August 1984. Front Page. Title is: 'US Spends Fifty Million Dollars on British War Bunker'. 'Work has started on the new war headquarters for the Americans at Dawes Hill, High Wycombe,

Buckinghamshire, the Ministry of Defence confirmed yesterday. And the three-storey underground bunker, which was first constructed in the nineteen fifties as the American nuclear strike command, is being refurbished at a cost of nearly fifty million dollars to the Americans. It will replace the American peacetime headquarters at Stuttgart, Germany, in the event of war.' And what do you think is on top of that? Great Hampden. Underneath Great Hampden cricket pitch is the centre of nuclear operations in Europe. And underneath, when we play our cricket match, when every Sunday people play cricket out there, etc. etc., in the Chilterns, underneath them are thousands of people underground, and there will be more of them. And this is going to be the centre of nuclear operations in Europe. It already was a nuclear base. But it now is going to be the centre. So you have thousands of Americans, when you come down to it, walking about under the Chilterns, while we're playing cricket on the top. That's the story.

From the *Listener*

With Mountain Language *(1988), Pinter continued to make plain that his political theatre was directed at a British political culture, one that he considered too strongly under the influence of US policies and agendas. In a televised interview with Anna Ford (printed in the* Listener, 27 *October 1988) he emphasised the relevance of his play to the UK.*

AF: *Is* Mountain Language *written to shock?*
HP: I don't write in those terms. I have no aim in writing other than exploring the images that come into my mind. I find some of those images really quite shocking, so they shock me into life and into the act of writing. The image is there and you attempt to express it. I was jolted by the images and by the state of affairs they refer to, which I think are serious facts most people prefer, understandably, to remain indifferent to, pretend don't exist. One thing, when you meet people who've been through

these appalling deprivations and assaults on their system, you
realise that they're exactly the same as you and I. Just because,
for example, they're three thousand miles away, a lot of people
say, 'Oh well, why don't we look at England?' Well, we are
looking at England. By which I mean, 'Do not ask for whom
the bell tolls, it tolls for thee.' [. . .]

*Would you hope that people come away from the play thinking
about relating* Mountain Language *to what's going on in this
country?*
I hope audiences will perceive it in their own way and make up
their own minds. I haven't written a theoretical piece of work.
It's not an ideological piece of work, either. In a sense it's hardly political. It's simply about a series of short, sharp brutal
events in and outside a prison. Whether that prison in that
location and what actually takes place is at all recognisable as
being possible in this country is up to any individual member of
an audience to make up his own mind about. I believe it's very
close to home. [. . .]

You say that Mountain Language *is not specifically about the
Kurds, or about their situation, although that's what prompted
you. Wouldn't it be more useful if it was specific, so that people
could tell exactly what was happening there?*
Well, I'm not writing a play simply about Turkey; in fact the
play isn't about Turkey at all. I think the play is very much closer to home and I believe it reflects a great deal that's happening
in this country.

What sort of things?
Well, my own view is that the present government is turning a
stronger and stronger vice on democratic institutions that
we've taken for granted for a very long time. It's embodied in
things like Clause 28, the Official Secrets Act, police powers,
and it's happening quite insidiously, but happening nevertheless in a very strong and purposeful way. I believe most people

don't seem to realise that the dissenting voice and the minority are in great danger in this country.

In 1999 NATO forces applied Operation Allied Force to implement the liberation of the region of Kosovo from Serbian control. This involved bombing of key sites in the Yugoslav capital of Belgrade in May of that year. Outraged by this action, Harold Pinter presented a television programme against the action (Counterblast, May 4 1999, Channel 4 Television). On 25 June 1999 he gave a lengthy speech, from which the following text is extracted, to the Confederation of Analytical Psychologists. The text is published in full in Masters of the Universe: NATO's Balkan Crusade, *edited by Tariq Ali (London: Verso, 2000).*

The NATO action in Serbia had nothing to do with the fate of the Kosovan Albanians; it was yet another blatant and brutal assertion of US power.

The bombing was not only an action taken in defiance of international law and in contempt of the United Nations, it was also totally unnecessary. The negotiation process at Rambouillet is said to have been exhausted but this was not in fact the case. At the start of the crisis there were two main objectives: to restore substantive autonomy to Kosovo and to ensure that the Yugoslav government respected the Kosovars' political, cultural, religious and linguistic freedoms. The plan at the Rambouillet conference was to achieve these two aims by peaceful means. The Serbs had specifically agreed to grant Kosovo a large measure of autonomy. What they would not accept was NATO as the international peacekeeping force, or rather, an occupying force, a force whose presence would extend throughout Yugoslavia. They proposed a protectorate under United Nations auspices. NATO would not agree to this and the bombing started immediately. [. . .]

The United States has finally agreed to a resolution of the Serbian conflict which differs in no significant respect from that which the Yugoslav parliament was ready to accept before the violence started. Why therefore was this action taken? I believe the United States wanted to make Kosovo into a NATO – or rather American – colony. This has now been achieved. I shall return to this in due course.

Nothing else has been achieved. NATO gave Milosevič the excuse he needed to escalate his atrocities, thousands of civilians, both Kosovan and Serbian, have been killed, the country has been poisoned and devastated. The Serbian atrocities are savage and disgusting but there is little doubt that the vast escalation of these atrocities took place after the bombing began. To cite 'humanitarian' reasons, in any event, as NATO originally did, really doesn't bear scrutiny. There are just as many 'moral' and 'humanitarian' reasons, for example, to intervene in Turkey. The Turkish government has been waging a relentless war against the Kurdish people since 1984. The repression has claimed 30,000 lives. Not only does the United States not intervene, it actively subsidises and supports what is effectively a military dictatorship and of course Turkey is an important member of NATO. The revelations of the Serbian police torture chambers are horrific but the Turkish police torture chambers practise exactly the same techniques and bring about exactly the same horror. So did the Guatemalan and El Salvadoran and Chilean torture chambers before them. But these were our torture chambers so they never reached the front pages. Those torture chambers were defending democracy against the evil of subversion, if you remember. Turkey is still doing it, with our full support, our weapons and our money. [. . .]

NATO has claimed that the bombings of civilians in Serbia were accidents. I suggest that the bombing of civilians was part of a deliberate attempt to terrorise the population. NATO's supreme commander, General Wesley K. Clark, declared just before the bombing began: 'Unless President Milosevič accepts the International Community's demands we will systematically and progressively attack, disorganise, ruin, devastate and finally destroy his forces.' Milosevič's 'forces', as we now know, included television stations, schools, hospitals, theatres, old people's homes. The Geneva Convention states that no civilian can be targeted unless he is taking a direct part in the hostilities, which I take to mean firing guns or throwing hand grenades. These civilian deaths were therefore acts of murder.

A body of lawyers and law professors based in Toronto in association with the American Association of Jurists, a non-government organisation with consultative status before the United Nations, has laid a complaint before the War Crimes Tribunal charging all the NATO leaders (headed by President Clinton and Prime Minister Blair) with war crimes committed in its campaign against Yugoslavia. The list of crimes include: 'wilful killing, wilfully causing great suffering or serious injury to body or health, extensive destruction of property, not justified by military necessity and carried out unlawfully and wantonly, employment of poisonous weapons or other weapons to cause unnecessary suffering, wanton destruction of cities, towns or villages, devastation not justified by military necessity, bombardment of undefended towns, villages, dwellings or buildings, destruction or wilful damage done to institutions dedicated to religion, charity and education, the arts and sciences, historic monuments.' The charge also alleges 'open violation of the United Nations Charter, the NATO Treaty itself, the Geneva Conventions and the principles of International Law'.

It is worth remarking here that the enormous quantities of high explosives dropped on Serbia have done substantial damage to irreplaceable treasures of Byzantine religious art. Precious mosaics and frescos have been destroyed. The thirteenth-century city of Peć has been flattened. The sixteenth-century Hadum mosque in Djakovica, the Byzantine Basilica in Niš and the ninth-century church in Prokuplje have been badly damaged. The fifteenth-century rampart in the Belgrade fort has collapsed. The Banovina palace in Novi Sad, the finest work of art-deco architecture in the Balkans, has been blown up. This is psychotic vandalism.

Why were cluster bombs used to kill civilians in Serbian marketplaces? The NATO high command can hardly have been ignorant of the effect of these weapons. They quite simply tear people to pieces. The effect of depleted uranium in the noses of missile shells cannot be precisely measured. Jamie Shea, our distinguished NATO spokesman, would probably say, 'Oh come on, lads, a little piece of depleted uranium never did anyone any harm.' It can be said, however, that Iraqi citizens are still suffering serious effects from depleted uranium after nine years, not to mention the Gulf War syndrome experienced by British and American soldiers. What is known is that depleted uranium leaves toxic and radioactive particles of uranium oxide that endanger human beings and pollute the environment. NATO has also targeted chemical and pharmaceutical plants, plastics factories and oil refineries, causing substantial environmental damage. Last month the Worldwide Fund for Nature warned that an environmental crisis is looming in the lower Danube, due mainly to oil slicks. The river is a source of drinking water for 10 million people.

Tony Blair said the other day, 'Milosevič has devastated his own country.' [. . .] This is standing language – and the world – on its head. There is indeed a breathtaking discrepancy between, let us say, US government language and US government action. The United States has exercised a sustained, systematic and clinical manipulation of power worldwide since the end of the last World War, while masquerading as a force for universal good. Or to put it another way, pretending to be the world's Dad. It's a brilliant – even witty – stratagem and in fact has been remarkably successful. But in 1948 George Kennan, head of the US State Department, set out the ground rules for US foreign policy in a 'top secret' internal document. He said, 'We will have to dispense with all sentimentality and daydreaming and our attention will have to be concentrated everywhere on our immediate national objectives. We should cease to talk about vague and unreal objectives such as human rights, the raising of living standards and democratisation. The day is not far off when we will have to deal in straight power concepts. The less we are hampered by idealistic slogans the better.' Kennan was a very unusual man. He told the truth.

I believe that the United States, so often described – mostly by itself – as *the* bastion of democracy, freedom and Christian values, for so long accepted as leader of the 'free world', is in fact and has in fact been for a very long time a profoundly dangerous and aggressive force, contemptuous of international law, indifferent to the fate of millions of people who suffer from its actions, dismissive of dissent or criticism, concerned only to maintain its economic power, ready at the drop of a hat to protect that power by military means, hypocritical, brutal, ruthless and unswerving. [. . .]

NATO is America's missile. As I think I indicated earlier, I find nothing intrinsically surprising in what is essentially an American action. There are plenty of precedents. The US did tremendous damage to Iraq in the Gulf War, did it again last December and is still doing it. Earlier this year it destroyed a pharmaceutical factory in Khartoum, declaring that chemical weapons were made there. They were not. Baby powder was. Sudan asked the United Nations to set up an international inquiry into the bombing. The United States prevented this inquiry from taking place. All this goes back a very long way. The US invaded Panama in 1990, Grenada in 1983, the Dominican Republic in 1965. It destabilised and brought down democratically elected governments in Guatemala, Chile, Greece and Haiti, all acts entirely outside the parameters of international law. It has supported, subsidised and in a number of cases engendered every right-wing dictatorship in the world since 1945. I refer again to Guatemala, Chile, Greece and Haiti. Add to these Indonesia, Uruguay, the Philippines, Brazil, Paraguay, Turkey, El Salvador, for example. Hundreds upon hundreds of thousands of people have been murdered by these regimes but the money, the resources, the equipment (all kinds), the advice, the moral support as it were, have come from successive US administrations. The devastation the US inflicted upon Vietnam, Laos and Cambodia, the use of napalm, agent orange, was a remorseless, savage, systematic course of destruction, which however failed to destroy the spirit of the Vietnamese people. When the US was defeated it at once set out to starve the country by way of trade embargo. Its covert action against Nicaragua was declared by the International Court of Justice in The Hague in 1986 to be in clear breach of international law. The US dismissed this judgement, saying it regarded its actions as outside the jurisdiction of any international court. Over the last six years the United Nations has passed six resolutions with overwhelming majorities (at the last one only Israel voting with the US) demanding that the US stop its embargo on Cuba. The US has ignored all of them.

Milosevič is brutal. Saddam Hussein is brutal. But the brutality of Clinton (and of course Blair) is insidious, since it hides behind sanctimony and the rhetoric of moral outrage.

9

Views on Pinter: Friends and Collaborators

This final section of the book contains reflections on Harold Pinter given by those who have worked or been associated with him. Many of these interviews are new, and others have been collected and collated from various sources. The first words are from Margaret Atwood, who tackles that awkward adjective 'Pinteresque'. (This article was originally published in The Pinter Review: Collected Essays 1999–2000, 2000, p. 5.) *Atwood's* The Handmaid's Tale *was adapted for film by Pinter in 1987.*

Margaret Atwood: 'Pinteresque'

Harold Pinter was already a strong presence, when, at the age of seventeen, I moved out of the Victorian penumbra of the high school curriculum and into the world where people who were actually alive were writing. There, in the bookstore where they sold exciting volumes with modern-looking soft but glossy covers, were Beckett and Sartre and Ionesco and Camus, and Pinter. Of course I thought Pinter was very old, considering the company he was keeping, but he was not. He had only started very young.

And what an astonishing trajectory it has been ever since. A comet, but a comet shaped like a hedgehog or a burr. Not a cosy presence: not comforting, not cuddly, not flannel. Prickly, bothersome, mordant and dour. Always unexpected: coming up on you sideways with an alarming glare.

But always itself, this body of work we now call *Pinter*. A singular accomplishment. It has spawned its own adjective: Pinteresque.

I was trying to think what we might mean by this adjective, or what I might mean, and two things came to mind. One was deafness, and the other was silence. In Pinter, people don't hear one another, or they mix-hear [sic], and sometimes this is deliberate and sometimes not. Paradoxically, Pinter thus makes us listen; he makes us listen very carefully, and very hard. As for silence, no one has ever used it better. The long pause, the reply that isn't there, the absence of expected speech. Pinter's characters are frequently at a loss for words, and this loss stands for loss in general.

I said *Pinteresque* to myself again, just to see what would come up, and two figures presented themselves. One was Job, who has had everything taken away from him and who is complaining quite rightfully to God about God's injustice towards him. *Why Me?* says Job, *I don't deserve this*. God doesn't answer the question. Instead he comes up with a bunch of questions of his own designed to show how great he is. The deafness of God: man outraged by a universe that either pays no attention to him or squashes him like a bug. Not to mention the other men in this universe, who are equally deaf and frequently shits as well.

The other figure is Abraham, especially the Abraham in Kierkegaard's essay about him. Abraham is ordered by God to cut his only son's throat. In the face of this cruel and unnatural request, Abraham does not protest. Neither does he agree. He is silent. But it is a huge surprise with a haunting echo.

One of these echoes is Pinter – the silences of Pinter.

Reverberating silences.

Pinteresque.

Directing Pinter

Peter Hall

Pinter's dramatic writing bewildered many when it arrived on the British theatre scene in the late 1950s. He became renowned for plays that refused to clarify the conundrums they projected, and actors and directors were faced with the task of making sense of material that resisted traditional modes of rehearsal and presentation. Peter Hall was Pinter's director of choice for much of the 1960s and 1970s and set a standard for the approach to Pinter's language and atmospheres. He was responsible for the stage premières of The Collection *(co-directed with Pinter),* The Homecoming, Landscape, Silence, Old Times, No Man's Land, Betrayal, Family Voices, Victoria Station *and* A Kind of Alaska. *The following is a selection of extracts from an interview Hall gave in 1974 to Catherine Itzin and Simon Trussler. The full interview was published in* Theatre Quarterly *(vol. 4, no. 16, 1974/75).*

CI/ST: *You're now the director one associates most closely with Pinter, but actually the association began relatively late in his career, didn't it?*

PH: In practice, yes. But Pinter had seen my production of *Godot* back in 1956 or 1957, and Michael Codron sent me *The Birthday Party* when it was first going to be done. I didn't know who Harold Pinter was, but I liked the play enormously. I couldn't do it though, because I had commitments in New York that year: and then when *The Caretaker* was sent to me, I couldn't do that, either, because I was just setting up the new companies at Stratford and the Aldwych. But I did put £250 into the production of *The Caretaker* at the Arts, which I think was capitalized at £1000 or something very low, and it earned me a surprising amount of money – it's one of the few times I've made money out of investing in plays, a hobby I've long since given up! I then put most of the money back into the film of *The Caretaker*. So there were these very early possibilities for association with Pinter, which didn't come to anything.

Can you remember now how you reacted when you first read The Birthday Party *by this unknown dramatist?*

Well, I heard the voice of Beckett, without any question, and the voice of Kafka – the horror, the terror of the unknown. But I did think the play was rather too bound by its own naturalism: you know, the three-act structure, the French's acting edition set. That was why I was so thrilled when I read *The Caretaker*, which seemed to have reached a point where the form was uniquely the dramatist's own. I don't think *The Birthday Party* is quite free from being a 'rep' play.

You didn't see the short-lived first production, presumably?
No – I remember actually coming back from New York on the Sunday morning after the opening, and reading Hobson's review. He was the only one more or less to get *The Birthday Party* right, and there in the same paper was the news that it had closed the previous night. [. . .]

By the time you eventually co-directed The Collection *with Pinter for the RSC, he had written quite a few other radio and television plays – why choose to stage* The Collection *in particular?*
He hadn't got a new play ready at that time, and we were trying to find something from among the other pieces which would be viable on stage. We decided to do it together for a number of reasons. I think it's true that Harold actually wanted to learn to be a director, and thought that collaboration would be a sensible way to begin. And I was very involved at Stratford that year, so I couldn't have considered doing a full-length play, even if there'd been one. I think, too, he also wanted to see how I responded to his stuff directly.

And how did you respond to The Collection?
Well, working on Pinter's plays over the years, I'm conscious, retrospectively, of having developed a technique, an approach, a way of going about things. I certainly didn't have that when we began *The Collection*. I don't think I was fully at home with it as a technique until about halfway through the rehearsals for

The Homecoming. But it was very much part of the same world as working on Beckett – making the actor trust what is given, making him accept the premise of the words. That goes as much for the architectural shape of the words as it does for any resonance that they may have for the actor emotionally. And since you cannot actually ignore or change the words, you may as well start from there. The parallel to me is with music – don't get me wrong, I don't think if you merely sing the right notes, you make sense in any human terms. You don't in opera, you don't in Pinter. But if you sing the wrong notes you are going to make nonsense. And certainly, even in *The Collection* there was a great discipline required of the actor, to trust the text. [. . .]

Can you describe the process of work on the play?
I can speak about how I work on a Pinter play. It doesn't mean to say this is *the* way. And I must make absolutely clear that although Harold and I have had a long association and I've directed a number of his stage plays, and we've worked together on films and so on, it is a totally pragmatic situation. I would hate anybody reading this to think *this is the way to direct Pinter*. This absolutely is not true: it's the way I direct Pinter. Having said that, my working arrangement with him has been, over twelve years, that in front of the actors – and I stress that – he can say anything he likes about what I'm doing, and the production, and the rights and wrongs of it. And in front of the actors I can say anything I like about the text, and the rights and wrongs of that. But I am the final arbiter of the production and he, obviously, is the final arbiter of the text. I think this has, on occasion, been very tough on the actors, because we do develop a kind of Tweedledum and Tweedledee act, and we are, I think, very good for each other. But that doesn't necessarily mean we're very good for some of the actors surrounding us. It's all a bit high-powered, it's very wordy, and we split hairs with great glee. The scrutiny can get a bit much. But Harold will never say, 'You should do that.' He will say, 'That isn't right,' which is something quite different.

Is there an example of that you could give?

Well, let's take *The Homecoming*. The problem there is that the biggest bastard in a house full of bastards is actually the man who at first sight appears to be the victim – that is, Teddy, the brother who brings his wife home. He is actually locked in a battle of wills with his father and with his brothers and, of course, with his wife, during which, in some sense, he destroys his wife, and his family, and his father, and himself, rather than give in. He is actually the protagonist. Now, it's very easy for an actor to fall into the 'martyred' role in that part, because Teddy says so little – just sits there while all the other characters are speculating about his wife's qualities in bed. But this is the point – it's a tremendous act of will on his part and if he was actually feeling anything uncontrolled, he wouldn't be able to do it.

It wasn't until Michael Jayston did it in the film that I realised how hard Teddy actually had to be, and how much in control he was. I'd felt it, but I hadn't pushed it far enough. [. . .] So my approach to a Pinter play is first of all to try and expose the underlying melodrama of the text. I try and find out who does hate who, and who loves who, and who's doing what to whom, and in the first stage of rehearsals play it very crudely.

Does this mean that you have to find what is actually happening, in fact, in so far as there might be a fact?

Yes. There is a fact. Certainly there is a fact. Why, in *The Homecoming*, is Lenny so obsessed from the word go with destroying his father? Talking about his cooking and his rotten meals and so on. Now that must not, in my view, be played with any kind of heaviness: but the underlying feeling is one of absolute naked hatred. Because I think at the base of a good deal of Harold's work is the cockney game of taking the piss; and part of that game is that you should not be quite sure whether the piss is being taken or not. In fact, if you know I'm taking the piss, I'm not really doing it very well; and a good deal of Harold's tone has to do with that very veiled kind of mockery.

Now, actors can't play veiling until they know what they're veiling, so we play mockery, we play hatred, we play animosity, we play the extreme black-and-white term of a character. That stage of rehearsal is very crude, but it's a very important stage, because unless the actor understands what game he is playing, what his actual underlying motivations are, the ambiguity of the text will mean nothing. People who think that all you've got to do in Pinter is to say it, hold the pause and then say the next line, are wrong. The mystery to me is that there is a communication in the theatre which is beyond words, and which is actually concerned with direct feeling. An actor who says to you, 'All right, I may be feeling that, but unless I show the audience that I'm feeling it, they won't understand,' is actually wrong. If he feels it and masks it, the audience still gets it. [. . .] But, very early on, one felt actors making Pinter patterns, and that's really dreadful – though I suppose it's better than actors trying to 'normalise' Pinter's speech rhythms, because the first thing I say to actors when we're beginning a Pinter play is: 'Look, don't mislead yourselves into thinking that if there's a pause there, there shouldn't be a pause there, or if there's a silence, there shouldn't be a silence, because there should. Our job is to find out why. And don't, in order to make it comfortable, turn a full stop into a comma, or break it up in a colloquial way different to the way he's written it.'

I actually believe that Beckett and Pinter are poetic dramatists, in the proper sense of the word: they have a linear structure and a formal structure which you'd better just observe – don't learn it wrong, don't speak it wrong, you can't, you mustn't. But there are various things that you can exercise. One of the greatest influences on Pinter, obviously, is the early Eliot – particularly in the repeated phrase, the catching up of a phrase and repeating it over three sentences, keeping it up in the air, like a ball. Now, that is often written in three separate sentences; but it has to make a unit, and you don't find that unit till about the third week. So at the beginning it is better just to observe absolutely accurately what he's written.

I also know that the intensity of the feeling underlying Pinter's text is so very extreme, so very brutal, that you have to explore this melodramatic area that I was speaking about. And this of course raises the question of where the actors live in relation to each other, physically, because until you start letting loose the naked feeling you don't know the answers to the basic questions, such as, are eyes necessary, or are they not? Are they part of the weaponry?

My vocabulary is all the time about hostility and battles and weaponry, but that is the way Pinter's characters operate, as if they were all stalking round a jungle, trying to kill each other, but trying to disguise from one another the fact that they are bent on murder. And whether you can see a character's face or whether you can't, whether you hold his eyes or not, is absolutely critical – and that to a very large extent comes out of the actor's psyche, once the feelings are being generated. So I wouldn't have anything to say about the physical life of a Pinter play until the emotions had been released, because I wouldn't know what they should be. Equally, Pinter deals in stillness, in confrontations which are unbroken, and I think it is mandatory to do as few moves in a Pinter play as possible. You don't want moves up to the drinks cabinet, or across to the table, in order to 'break it up', or to make it seem naturalistic. It isn't naturalistic. [. . .]

Do you find improvisation is of any value in trying to get at the nature of the underlying tensions?
You can't improvise easily as an aid to acting Pinter, because at the end of the day you still have to speak a very formal text. But you can improvise feeling patterns, or you can play the opposites – say, 'Let's play this scene with you hating instead of loving.' Or you can increase the obvious underlying tensions, you can swap roles – you can do all the things that make people aware of the underlying tensions. To that extent improvisation is helpful.

[. . .] the second stage is to find how to disguise the emotions which are quite evidently being felt. When Ruth returns with Teddy and comes downstairs in the morning and the father is so dreadful to her and to his son, 'having tarts in the house at night', the obvious realistic response would be to break down left and bury your head in the sofa, or whatever. But he beckons her over to him, the father does, and she crosses and looks him in the eye, and he says to her, 'How many kids have you got?' 'Three.' 'All yours, Ted?' Now, by any normal standards of improvisation, Ruth should he playing that scene hysterically, but she isn't. The alarm is underneath, but totally masked.

And the actress knows why she isn't hysterical?
Oh, of course. Because she's taking the old man on. If the old man is making that kind of challenge, she is accepting it. It doesn't mean to say she's not upset, underneath her mask, just as in the last section of the play, when Teddy is deliberately pushing the family, they retaliate with the proposition that his wife should be put on the game, as a dreadful joke at first, to see if he'll crack. And he is saying throughout the last twenty minutes of the play, 'You have your joke. Go on. You want to put her on the game? You needn't think I'll object. Put her on the game.' He's dying inside, because he doesn't, of course, want to lose his wife. But again, the mask is not allowed to slip.

There's one little crack at the end of the play, the most difficult moment of the play, when he's leaving the room, and Ruth says, 'Don't become a stranger.' It is very difficult to play. It's the first and only time she calls him Eddie, which is obviously the intimate and familiar name. It is all there, and it's all very . . . calculated is the wrong word, because I know Harold to be a deeply instinctive writer, who writes very quickly once it's there to be written, and it would not be true to say that he works it all out like an intellectual game.

It's almost as if you have to direct two plays each time you direct a Pinter play . . .?

Yes, you do. You certainly do. And I think the achievement of a Pinter production must be that the two plays meet. Because what stirs the audience is not the mask, not the control but what is underneath it: that's what upsets them, that's what terrifies and moves them. In that sense Pinter's is a new form of theatre. [. . .] And where Pinter on the stage goes wrong is if the actors stop playing the game, it they actually show what they're feeling, because it becomes ludicrous – you know, those unfortunate laughs you can get in Pinter when it's played without underlying truth. Suddenly, something quite apparently serious is said, which pulls the rug away from everything. Now, Pinter is very funny, mainly because you can't believe people can maintain these signals, these masks, and it's so shocking, it makes you laugh. But if an actor indulges himself and actually drops the mask, and says, 'I want to show the audience that I'm breaking my heart,' the whole scene collapses.

I think it's at this point, as you manufacture the masks, that you have to verify, in a very particular way, that you are saying what Pinter says, and hitting the rhythms that he wrote. [. . .] There is a difference in Pinter between a pause and a silence and three dots. A pause is really a bridge where the audience think that you're this side of the river, then when you speak again, you're the other side. That's a pause. And it's alarming, often. It's a gap, which retrospectively gets filled in. It's not a dead stop – that's a silence, where the confrontation has become too extreme, there is nothing to be said until either the temperature has gone down, or the temperature has gone up, and then something quite extreme happens. Three dots is a very tiny hesitation, but it's there, and it's different from a semicolon, which Pinter almost never uses, and it's different from a comma. A comma is something you catch up on, you go through it. And a full stop's just a full stop. You stop. [. . .]

On the whole you've tended to talk about Pinter's work as if it were a unified entity – do the production problems actually not vary a lot from one play to another?

've been talking very much about *The Homecoming*, actually, which I personally regard as his greatest and biggest play. I think that what happened in *Landscape* and *Silence* was a very exciting herald for the future, which hasn't yet quite developed, although I think the Proust film he's recently done is well on the way. We've spoken a lot about hostility and jungle warfare and all the rest, but the other fascination, the obsession in Pinter's world, is trying to pin down reality, trying to pin down memory, trying to pin down truth: which is why Proust is to important to him, and why he's managed to reduce those twelve novels to 212 pages of images, which actually do work. It's the most extraordinary thing to read. And *Silence*, particularly, was a beautiful, heartbreaking evocation of the contradictions of memory. I would think that the problems of what is true, what is false, are going to go on being an obsession with him.

That particular theme was much more explicit in Old Times, *was it not?*
Much more literally explicit, yes.

I think it was because of the literalness that I didn't like it as well as Landscape *and* Silence. *In those plays it almost doesn't matter at any stage what version of reality is valid.*
No, but I think what is remarkable about *Old Times* is that Deeley's own sexual insecurities, personal inadequacies actually make him invent relationships and happenings which were not, in my view, true at all. The play is not about two lesbians, in spite of Visconti. They are not lesbian.

I personally think *Landscape* is a little masterpiece. The problem of *Landscape* was not knowing, knowing and not knowing – a very fraught acting exercise. I rehearsed *Landscape* for about five weeks, I think – it was one of the most difficult things I've ever done, and it's not because of the physical life, because there isn't any. I think, again, you see, it's a fascinating theatrical image – a man talking to a woman, and she utters her thoughts and he doesn't hear them, and she apparently doesn't hear what *he* says. [. . .]

I suppose that the other development I sensed in Landscape *and* Silence *was that whereas previously people were antago-nistic towards each other, in conflict with one another, here were a couple and a trio whose lives almost couldn't have been lived without one another . . .*

Dependence on each other . . . yes, I think that's true. But equally I think one could make a case that in *The Caretaker* and in *The Homecoming* the hostility *is* the dependence. [. . .

Is there such a thing as a Pinter world-view?

Oh, Christ. Speaking personally, I get a very bleak, very uncompromising, very hostile view of life out of him. Counterbalanced by a longing for contact and relation and . . not getting into a situation of deep regrets, which is very painful. Because all his characters do have regrets, do crucify themselves, and everyone else. But I think what is for me won-derful about Pinter is that in an unblinkingly hostile situation where everybody does go wrong in some way or another, there are little moments of light and tenderness which are cherished. He is a very pessimistic dramatist; but I don't really understand how anybody could honestly be writing the 1960s or 1970s and be particularly sunny. People are always saying to me. 'Why don't you do happy plays, that are life-enhancing?' to which the answer is: 'Well, why don't people write them?' But I find the great thing about him is that his tenderness and his compassion are not sentimental, but absolutely, unblinkingly accurate.

Nor cynical . . .

Not at all, he's not cynical, he's unblinking. He scrutinises life unyieldingly, and I think it's my job as a director to scrutinise it, if I can, as carefully as he has.

David Leveaux

David Leveaux was the director who became associated with Pinter's plays in the 1990s, and Pinter thought highly of his approach following his work in 1991 on Betrayal at the Almeida. He was approached to direct the 1993 revival of No Man's Land at the Comedy Theatre. He directed the première of Moonlight at the Almeida in 1993 and Betrayal in New York in 2000. This interview with Georgina Brown, entitled 'Because it's not quite Cricket', was published in the Independent on 1 September 1993.

Beyond politics, beyond situation, beyond narrative. I see it as the first play of Pinter's middle period,' is what David Leveaux allegedly said about *Moonlight*, Harold Pinter's first full-length play for eighteen years. Before writing the play off as probably also beyond the pale, however, it's worth chucking the comment back at the director. He squirms. It's partly the tendentiousness that makes him wince, but mainly the fact that he insists he said nothing of the sort.

'It's just not a trustworthy remark. The play is certainly not beyond situation. The thing about the middle period came out because the question implied that it was Harold's swansong, which irritated me. It's deeply, *deeply*, deeply political. Harold isn't a political writer; he's a *deeply* political writer – like all radical imaginations. He understands politics in the relationships between individuals. But the play is beyond politics in that it's beyond polemic. As for narrative you can't apply Leavisite methodology in the way some critics demand.'

Leveaux ought to know. This is the third time in three years that he's been up to his eyeballs in Pinter. The first time was pretty low-key. When he was asked to stage a revival of *Betrayal* at the Almeida in London, he didn't meet the writer until he turned up to a rehearsal. The second time, things heated up. Pinter had liked enough of what he saw in *Betrayal* to ask Leveaux to direct *No Man's Land* with himself playing

Hirst, the belligerent writer, the part played by Ralph Richardson in Peter Hall's original production. At that stage Pinter became Harold. 'As Harold himself said, he was never going to be Ralph Richardson, but he was going to be something else that would bring a kind of compelling central figure to the play.' He was right, though Paul Eddington also had considerable pulling power in John Gielgud's role of the minor poet Hirst brings home from the pub. *No Man's Land*, a theatrically fascinating but somewhat opaque and never easy piece, romped triumphantly into the West End.

When word was out that Pinter had written his first full length play since *Betrayal*, it was odds-on that Leveaux would be the first director to get his hands on it and that the Almeida would once again be the chosen headquarters for Pinter's renaissance. Leveaux isn't thrilled about the label 'Pinter's anointed son' that has attached itself to him ('It suggests a proprietorial attitude to his work and its interpretation'), but he accepts that that's the impression given. He says they are friends but he describes their relationship as a working one: 'We don't have long-drawn-out discussions; much between us remains completely unspoken.'

The collaboration is all the more intriguing since Pinter might have taken his pick of any one of Britain's senior directors. If Leveaux was a cricketer, all might be explained, but he's the last man to know a wicket-keeper from a back-stop. Toss him a particularly tricky full stop, on the other hand, and he'll talk phrasing and timing for a very long innings. And that, presumably, is something Pinter really appreciates.

To judge from his productions so far, Leveaux appears to have a way with Pinter, both the man and the work. One critic observed that he released the humour of the plays and so relieved the audience of the anxiety of interpretation. 'If the audience are sitting there thinking this is all very clever but don't actually understand it, they are not being made free to experience the play,' says Leveaux.

The first thing he discusses with a cast of a Pinter play is the importance of not being swept up with a received notion of what is 'Pinteresque'. 'That sort of slowed-up naturalism that people understand it to mean may be very different from what Pinter actually is.' Instead, he points out his natural lineage from Noel Coward. 'Thinking about *Betrayal* in Cowardesque terms released a sinew in the language and a range of expression that revealed the play in a different way. The wit burst out.' He also believes that his extensive experience of directing Strindberg and O'Neill has been the ideal preparation for coming to Pinter. 'Like him, they're dealing with intense invasions of human behaviour which tell you something larger than what you seem to be looking at.'

He claims he was unfazed either by having Pinter looking over his shoulder in *Betrayal* or by having to direct him in *No Man's Land*. 'There isn't a status thing between us. Harold came emphatically with his acting hat on. He didn't bring a dogma or a doctrine about how a play should be done. As an actor he had a need to know that something would probably work. If you say something he doesn't understand, he says so – he doesn't mean it rudely – he goes straight to the heart of something. But in the arguments we had about *No Man's Land*, I'd say fifty per cent went his way, fifty per cent went mine.'

This equable strain would appear to contradict the reputation created by Pinter's friends who've said if you don't agree with him you might as well leave the room. Leveaux doesn't pretend he's a pussycat, but he doesn't find him difficult. 'A difficult person is one who's tricky. He's not tricky – or vain. If he was vain, he would never have exposed himself in *No Man's Land*. He could have retired years ago to Holland Park and never been seen again.'

While his association with Pinter has brought Leveaux noisily into the public arena, Leveaux refuses to take any credit for helping to unblock the writer at a time when so many had decided that his plays were getting so short that the rest would be silence. 'He would have written this play if I'd decided to go into the Foreign Office. Quite simply being part of the lifeblood of the theatre enabled him to come back to it again.' And come back with a vengeance. According to Leveaux, *Moonlight* enters territory Pinter has never before explored and has a technical mastery the director finds thrilling. 'It's a very economical telling of a very big story.' *Moonlight* concerns a dying man and the ties that bind him to life and in it Pinter is as cussed and aggressively riddling as ever. What is most remarkable about the play are its moments of tenderness. 'It's not a comfortable play but it is a compassionate one,' says Leveaux. 'It may treat the subject of death but it has got the funniest lines in it written in the last twenty years.' And that's about as far as Leveaux can be drawn on the subject. 'I want to preserve the experience for the audience rather than prescribe what it should be.'

He has a larger mission, however. 'If I do anything, it is that remove the curse of enigma from Pinter. I'm not saying *Moonlight* is easily experienced in the theatre, but it isn't an intellectual crossword puzzle either. Pinter doesn't set out to confuse his plays deal with confusion itself; they become active dramatisations of a confusion we all feel. The plays aren't a code for something else. If you think that, the production isn't working.'

Quite how playful Pinter is being in his plays, however, is harder to judge on the page than the stage. Once a director has imposed a dramatic solution, it becomes much clearer. Pinter who is himself an experienced director (his production of Mamet's *Oleanna* is transferring to the West End next week) has said that the director should treat the writer's work as sacrosanct, and Leveaux is happy to follow this direction. 'The reason for Harold's insistence is not obstinate pedantry. I start with the premise that what is down there is meant and if you think about that long enough it will make theatrical sense. It's easy to fall into the trap of imagining what's written instead of seeing what precisely is written. If he hasn't written a pause and you stick one in, it won't work.

'The act of writing seems to have been accomplished by having an open channel between his unconscious and the page

When he's finished, that channel is no longer open. He does almost look at the play as written by another, so rightly he resists rewriting a line that seems difficult because it obscures the original source of the thing. He comes as an inspired visitor to his own material. Sometimes he will say, "It seems to me that what's happening here is the beginning of some aggression. I don't know what it is." What Harold doesn't do is bring in his briefcase the secret solution to *Moonlight* and then keep it from everybody.'

Gari Jones

Gari Jones is a director and writer. He has collaborated with Harold Pinter on numerous projects both as Director and Associate Director. These collaborations include the productions of Simon Gray's Life Support *(1997) and* The Late Middle Classes *(1999), Pinter's* Celebration *and* The Room *(2000) and* No Man's Land *(2001). He also directed a series of Pinter sketches for the 2002 National Theatre Pinter platform. I conducted this interview on 17 January 2001.*

MB: *How did you come to work as associate director to, and collaborator with, Harold Pinter?*
GJ: The link with Harold was, indirectly, through Nick Ward, who was the first person to take me under his wing, and he and Harold shared the same agent. Harold had a real admiration for Nick's writing. I ended up directing Nick's work and that same sense of collaboration has developed since with Harold.

The first work you did with him was on Simon Gray's writing, wasn't it?
Life Support *and* The Late Middle Classes. Then I directed *Look Europe* at the Almeida followed by a Pinter evening at Soho for PEN and then the Sketches at the National, all of which Harold acted in.

Was your first exposure to Pinter's work, then, knowing him as a director? How well did you know his writing?

He was a major influence on me when I was at school – him and Berkoff, believe it or not. Both of them had, for me, a real dense imagination and there was something almost 'other-worldly' about their work. I don't feel the same now because my understanding of it has changed. At the time there was something very sinister and 'spiritual' about it. I think I felt that I was tapping into something very special. It wasn't something I wanted to share particularly, only with a few people who were working on it together with me. We used do *The Dumb Waiter* in our lunch hour, off our own back. I read everything and would practise it somehow, and try to understand it. This is when I was fifteen to eighteen. So, there's something quite solitary about it in a way. And I think with Berkoff, there was an anger there which doesn't quite come out in the same way in Harold's work. It was a sort of cult thing, but they both really struck a nerve, definitely. I hadn't really had the chance to touch any of his other work and then I was asked to work with him on *Life Support*. To suddenly get a phone call from someone that you admire so much is such a strange thing to happen. Nick took me on a little bit but working with Harold was a big deal. For someone like him to put that trust in me was extraordinary. You always want to get to that point where you can really help and nurture people and I like to feel I'm getting the chance to do that now myself . . . but to hand over your West End production! I was left in charge of it and was giving Alan Bates notes.

Pinter hadn't really worked with an assistant director before, not with the same kind of relationship that he seems to have developed with you. Can you explain what your function is in support of him?

There was a definite sense of understanding where he is as a director and how he deals with text and with actors. And I was respectful of that, because it's very different to me when I'm directing.

How?

Well, for example, the environment: there's always a very focused environment in Harold's rehearsal rooms, and a quietness about it. My rehearsals, however, are, for want of a better word, very laid-back.

But when you started working on Life Support *you had to adopt, or accept, this different approach of Pinter's. Was that difficult?*

Well, I just went in with eyes open. I had no idea what it was going to be like. To be honest, everyone was so lovely it wasn't intimidating, but I really had to learn on the spot and constantly adapt to the situation. I wouldn't say anything unless I really thought it was valid, particularly at that stage, when I was trying to find out what this relationship is. I've never felt since then I've suggested anything that's not been fulfilled, to be honest. I got more and more confident, to the point now where I feel like we're co-directing.

There's much more of a collaboration about it, now?

Yes. With *No Man's Land*, I took rehearsals for a week and I gave the cast all their notes, and I took the show out on tour. That's complete responsibility. I was involved in the casting on that one and *Celebration* and *The Room* as well. I was in on all the auditions or certainly conversations about whether to put the call out to people or not.

I'd be fascinated to learn about Pinter's relationship with his own texts. What did you witness, for example, in terms of his relationship with Celebration *and* The Room, *and how it made a difference in terms of coming to them and making them live again? Live again in terms of* The Room *at least . . .*

What always strikes me is that there's a real sense of him not really knowing what he's written. He says that and I do believe it. He might understand something on an intuitive level, but no more than that.

173

Which is the same as what you or I, for example, would brin
to the rehearsal room?
Yes, absolutely. The rehearsal process for him has reall
become about exploring the play with the actors and not eve
trying to reach conclusions necessarily. It is about finding
clarity in stating what these plays are saying, and to let tha
speak for itself and not necessarily reach any conclusions at a
about them. Occasionally he has them, but he doesn't do thos
conversations of character background. He doesn't really go i
for that. So I do that stuff instead and have those conversation
with the actors.

You provide that 'comfort' for the actors?
Yes. I listen to the making-up if that's what's needed, and h
knows I do that. I think people know sometimes he doesn'
really want to have those conversations because he finds ther
slightly pointless. Although at the end of *The Room*, when th
blind man comes in – 'Who is he?' Having that conversation i
tricky, but you have to have it in order for that connection t
happen between Rose and Riley and be resonant. And it wa
stunning. I remember when we were rehearsing, it was extraor
dinary, and that came from having to have that conversation
ultimately.

What kinds of conclusions were raised in that discussion abou
Riley in The Room?
We had a conversation about Rose's background; about wha
their connection was, and agreed that he wasn't her father
there's an implication of that. It was ultimately a spiritual con
nection, from a past that she's left and wanted to forget. It'
quite a simplistic kind of point of view.

So it's not a matter of pinning it down to facts, and dates?
No. It was a sense of saying that what you feel is from a ver
long time ago; you were in a very different place to this, an
there was something very spiritual attached to that place, an

174

hat's ultimately where your roots are. And there was a tremendous amount of love there. Something happened, and you had
o leave it. It's been forgotten, it's not even something you carry
around in you any more. And I think that by allowing that to
happen then the stakes become even higher. Because if it is
actually forgotten then the whole thing becomes much more
shocking, there's no sense of yearning for it any more, so when
he comes in there is that sense of going 'I don't want to go
here'. Just a tirade of abuse comes out: that's the first reaction,
that's the immediacy of it.

*Was Pinter participating in this discussion? He wasn't resistant
to that conversation happening?*
Not at all resistant. There was just the four of us there and
there was a sense of it being quite delicately, gently handled. I
think that's a prime example of that kind of conversation having to happen – it did have to happen. Whereas, with
Celebration for example, all you can really do as far as he's
concerned is go from what it says in the play. And he does trust
actors implicitly, trusts that they're going to do their work, and
really get to the essence of a character and allowing these facts
to be taken on board, so you can start to build up a bigger picture. There are lots of pointers in *Celebration*, particularly
about the two couples: what their home lives are like, what
their relationships are like with their kids, what their marriages
are like. All those things are in there but they're like snippets,
moments, and once we started playing it those things start
coming out. You have to hang on to those moments because
that's what there is. If you cast well then half the job's done.
Then you're really just looking at shaping it, with delicacy,
clarity and precision.

*And as far as casting is concerned, then, obviously he chooses
actors that are happy to work within this framework of eking
out a performance without emphasis on the characters' back-
grounds and what have you.*

That's the plan, yes, but often people find it very hard as ther
is something very organic about the process, which often h
might really sit back on, sometimes for quite a long time and s
sometimes there can be a sense of 'We're just doing it again?'
And then Harold will go: 'Very good. See you tomorrow.' I
might seem like you're just repeating it, there's the element o
familiarity which is important for him, and he thinks ther
should be that happening for the actor as well. He's the sam
when he's acting. You reach the end of something and he ha
this pause for thought and says, 'Can we do it again?' We do i
again and go, 'Yeah good, see you tomorrow!' Some actors d
really struggle with that approach. But, I can't help feeling tha
he puts so much trust in them and their craft, that it's some
thing that he really cherishes, and doesn't want to infring
upon.

*How would you describe him as an actor? How would yo
characterise his own approach to acting?*
There's similarities to his directing; something very methodica
about it. I know he really believes in a sense of discovery, an
discovering with other people, and that's why he's such a col
laborative man and loves these relationships and nurture
them: with me, Eileen Diss, Mick Hughes and Dani Everett an
all the actors that he's worked with time and time again. He'
one of the most collaborative figures I know. Whatever he'
doing, there is that sense of wanting to discover it with a grou
of people. I think you probably reach personal conclusions bu
not group conclusions, it's just that there's an understandin
that's unspoken within a group of people by the time a pla
opens. It's similar with his acting and with his writing, allowin
things to resonate, to be what they are and not question them
If I've asked him to do something he's never questioned it;
don't think he's ever questioned anything I've said. That's th
same when I'm sitting next to him in the rehearsal room an
the same with him as an actor: you ask him to do something o
give him a note and he just takes it on board. It's then how h

takes that on board, and what he then does with it. It might just sit inside and be there, as an idea or a presence, just something that keeps ticking away. And it might come out in a few different ways over a period of time. You never, never, ultimately go, 'That's it,' and pin it down, and then later go, 'Oh no, you didn't do it that time.' I find that really interesting. That's how I see all these roles: they're all similar. You take something in, trust your own self, your own instinct and your own intuition. And, of course, trusting everybody around you as well. When I was asked to direct *Monologue* for the Lincoln Centre in New York, and the *Sketches* at the National – even though I directed those myself – the relationship still continues.

Was there dialogue with Pinter about what was going on in rehearsals?
Yes, daily.

What's the nature of that dialogue? Is it concerned with the text or with your revealing what's going on in rehearsal and getting advice on it?
I felt really confident with *Monologue* and the *Sketches* that I could do my own thing. We went and had a chat about *Monologue* before I started rehearsals, and I kind of tested the water a little bit about a few ideas I had for it.

Including the insertion of music?
That was the main thing ultimately. I just wanted to really root it in a reality, because in the piece the situation itself is surreal, and so I wanted to give the character a proper space, and give him an environment for it to happen in – that was something me and Eileen Diss wanted to do – rather than it just being these two chairs floating in air, which in itself becomes quite symbolic. The piece does that anyway. So by making him do those things – and he does believe the person's there, he has to. It's just a matter of saying it's just normal, why shouldn't he give him a glass of beer? The idea that they used to drink

together, and maybe had too many, and that was part of their friendship. Rather than it being after tea in the afternoon or something, which kind of roots in that 1950s highbrow Pinter-thing I've always wanted to get away from. So we made it in the middle of the night. The memories came out of a lack of sleep in a way. Maybe he does this every night. The same with the music: there's no mention of music in the script. That music can trigger off memory and emotion in such an immediate way is such an important part of our lives. And so that was something that I just had to, I was going to do it, so, I had to know that he was going to go, 'Yes it sounds really interesting.' I think with a piece like that it was quite a bold thing to do. We ended up with two pieces of music, but there was a third. Harold saw our dress rehearsal in New York and asked if I'd cut the third piece. We cut it, and it was better without it. The light really, really, slowly dissolved leaving the two chairs, and then finally the empty chair went out. It was like he switched off, that was the idea of it. And so that happened to this piece of music, and to be honest it was so much more resonant in silence, I just remember going 'Oh God, that hurts' when I saw it without music there, it was much more telling, it was absolutely right.

So you find Pinter can actually be quite flexible with his own text from that point of view, in terms of people bringing new angles to it?
Absolutely. He's talked to me about some very obscure productions that he laughs about just because he finds them slightly ridiculous. He was talking about a production of *The Homecoming* where in the middle of the night the mother comes on and they have a dance in this production, and they're dancing in the night. You can see the difference. There must be a point where you go, 'No hang on a minute, you can't do that.' But at the same time I think he loves it. I think it's just finding the reality in things more than anything. That's what I mean about talking about reinterpreting things and not doing,

it for the sake of it. I think one thing that I've always felt is that because his work is so revered, everyone has to frown a lot whenever they talk about it. I know that he doesn't, he doesn't treat it like that, and so he finds all that quite funny. I mean a lot of the old tapes I've seen, and, to be honest quite a few productions, since I've been doing this, are far too alienating. All reality is gone. It's not real – and that dialogue is as real as it gets. And I always just wanted to go right against that and root it in a reality. It has to come from a real sort of emotional place in terms of where the characters are at.

You're not talking about clarifying the plays, you're not talking about making it clear exactly what's happening and what they're talking about. You just need the actors to know how to 'inhabit' the character.

Yes, but then, theatrically you can go off on little fantasies which might seem surreal in themselves, but all they're doing in a way is showing what a state of mind is like. He writes the essence of the human spirit, he does it brilliantly, so you don't need to make it weird.

What motivates him now, would you say? He has nothing left to prove, it would seem, nothing more to accumulate. From talking to people like yourself, I gain a sense that he just simply loves the theatre, and loves doing it.

Absolutely, though I do think he does still have things to say. *Celebration*, in comparison to his fifties, sixties plays, is like classic slice-of-life sign-of-the-times. And it does cover so much material. Those little moments, it's all there. He really has got a voice, I always think there's that sense of a need, dare I say it, a need to make himself heard.

There's a bit of bile in Celebration, *political bile. More than a bit. This notion of this is our 'new world order'. These are the people with power.*

It's social bile as well – the state of us! It's dark. It reminds me of all those elements of 'New World Order' and 'Press Conference'. They're only really snippets but it's a combination of those sort of things, isn't it? There's a passion and an enjoyment, but it seems like he's always got his bit between his teeth, and a need to get something out. I think that's where the writing comes from, isn't it? It's so sporadic: when he just writes and it's done, it's like a splurge, so that's why you always feel it's written with quite a darkness.

Would you say that that energy, that motivation, is a kind of enjoyment of the possibility of being subversive, or is it directed specifically at making a point, making something known. There's a contradiction, it seems, between his being articulate and precise on political matters and his choosing to be less revealing within his writing.
The way he perceives people interacting, that's in all the plays. That in itself is quite a unique kind of mindset. That in itself is seeing beneath the surface.

I wonder if the enjoyment he gets from 'rattling cages' comes through in how he wants his plays to operate. Is there any discussion in rehearsals of the audience? What's the relationship of this play to the audience? What do we want to do to them, what do we want them to take from it?
No; he says, 'Oh fuck 'em!' Of course he cares but if an actor says, 'Maybe the audience won't get that' – or a practical thing: if anyone mentions sight-lines! 'You know what I say: fuck 'em.' I think that's to do with making a piece of theatre and going, 'Well if they can't see a bit that's fine,' and I kind of think that's fine. But he does care about what they think.

It is funny, that attitude seems to suggest that the audience's responsibility is to come to it, confront it, and make of it what they will. Which is fair enough. But if that's how you operate in rehearsals there's no sense of attempting to allow the audience to invest in it, it's almost like setting up a barrier for the audience.

It's only ever mentioned if the audience are mentioned. He's like, 'Oh we don't worry about them, we're just doing our thing, and they're watching it.' So I don't think there's a sense of confrontation. It's more to do with practicalities or him not feeling he has to excuse what he's written because the audience might misinterpret it. If those conversations ever come up – 'But won't the audience think x-y-and-z?' – he says, 'Well, I didn't write it for them!' He does want people to get it because I know when we talked about *No Man's Land* he said to me that he wanted to make sense of it. He really did. And he hadn't felt like that had been done before.

And what was the sense he was trying to make?
Just to really tell the story. And not allow it to be this slightly ambiguous work: why is this man here, why is he being allowed to talk? All the 'whys' that come up from that play. And I think if it is presented, as I was saying earlier, with a certain acting style and a certain sort of directorial hand, then it can be completely alienating, and people will come away thinking it's just another weird Pinter play.

So it's not a matter of pandering to the audience, it's not a matter of worrying about their sensibilities, it's more a case of sculpting something that will have an effect upon them? It's their job to come and sit and watch it.
Yes. And of course, I think with anything like that there are going to be ambiguities, people don't understand things as other people do, and that is just par for the course, isn't it?

With the more politically orientated stuff he clearly wants to have an effect, clearly wants to change attitudes. He doesn't tell you, 'This is what's wrong in the world.' It's more a matter of inculpating the audience.
Well, it seems always to me that there's a sense of letting that speak for itself and not ever preaching. It's cleverer than that. And even if it's showing us a side of society that is despicable,

that is the representation. It's hoping that people are intelligent enough to get the point. Something like *One For the Road*, when I went to see it, people were coming out really wanting to pin it down. 'Oh that must have been about the recent events in . . .' Or, 'Who do you think that man was?' 'Who do you think he's based on?' He's based on many, many, many people.

When he himself played that role last year it was very clear I thought. You tend to see that role being performed very brutally. The humanity that he brought out in it makes you see that is already there in the text.

Nicolas doesn't think he's doing anything weird. He's just enjoying himself. I think it's often finding the contradiction. And so you don't do the obvious, you let the words do that. I thought he was amazing in that. I remember him saying he was going to do it, and that he was quite scared. Because he understood the implications of playing that part. How revolting that man is. And how upsetting, and how many people are like that. So it was really interesting to hear him say, 'I can't quite believe I've got to get a handle on that.'

Because those people who have that attitude, that power, are the kernel of everything he despises.

Absolutely.

It motivates him?

Yes, and then to turn him into someone who's actually quite normal and enjoying the time in their office and enjoying the game and enjoying their power.

That's what that play offers, isn't it? Once something is normalised we accept it too readily and we're prepared to put up with a great deal.

It's putting ideas into the audience's heads, and the other people's, the other characters' heads. But not knowing, you put the idea there, you plant the seed, and the whole thing just builds up into this utterly, utterly despicable state. Which, yes, it's daily, universal. Just this utter gut feeling, a gut reaction, which I think he does so brilliantly.

The Actor's Experience

Henry Woolf

Henry Woolf's friendship with Harold Pinter dates from their days together at the Hackney Downs Grammar School in the late 1940s. Whilst studying for a postgraduate degree at the Drama Department in Bristol University, in 1957, Pinter told Woolf of an idea he had for a play. Woolf asked him to write it for him to put on at Bristol, inadvertently instigating Pinter's career as a playwright. In 1973 he performed in the première of Pinter's Monologue. *Though he today lives in Canada, he returned to England in 2000 to perform in the revival of* The Room *which was performed alongside Pinter's latest work,* Celebration, *in a double bill at the Almeida Theatre, Islington, transferring to New York's Lincoln Center Pinter Festival. In 2002 he participated in the National Theatre's Pinter Platform, taking a number of roles in a series of sketches and reviving* Monologue *under the direction of Gari Jones. This interview was given on 16 January 2002, and is followed by an article Woolf had written for the* Guardian *that week ('Pinter and I were Kings of the World', Henry Woolf, the* Guardian, *Monday, 14 January 2002).*

MB: *I must ask you about* The Room. *It's a play you have an investment in, you might say, as you were the person who commissioned it. Pinter's first play.*
HW: Yes, I said, 'Do write this play, I've got permission from the drama department to do it.' And then he said, 'I can't write a play in under six months.' But he did. He did it in two days – he says four days but I remember it as two. And the main requirement at Bristol was that the production would cost one-and-ninepence. It cost four-and-six in the end, I think.

You revisited it a couple of years ago, acting the role of Mr Kidd once again. That was the last time you were directed by Pinter.

The only time, except when we did *The Room* in 1960.

A play written so long ago must have been fresh to your and Pinter's minds when you came back to it together. Obviously he knows it well, he's written it, but to return to it after forty-odd years, must, in some way, have been like dealing with a play by someone else.

He has an extraordinary quality of being surprised by productions of his own plays, which is still true and really touching in a man of his age and achievement. There's still surprise, and that, for me, is quite remarkable. He actually has a wonderfully innocent quality of welcoming discoveries by his actors and the directors of his plays. I think sometimes this has led him astray. I think sometimes he has let himself be conned a bit by people who flash brilliant productions in front of his eyes, which are reverential without having any art. The only time Harold and I had an argument about his work was over a production of *Night*, which was all so beautifully middle-class. But it wouldn't be much of a friendship if we didn't disagree from time to time.

How does this surprise he experiences in relation to his own plays manifest itself in his directing?

I've been in the game a long time now, and the kind of directors I can't bear are the control freaks, however much they disguise it with charm, however much they pretend to be democrats. Do me a favour! Harold's not a control freak, he's prepared to accept departures by his actors and by his characters. I know playwrights who religiously control what their characters are doing, they refuse to admit that their characters have a hidden life. But Harold seems tickled pink by what his characters get up to. It's as if he's pulled a cork out of a bottle. He's said in the introductions to his work how you can't control your characters, how they take off. And this has a direct bearing on the way he directs. He's entranced by what people do with his characters. He's delighted, and it's wonderful to see him absolutely bowled over by things. At the same time he will say, 'No, no, you have to be exact with words, exact with the techniques.' When I say he's willing to be surprised I don't mean he's one of these smooth, raw, 'no preparation' directors. He's highly focused, he wants the goods, but at the same time he's prepared to let the bloody horse run. That's very rare, you know. He could easily have settled down on his theatrical backside, but he hasn't. He's still at the cutting edge of theatre, he's still earnest. He's just written a new sketch for the *Sketches* here at the National. And he's still delighted. I can think of people for whom theatre is a curse, because they went into the theatre thinking it was a wonderful chocolate factory, and then they got sick of the taste of chocolate. But they couldn't get out of it, it was too late. By the time you are thirty-five or forty you can't do anything else. It isn't like that for him. He's still excited by it, and loves it. And it's very nice that he's fresh – fresh as a daisy, really.

What was your own experience of performing in The Room *again, after all those years?*
Well it was very strange. It was unearthing something, and not only the play but me. Oneself. It wasn't just the play that was forty-three years older – I was! But at least I was the right age for the part and I sort of fell into it rather. What was nice was that Harold took a bit of a chance, having an old boy who just happened to be his friend doing it. It went well. And it was rather funny, not having been directed by Harold since 1960. He was very good because I was a bit stiff. I'd been a lecturer for years, and directing: I ran a Shakespeare festival, and directed a lot of plays with the students. I hadn't done a lot of acting for a long time. They were a very good cast – Lindsay Duncan, Lia Williams, Keith Allen, George Harris and Steven Pacey – and I was all right actually, if I do say it as shouldn't.

All right in the end. Partly because I knew what was in the play.

What was the experience of working with Pinter again as a director, and as a friend?
It's a great advantage having an actor and a writer as a director in the sense that he understands actors, what the acting process is, what they're up against. A lot of directors have succeeded because they deliberately refuse to acknowledge actors and their problems. They bulldoze their way through them. Which is very convenient for them because the actor has to do all the work, and have all the solutions. They refuse to accept that there is such a thing as an acting problem, they don't want to know about it. Harold does know, so he's very nice and generous with actors. And he's particular, very punctilious, very exact when it comes to rehearsals and stage management. But he's a humane man, he's got a big heart. So, he's very nice to work with. You know one of the nicest things about Harold, he really likes younger people, he likes to hand things on – he loves people like Danny Dyer and Gari Jones, because Gari understands what Harold's after – so he's not an old bull protective of his patch. He's a generous bloke. He's often angry, of course and people get frightened of him. Very frightened.

That reputation is odd. I've always found him very generous, very welcoming and open.
He *is* generous. If he thinks you're genuine. If not, watch out. He's a courageous person, and I'm really upset, actually, that he's so ill.[1] He's always been as strong as a ox. Do you know Virginia Woolf's *The Waves*? Remember how they talk about Percival? Their focus, their dynamo. The idea of Harold being ill is strange for us all, because we all bowled around together you know. And he was our Percival.

Your friendship is bound into his career, as are other of his friendships, it seems. His creative writing seems always to be grounded in real relationships and experiences, however obscure the writing seems to some. He wrote Monologue *specifically for you to perform, and that's another text you've now revisited together. You first performed it in 1973, twenty years ago.*

When he wrote it, I know that he said to his secretary, 'That's for Henry.' He never said that to me. Which is how we are with each other. There's a bloke who puts his money where his mouth is, because he could have had anyone to do that play. Can you imagine in 1973 being offered a solo Pinter play on BBC world-wide television? Do you think a few people would have said no? No. And he chose me. I was, you know, not well known at all.

Was it good to revisit it after all these years?
It's a great play.

I thought it was very light, your performance of it tonight. It had a lot of hilarity in it. For a long time people felt obliged to do Pinter in a serious, grave way. Gari Jones approaches Harold's plays in ways that the author himself would perhaps never do, but still in a very Pinter spirit. One of the qualities of Pinter's own productions of his own plays is that they do seem to undermine expectations sometimes. No Man's Land *here at the National, for example, to my mind, undermined expectations of what Pinter directing Pinter might be. Some of the known, famous lines from that play which are quite bleak – 'No man's land does not move or change . . .' or 'I'm a man on the brink of . . .' – they were given almost as throwaway, funny lines, which made you listen to them differently. Anyone else would have felt that these are serious lines and they have to be said seriously.*

It was the best production of No Man's Land I've seen. One of the reasons I liked it was Corin Redgrave's Hirst. Harold himself and Ralph Richardson were both very good in the part, they played Hirst off the back foot, but Harold must have encouraged Corin Redgrave to play him off the front foot. He was very lively. He came out sparking, to use a Pinter word, in the second act, just sparking.

That aliveness, that sprightliness gave the production a perhaps unexpected levity. Many people expect, and perform Pinter plays in a very dour way.
I hate that. Did you read my piece in the *Guardian* about him and me? You know what I meant – 'the grim hand of reverence'. It's deathly.

From the *Guardian*

It's been really inconvenient, Harold Pinter becoming famous like that. A great playwright, a cultural icon. If he hadn't, we might still be bowling about Hackney together, two lively old gents toddling off to the Sally Ann Sunset Home to be safely tucked up for the night. What with all his writing and acting and directing, I haven't seen half as much of him as I'd have liked over the years. Not to mention marriage, family and other friends – sizable interventions, you'll admit. And me? Well, yes – the world I thought to have stuffed securely up the fathomless recesses of my most trusted orifice suddenly turned nasty, and before I could say 'solipsist' I found myself married, with a family in tow, a working actor and, of all things, a professor. Cor! Up to my ears like everyone else in what is laughingly called life. Ah well.

I might have known the old order wasn't going to last when, by a bit of luck, I got the chance to direct the first production of Pinter's first play, *The Room*, way back in 1957, at the Bristol University Drama Department. On the first night the audience woke up from its polite cultural stupor and burst into unexpected life, laughing, listening, taking part in the story unfolding on stage. They had just been introduced to Pinterland, where no explanations are offered, no quarter given, and you have the best time in a theatre you've ever had in your life. After that, despite the efforts of some skilled theatrical assassins (you should read some of the reviews for *The Birthday Party* from 1958 – pure poison), there was no stopping Pinter. He was away.

However, there are more insidious ways of nobbling a favourite than strangling him at birth – the grim hand of reverence, for instance. The first night of *The Room* in 1957 glittered with laughter and menace. (Good old Martin Esslin – what a wonderful phrase he coined: 'the comedy of menace'.) And the second production? Directed by someone else. Pompous intimidation of the audience: 'No laughs please, this is art' – that sort of thing. The grim hand was already at work. It should never be underestimated. Look what it has already done to some wonderful playwrights – Chekhov, for example. Remember the awful, mummified productions, taken move for move from the original Stanislavski prompt books, that the Moscow Arts Theatre used to bring to London? Dead as mutton. Great actors sleepwalking through yesterday. Embalming fluid has been tried on Pinter often enough, but forty-five years after his first production he still comes up fresh as a daisy. He will never become a museum piece.

Over the next couple of weeks I will be performing Pinter's *Monologue* (at the National Theatre, no less – better than the end of the pier, eh?). It's an unbelievable treat. Pinter first asked me to do it in 1973 for the BBC. He could have had almost anyone play it. A world première of a Pinter play on national television – and a solo part to boot? Quite a few takers, one would think. But no, he asked me. Typically generous. Blindly loyal, some would say. He's the most loyal bloke I've ever met, especially to his old mates. He could have affectionately dumped us years ago, with no hard feelings and no visible bruises. But far from it – fifty years on we are all as close as ever, despite life's vicissitudes.

Playing the Man in *Monologue* is like being on both sides of the mirror at once. The character's world of memory and regret is alive with echoes of the life we once shared as friends: 'You introduced me to Webster and Tourneur, admitted. But who got you going on Tristan Tzara, Breton, Giacometti, all that lot? Not to mention Louis-Ferdinand Céline, now out of favour, and John Dos? Who bought you both all those custard tins cut-price?' Pinter introduced us to them all, of course. I don't know about the custard tins.

Monologue may share locations ('Balls Pond Road . . . the rain in the light on the pavements in the twilight') and situations ('The sweet, the sweet, the sweet farewell of Paddington station . . . nothing like the sound of steam to keep love warm, to keep it moist, to bring it to the throat') with the real world, the bygone world, but the play itself is something quite other – an extended dramatic poem, very funny and very sad. It is a little masterpiece written by someone at the top of his form. Each time I play *Monologue* I hear echoes of other times and other places, but they come from far away. I'm on the other side of the mirror now, alone in a vivid landscape, wandering in Pinterland.

Lindsay Duncan

Lindsay Duncan has been one of Pinter's trusted female actors since she first worked with him in Robert East's Incident at Tulse Hill *in 1981, which he directed. She took the part of Ruth in* The Homecoming *in 1997, created the roles of Rebecca (*Ashes to Ashes, *1996) and Prue (*Celebration, *2000) and took the lead role of Rose in the 2000 revival of* The Room. *This interview took place on 20 July 2001.*

MB: *I'd like to discuss that which makes Pinter distinctive as a director. I would imagine, for example, that he is not the sort of director who works by giving a lot of instructions to his actors, detailing their every move and motivation?*
LD: No, not at all, no. He's very spare. His input is minimal, as you can imagine. One of the things he doesn't ever do is back-story. You don't sit around doing anything like that; you just get on with it. What works is what's on the page and the

relationship between that and the actor and the designer and everybody else. The mystery element in his work is for you as an actor to 'meet' somewhere in your own imagination, I think. He doesn't always articulate things, and even has said about certain things in his plays that he does not know. Personally none of that has ever bothered me because I know something's happening and I know in performance that an audience understands something which, sometimes, is beyond being articulated. And, of course, Harold knows that too. So really he's very practical about it. He's not a time-waster and I think that's evident in both him and his work. He can be delightful, socially: he likes good craic as much as anybody, but in the rehearsal room it's very disciplined. His presence informs the rehearsal room and everyone focuses on the work. I think he also likes to just get on with getting to the point. He likes to raise the stakes quite early on, I think, and that can sometimes feel like a pressure. I remember on the double bill that we did, he made a decision that by the end of the first week we should all be off the book. And then he said we were going to run it and I again felt anxiety and that he was pushing me, and I expressed something along those lines, and he said, 'My feeling is that we will learn a lot by going through this process and that's why I'm doing it,' and that's simply what it was. Of course, he was absolutely right, he knew that it was important to push beyond the embarrassment, the exposure of not being ready, of not knowing the lines terribly well. He knew it was important, because then, by going through the arc of the play, he would learn something and I would learn something because I was the one character who goes all the way through. That's where his understanding of the rehearsal process helps. Does that come from his having been an actor? I don't know, but it is directorial in that he's the one who's taking responsibility for where we all get to at the end of rehearsals and he was very clearly taking the reins there . . . as I remember on *Ashes to Ashes*, there was such an intimate process because it was just Stephen Rea, Harold and me and one stage-management person.

Wasn't Ashes to Ashes *also a performance that really developed while it was running? It wasn't really finished at the end of rehearsals but . . .*
Oh, it'll never be finished. No, it's a play that really haunts me.

But confronting a character like Rebecca and trying to absorb and project her dilemma, and make emotional sense of it yourself, that's quite a chore.
I don't have any difficulty making emotional sense. It's hard to talk about it, because it really affects me. It's a play that I don't think will ever leave me really and I suspect Harold feels that it was unfinished business, that first production, and maybe Harold didn't know quite how to hand it over to an audience. I don't think any of us knew. It was much easier to be in the play and to connect with Rebecca and her journey from that sitting room to that other place. Of course I feel passionately about making it possible for an audience to receive it on some level and I think Harold was maybe chasing that himself when we were doing it. And because it is such an intimate piece and there were just the three of us working on it, it was very hard to get a kind of objectivity, hard to get down to that practical matter of 'What does this mean? How do we get them there? What is confusing in the play?' I think Devlin is the audience's point of access and you have to have a point of rock-solid determination in that place for Rebecca's thing to float away, but that's not to make it light in any way, I mean, where she goes is palpable. But, you know, he is determined – an intellectual thug – to keep her in that room to keep her with him, amongst other things that are going on. Testing the nature of their relationship, testing the level of sexuality between them, all that stuff is going on. I'm curious about where Harold's understanding of the dynamics lies. I've always wanted to do the play with Harold as Devlin, because I think he'd be a fantastic casting for that part. I've seen him quite a lot on stage, in recent times. Seeing him in *One For The Road*, it informed everything. I always remember a piece of direction Harold gave me for *Ashes to Ashes*: it's the

end of the play, Rebecca is isolated and her words are loaded with tragic implication. Personally, I find it devastating. I tried it in different ways and then, in previews Harold said, 'You know really it works when you just drive it through like a truck.' He was absolutely right. Not rushed, but remorseless. You can be drawn as an actor to the murky waters of sentiment, deeply felt emotions etc., but Harold's writing and directing demand something more rigorous.

This suspicion you have about Ashes to Ashes *being unfinished business, and curiosity over Pinter's own relationship with the work, is revealing in what it indicates about his own relationship with that creation, and his writing in general. He himself was still tackling it, coming to terms with it, long after the ink had dried.*

Yes, he was still tackling it. On day one of rehearsals he said – as you know he always gives new plays to close friends and collaborators to read – he said to me, 'Some people have suggested to me that Rebecca may have been pregnant and lost a child and I'm asking you what you think about that.' And I felt then and still feel, for me, that that was too specific. I couldn't use it. I didn't need that information in order to play Rebecca. But he did ask me what I thought of that . . . and obviously he chose to share the fact that this had come up. He was floating a notion, and it's interesting, isn't it, about what he's written. Of course he can quite rightly be very firm about certain things, but he has a very touching openness about certain things. So, if this had occurred to people, was that indeed something that should be part of the thinking, should be almost part of the play? Not that he would write it in, but almost asking, 'Is that what's happened to Rebecca the character I wrote?' We had this very brief exchange about it and that was that and it was never referred to again.

So, he watches your process as you inhabit a character. What kind of things does he do to intervene?

He's quite gentle with his interventions. He might pose questions. I suppose, like all good directors, he'll see where you're going and then he'll use what you are evidently beginning to achieve – it's almost an editorial job – then maybe encourage you to go further. He's not controlling in my experience at all, but he's very, very watchful. His concentration is extraordinary. So he does sense quite acutely what you're doing and where you're going. He is capable of talking so freely about something as if he hasn't written it, which is where he's able to let you discover things for yourself, because he knows there's stuff in his writing which can only be recovered through the process of performance. Sometimes, as I think with all writers, there will be surprises in there which are to do with a sort of chemistry between an actor and a piece of writing. Now, he recognises that absolutely, so you don't feel constrained because he's written it. He can be quite amusing about himself and talk about the author ironically, as if he weren't actually standing there.

Does he never 'blow the whistle' and veto ideas, as the author? Is there ever a point where he says, 'That is simply not what I wanted,' or 'not what I intended'?
I don't think I've had that experience. He'll select his actors to meet his work and his way of working. Obviously, he's not going to ask actors who are known for their longing to improvise, because that would get everybody absolutely nowhere. It's my way to sort of creep up on the text and just slowly immerse myself and to some extent that's in tune with the way that he works, though he would be inclined to push the pace. I'm not suggesting any kind of smug, perfect agreement, because neither he nor I know what the end result will be. I think it's quite important to remember his sense of openness about what happens when the actors begin. And I think even with plays that have been done before, there is an absolutely genuine sense of him being very open to all possibilities. It's not a real sort of tug about what he wants to do against your own impulses.

There's no sense of him pushing you in any particular direction.
It's an exploration.

It sounds like a collaboration, really . . .
Yes, absolutely . . . Some people employ a certain kind of method. I just worked with someone who gave me a book of notes on the background of this character, and everybody else, and how much they earned and so on . . . Almost Mike Leigh territory. And then I was back with Harold, who just doesn't do any of that.

Have you ever witnessed any kind of conflict between people who need to know background, who find some need for assimilating the motivation of their character, for example?
Well, with *Celebration*, we did feel, initially, a little bit exposed, a little bit bewildered. We weren't quite sure how and where to pitch these people, and I thought, 'Oh God, we're actually going to get to that point where we'll have to pose questions.' I've never felt the need before, but we weren't quite sure. It's very much an ensemble piece, you can't chart your own course through it, not that you ever do really, but these characters have a thin emotional life and so probably that was one of the reasons why we felt exposed and started really wanting to ask the question that we knew we would get short shrift with. I think I was chosen as someone who had a good relationship with Harold to ask something like, 'Where did they come from, how common are they?' He said, 'I refer you to the text and I think you'll find the clues are there,' and of course they were.

How do things pan out over the few weeks of rehearsals?
With *The Room* particularly, and maybe even *Celebration*, but certainly with *The Room* he was very keen to get off book and capable of running sooner rather than later. And then he'd go back and work through it. He thinks you learn by doing the whole and you need to do that fairly quickly, otherwise you lose sight of it. You know, of course, there are no resolutions,

no solutions. With these plays, you're just opening up more questions. I think he understands that you need to get to that end point and you have to feel that process in order to get the arc of the play, because the characters just tumble, they free-fall through their lives, their situations and you have to let go. I haven't asked him why he likes to run early, but I think he knows that it's important for the actors and presumably it's important for him as well, that he can see the whole before going back to detailed work. But on the other hand, rehearsing *The Room*, he was very calming and at pains to take the pressure off me and for me to just settle into it, not feel this awful pressure. But having gone through that kind of work, then his foot goes down on the gas, as it were, and he knows he's got to then put some pressure on, otherwise you won't be able to move on.

Is there then a scrutiny of detail once he's got the whole thing together?

Once it looks real and he can tell that the actors have stopped being self-conscious and are actually settling into it, then, only at that point, will he gently remind you of the emotional aspects of the character: the fear, the anxiety. And then, again, he'll encourage you to let that happen, to not gloss over it; he won't let you go for ages through the stuff at a superficial level. If it's practical stuff you do it until you're comfortable, but then he will remind you – as when Rose says, 'Can you hear the wind?' – that it's very important that we sense the wind and her anxiety with the outside world. He will be onto that right away, saying, 'Let that happen.' Those anchors go down and if you go on for too long without doing that with commitment, then it's not going to inform the next piece, you know. The thing about Harold is he's very spare. It's deceptively simple, I think, because he takes huge responsibility in his attentiveness to see what you're doing and so there isn't a great deal to be done, but he just encourages you to go deeper there, take your time there. Sometimes, with other people you stop and you talk about things for ages and, of course, actors are very good at spinning out the talking because it delays the moment where you have to get up onto your feet again and do it, which you both love and hate. But that would never occur with Harold.

Would you say, then, that he acts as a sounding board for you, rather than someone who literally directs you?
Yes. At least, that's been my experience, really.

As an approach, that sounds like it gives you a great deal of freedom and involves a great deal of trust in you as an actor. To what degree do you get support in that from Pinter striving to make sense of these characters, or to get into them? Because it sounds to me more like a process of decreasing doubt than increasing knowledge. He must be validating you in some way as you move on?
Yes. In the most general terms. Harold is without any doubt on your side. I've never felt as if I have to prove myself to him, I've always felt that the rehearsal process was embarked upon in order to discover what's in the play and hand it over to an audience and that as the actor I would need and get his support. He's not sitting there like some judge, and all his notes are given always with not a critical sense but a supportive sense: 'You may find it helpful to . . .' 'You might find it easier . . .' I think he does see himself as, several things, yes, a leader, an enabler, a supporter, an editor. All skills that I think you do need as a director; the prevailing sense in the room was discipline and support for the actor.

I imagine that a difficulty of acting in his plays is the amount of exposure you experience as an actor; there aren't many words to hide behind, are there?
I think it's fantastic, it's just the greatest satisfaction because those words have been chosen with such precision and you have such a fantastic sense of knowing that you've just got

everything you need. You just have to make that leap of faith – as you always do as an actor – about just inhabiting character and getting that language in your mouth. You can't sidle up to it. And when you do that you've got so much information already. It's the same with Shakespeare, technically, maybe more difficult to get your lungs going and just thinking longer thoughts with Shakespeare, but you know there are dense images; it's the same with Harold. These words just go (*imitates a machine gun*) reverberating, don't they? Things that just give me goose pimples because he is a great writer, so his selection process is brilliant. Once you've made that commitment, that's why he knows you need to do that because until you really let yourself go into the play and the writing, you won't have what he's giving you. You've just got to jump in and then of course you will emotionally discover more and more and more. But he's given you everything you need. His writing is the most comfortable I've ever been in, I think. 'Comfortable' – it's so funny to use that word, you know, as an actor, because of course it's the most uncomfortable world, most uncomfortable. And he, of course, understands that. He said to Stephen and me before we performed *Ashes*, literally before the first performance, he said, 'You know that a lot of people hate my work. I mean really hate my work and you're going to be in the firing line.' He must have known how elusive *Ashes*, particularly, is. But that's him saying, wisely, 'This is what it's going to be like, there's nothing I can do about that,' and you know, it was quite bumpy, often. And of course you knew that, he didn't have to say it. But it's generous, it's generous because, again, without being remotely sentimental, he was saying, 'We're in this together,' and sort of, 'I'm sorry, I can't do anything about this, this is where we are and this is what's awaiting you,' and it's great, it's just great.

Lia Williams

Lia Williams also has a long-standing association with Harold Pinter. She first worked with him, playing Carol, in the UK pre-mière of David Mamet's Oleanna, *which he directed at the Royal Court Theatre in 1993. She acted alongside Douglas Hodge in* The Lover *and Pinter himself in* The Collection *in 1998. In the 2000 New York Pinter Festival double bill of* The Room *and* Celebration *she played the roles of Mrs Sands and Suki, respectively. She played the part of Ruth in the 2001 revival of* The Homecoming *alongside Ian Holm as Max. This interview took place on 27 April 2001.*

MB: *You have become one of the Pinter 'family' of actors with whom he has worked on a number of occasions. How did you first come to work with him?*
LW: I met him as a director, before I knew him in any other way. He was asked to direct David Mamet's *Oleanna*. I think I'd be right in saying one of Mamet's greatest influences was Pinter. Mamet asked Pinter to do *Oleanna* and out of the blue I was pulled in to meet him, and read for him. I think it had been sug-gested to him that he met me. Harold meets very, very few peo-ple when he is casting; he is unlike most directors, and he is absolutely brilliant at knowing exactly what he wants. His abili-ty to cast correctly is a huge talent in itself. So, I went to meet him for *Oleanna*, only knowing his plays. I had fallen in love with him as a writer from the age of seventeen, when I first started reading him, but not knowing why. I just loved the muscularity of it and the rhythm, the musicality of it, without really under-standing it. So then to meet this man who had become my hero at seventeen and to go into his writing studio was an extraordi-nary experience, but the thing that surprised and delighted me was how full of humility he is, and how kind and encouraging.

Is acting Pinter different from appearing in any other writer's work?

I understood exactly what he wanted very, very quickly. It's a sort of innate understanding really. Which I think a lot of his actors who work with him regularly have. I think as an actor you can either do Pinter or you can't. It is like trying to teach an actor to be funny if they don't naturally have a sense of timing.

When you say some actors have an innate understanding of Pinter's world, do you mean they don't question it? They just involve themselves in the script without trying to intellectualise it or absorb it . . .
Partly that, but it's really – it's just an instinctive reaction. That it's just a feeling you have for it instinctively. And if you don't have that with Pinter's work as an actor, you are pretty lost. That's why I think it is quite hard to do his work well. Look at *The Homecoming*. I don't know what it is about his work, but I start reading it and instantly the hairs on the back of my neck go, and I just don't get that with many writers. He has this brilliant way of writing women, which I find really exciting because not many writers do it. It is something to do with the hidden agendas and the duality within his characters, and the less-than-conscious workings within them. He seems to write it brilliantly, I think. I never understand people who say he is a misogynist.

The Homecoming was the first play to properly disprove that theory, I would have thought. It's not a feminist play, in my view, but you do get this one character, this female character with various different perspectives, who works . . .
She controls all of them, doesn't she?

Yes, and she also has control of how she is perceived by people. Even if that perception isn't always particularly pleasant.
She teaches them to behave with her. And then she uses it to control them. A lot of people would say that's misogyny, but I just don't think it is, I just think it's thrilling theatre, brilliant

character writing. It's about conflict. His characters have conflict with each other, but they have conflict with themselves and that's what's really exciting.

What was your experience of being directed by Pinter in one of his own plays?
He has this ability as a director to be able to say one word to you or a very short sentence and suddenly it is as if the whole part can unfold before you. He might say, 'OK, well, what if she does that this time?' and then suddenly, for some extraordinary reason, whether it's the body language or the distance or how it relates to the audience or the space of the room, whatever the conflict is between the two characters, it just finds itself and opens up immediately. And you don't need to discuss that. It's there.

No, it's a spatial understanding as much as anything else. What is the proximity between the two people? Where does the eye contact happen and not happen? It's those kinds of questions which you can't codify.
It is often to do with beat and rhythm, it is never intellectualised. And he'll never ruminate. He will often do it in terms of hearing . . . if it is rhythmically wrong, he can say, 'Just come in a beat quicker there,' and you'll do it and not only does it work musically, it informs you about the character, the situation. And he is brilliant at knowing when something is not quite right and, as a director, he is not afraid of waiting for something to happen. I remember when I was doing *Celebration*, I was struggling in rehearsals, not with the musicality or anything, but with who this person was, who Suki was. And I had a line where I say, 'Oh I do,' and on this one particular occasion 'Oh I do' slipped out in a different accent and inflection and he said, 'That's it!' and we realised that she had to come from a different class. By the end of the afternoon, we'd got it sussed and we knew what we had to do. But until we heard that sound, he couldn't say how he thought that character needed to be. Which is fantastic,

because it means he comes into rehearsal with his own work, as a director, without any preconceived ideas.

So he is unravelling the mystery at the same time as you are?
Absolutely, he is. And you can never say to Harold, 'What's this bit about?' or 'What is the intention of the character?' because he will just say, 'Well, I don't know.' I remember one occasion when I was playing Mrs Sands in *The Room* and Keith Allan was Mr Sands and I said to Harold, 'Is there any way that Mr and Mrs Sands are consciously trying to remove Rose from this place? Are they threatening her? Are they a threat to her?' And this was all on day two of rehearsals or something. And he said, 'Oh no, no, no, I don't think so, no.' So, we, we sort of dismissed it, and we did all our rehearsals and I think on something like the second to last rehearsal before we went into the theatre, he just very quietly said to me, 'I think you could be right.' I was very moved by that because he is the writer, and he created it.

But you revealed something to him, or there was a sense of your having done so.
It informed me about him, how he is not aware sometimes of what he has written. He'll say that himself, he'll say he doesn't know how he does it, he certainly can't explain the process of it.

So you'd say that really when he's directing you, he's sharing the creative process with you, almost to composition, or re-composition of the original work?
Yes, he's sharing it. He said to us all on the first day of rehearsals for *Celebration*, 'This is a voyage of discovery for me as much as it is for you, I don't know what the bloody hell it is.' When he described it to me on the phone, when he asked me to do it, he said, 'Well, I don't know what you'd call it really, I suppose it's a farce, I'm not sure.'

Did you detect any difference to his approach to, say, Mamet's play than to his own work. Was there a different kind of investment at all?
No, none.

I think that's interesting in itself.
It's extraordinary. No, he walked in to *Oleanna* rehearsals with the same 'not knowingness', as he did with his own work. With *Oleanna* it was extraordinary because he just spent hours and hours and hours patiently watching us create it. Chipping in and pulling out and chipping in and pulling out, and it's like a sculpture really. Then he gradually refined us and pared our performances back to the bones. This created a knife-edge tension and made the play dangerously taut for the audience.

He strikes me as a relatively traditional director in many ways . . .
He's certainly not interested in actors' bonding games and pretending to be washing machines, so . . . Yes, he is he's absolutely text-based, and thank God for it. Of late, well since I've known him really, he really has kind of lightened up about his work, for want of a better expression. He would snort at me if he heard me say that! You know he'll even say things like: 'You don't have to do that pause if you don't want to!' But having said that he's absolutely rigid about words. I think one day he came in to rehearsals on *Celebration* and he said, 'I'm cutting a word!' and everybody went 'Ohhh!' I think it was an 'and' or 'a', and we all scraped ourselves off the floor in disbelief because he'd cut a word! But in terms of the rhythm of a thing he'll help, he'll say, very diplomatically, 'I don't think that's a three-dot pause, it's a two-dot pause!'

Being 'faithful' to a text is important to him, it seems to me. An obligation to recognise truths within a text and then make them manifest on stage, whether it be through design or within your acting.

Totally. He is an intensely faithful and loyal person, whether it be in his political beliefs or who he loves, or whose text he chooses to put on. And his actors, and people like you, you'll find that he'll be incredibly loyal to you, because once you have earned his respect, you will have it for ever. And I think that feeds through to every aspect of his life. And I think it feeds through to his texts, and . . .

Directing other people's texts as well?
Yes, absolutely.

Respect for someone else's creativity. Even to the point of arguing with them, as with Mamet. They had a dispute, did they not, over the use of Mamet's original ending to Oleanna, *which Mamet had replaced.*
Mamet changed the ending. He rewrote the ending to protect his wife, who was playing the role off-Broadway, and she was getting a really hard time from the audience, so, he rewrote the ending. I don't know if you've seen it, but, in the rewritten ending, he beats her up and she stands up slowly and she says, 'Well that's right.' Blackout, end of play. But in his original she gets up having been beaten up and continues her diatribe, saying he has failed in his responsibility to the young and so on. It's a crueller, much harder ending. But, Harold was absolutely convinced it was the right one. And yes, they did discuss that . . . there were a lot of faxes going between them!

Did you try out the other ending at all, or did you just simply stick with . . .
No, Harold really believed . . . he phoned me up and he said, 'Well, what do you think?' and he described the alternative ending, and I agreed with him totally and I said absolutely, it has to be the first ending. And I don't know if we spoke of knowing that the British audiences weren't going to be quite so vocal as the American audiences. I don't think it was to do with that. It was to do with the coda. It was to do with the structure.

And he really enjoys throwing something at an audience and letting them decide. Otherwise it didn't end itself properly. I think he enjoys anarchy, he really enjoys throwing something at an audience and letting them decide, and of course it caused enormous conflict. The audience would divide themselves. And that's brilliant, that's great, conflict is great drama. So it was good. But he will always say, you know, sod the audience, let them think what they need to think, whatever that may be it's fine.

So, it's not as though he wants to direct them through the play?
No, he's not trying to manipulate anybody. He'll just let an audience decide for themselves and often that really winds them up because people need to know, particularly now. They want to know how to feel and what to think because we are told all the time, by everything coming to us – advertising, television, film, everything. And he just won't do it and so audiences just get cross and upset. They need to know what *Celebration* is about, or what *The Room* is about, and they get upset when they aren't given clear answers. So you know, you often go into the bar after the show and there is quite a tense atmosphere, quite heated, even hostile. You can like it or loathe it but here it is, and he's not afraid of that. I don't think Harold has ever been afraid in his life. Except perhaps by his own mortality.

A Design Perspective

Pinter's 'family' of designers, whom he often employs on the productions he directs, and recommends for productions of his own plays, include Mick Hughes (lighting), Eileen Diss (design), her daughter Dani Everett (costume) and Tom Rand (design and costume). This interview, from 3 April 2001, is with Tom Rand, who discusses his relationship with Pinter as a director. He has designed the costumes for The French Lieutenant's Woman, *Ronald Harwood's* Taking Sides *and*

Reginald Rose's Twelve Angry Men *(which Pinter directed in 1995 and 1996 respectively), the 1995 revival of* The Hothouse, *in which Pinter performed,* Ashes to Ashes *in 1996, and the decor and costumes for* The Lover, The Collection *and* A Kind of Alaska *at the Donmar Theatre in 1998. This interview took place on 19 July 2001.*

Tom Rand

MB: *How do you get along with Pinter as a director with whom you collaborate?*
TR: You expect, of course, that he's going to be hugely perceptive, as a director. What you don't quite expect is his humour as a director. His plays are funny but you don't necessarily expect the man to be as funny. And also you don't expect him to be so incredibly theatrically attuned. Again, the plays are theatrically attuned, but it doesn't necessarily mean that the man is, but by God he is. A writer doesn't necessarily always make a very good director. He understands – and rarely do directors understand this – when to leave actors alone. He seems to have an ability – whether that's because of his work as an actor, I don't know – he seems to have an ability to realise exactly how far to push the actors at the right minute. I suppose it's because he's a very tactful man. And he's incredibly loyal to actors.

What is Pinter's creative process as a director?
He approaches the rehearsal process, the actual four weeks or whatever it might be of rehearsing the play, in a relatively traditional way. In my experience he's always started by the actors sitting in a circle reading the play. Which a lot of directors don't do; a lot of directors have decided that is traditional and boring and not helpful, and what we actually need to do first is, you know, discover how people lived in Eastern Europe in 1912 by doing a collage, and now let's play a game of tag, and now let's do exercises and so on and so on. And as all of those

things happen the actual text of the play gets shoved round the back somewhere. With Harold you start in a really sort of quite traditional way, and there's no doubt that actually hearing actors reading the words, whether it's good, bad, or indifferent, is hugely helpful. I think if he's directing a play of somebody else's he needs to get a sort of feeling of the shape of it. And if you just hear it in a bald way, you get a very good sense of that. And then he starts by working, from the start of the play through to the end of the play, and working sort of slowly, and usually working so that actors can bring a lot of information to it, which can then get chipped away. In a sense you start with too much, and end up with the right amount, rather than try and impose on nothing. I think that's a more truthful way of ending up with a production that has something to do with the play. And I don't think that's different whether it's his own play or whether it's somebody else's play, because I think he puts himself in that same position. I think he's very clear on doing that. Harold of course is an organised human being, which is very nice, and he's organised with his own time, he organises other people's time, and he realises that work doesn't happen from now to in ten minutes' time; work happens over longish periods.

What is his attitude to the work, as you have experienced it? What degree is it a collaborative process, and what degree is his word the law?

Of course, he obviously does have complete control, but he often doesn't choose to exercise that complete control. If he likes what you've done then it stays there. If he likes it seventy-five per cent it probably stays there a hundred per cent, because he thinks, well, this other person has chosen this object, they've chosen it for a reason, I'm not going to veto it. It was very interesting, working with him on Ronnie Harwood's play *Taking Sides*, which was a new play, and there was never ever a moment of Harold, certainly not saying but even implying, 'I can solve this problem.' Because of course with a new play there are moments when the play is in a rehearsal, when the author is there, when something perhaps doesn't work quite as well as it should. And there was never, in that instance, a moment of thinking that Harold was going to use his playwright card to be the doctor. He was the director; the fact that he was a playwright was almost incidental. He certainly never used that as a tool as a director. Of course, it informs him as a director, but he would never use it as a way of increasing his status or anything like that . . . I've never felt him even vaguely implying, you know, 'I'm a world-famous writer, my plays are done all over the world every week, why don't I solve this problem for you?' Not at all.

Harold, of course, famously doesn't like extraneous noise. The Theatre Royal, Bath, always has seagulls above it because it's relatively close to the sea, and I think it was at a run-through of *The Collection* which we took on tour that he said to somebody, 'Can't you shut those seagulls up?' I've sat in theatres with him when somebody's been eating a noisy box of chocolates and he was not happy about that. And now we're in the era of the mobile phone. At the first read-through of *Ashes to Ashes*, as Lindsay Duncan got to one of those very long speeches near the end – and I think there were only two actors, Harold, Eileen, one stage manager, and me, and that was it – and Eileen's mobile phone went off in the bottom of her bag. She, of course, went absolutely scarlet, desperately turned the mobile phone off, but there's no doubt that the atmosphere had completely gone for a moment. And, because he has such enormous respect and love for Eileen, she was all right, but I think anybody else might have been out of a job very quickly!

Is it possible for you to guess at why Pinter has been attracted to you as a designer?
It's because I do work in a character-driven way. All my discussions with Harold have always been about character, and one of the marvellous things is that Harold has never said, 'I think

she should wear pink or blue,' or anything of that nature, it's always been, 'What sort of person is this?' And therefore, how they look comes second.

So in your discussions of character with him are you being told what the character is like, is about, or – or is your opinion being sought?
We discuss it. Even if it's one of his plays. In fact probably more importantly if it's one of his plays.

Would you say the joint effort is primarily to serve the play, rather than apply a vision of some sort?
Absolutely. That doesn't mean that the end result can't be extravagant, flashy, hugely varied, hugely colourful, hugely dramatic. It doesn't mean that the end result is going to be beige and boring. Unless it needs to be beige and boring for that particular work.

And I presume you could actually challenge the work in some way, whilst serving it.
Often you undercut the work, or very often you can do the unexpected, which can enrich the work too. Harold's plays have a very strong sense of place always. Very often, I think, he's triggered by, a 'where': *where* this play is set. When I designed the sets and clothes for *The Birthday Party*, Joe Harmeston, the director, and I went to see Harold with this sort of preliminary model, and we'd already decided that it was a house somewhere on the south coast, and so on and so on, we knew that anyway. I don't think this had been done before, the set for that play showed the whole house. And, also, it was important to set it by the sea. And so you saw this skyscape, and it had a sense of being at the end of somewhere, but somewhere slightly isolated, slightly lost.

What I got from the design in that production was there was a sense of the characters being trapped at the end of somewhere, but with this potential for escape, but – but no actual escape properly sought.

Exactly. The walls were either transparent or they were opaque, and it depended where people were in the house, and went up the stairs, and all that stuff. Originally we were going to go through and see through to the back of the house, and see much more of the outside. We actually wanted the house to move and to be on a pivot, so that its point of view slightly changed, but we ran out of money.

The space of the plays is built into most of his plays, isn't it?

I think they are. Equally, you could imagine productions by certain directors in certain countries which might choose to set his plays in a sort of expressionistic or menacing or overtly twisted visual, which would be hugely unhelpful. Because any thing that is menacing or worrying, or any of those other words, in his plays, is usually implied by tiny nuances of lan guage; it's not *The Cabinet of Dr Caligari*. And the moment anybody starts doing that with his plays, and I'm sure they have . . . it must be just ghastly. Because you don't need all that stuff, and of course what is always more unnerving about peo ple is when they're in a relatively real place. You just don't need the rest of that stuff going on to make this person sinister.

One of the characteristics of Pinter's work, to my mind anyway, and I think it can get a little overlooked, is the fact that he is very rooted in the real world. And yet there is a relationship between a, shall we say, 'naturalistic' view and the atmospheric one which does in a way lend itself to a more expressionistic approach maybe, or one that in some way has visual motifs dominating in order to communicate beyond the verbal.

And I think the moment you start distorting those realities I think then you're on very, very dodgy ground. And I think you're in danger then of telling the story in the wrong kind of way.

Talking about the 'where' of a play, with Ashes to Ashes, *there's a great importance in that room, the domestic space, and the lighting of that room which dims . . .*

I think I was slightly in at the birth of *Ashes to Ashes*, in that Harold and I were having a meeting about *Twelve Angry Men*, and we were talking about the background of the various characters in *Twelve Angry Men*, and there was one of the men that we decided was from Europe. I mean the playwright had already decided, and we sort of built on that slightly. My parents came from Vienna in 1939 after the Anschluss, and we were talking about this particular character, and his age. The play was set in the fifties, and we decided he was in his forties so he was born in about 1910, which was the same year that my father was born. And I told Harold that this character had a slight quality of my father. So I told Harold a little bit of my family history, which he knew mostly anyway, because we talked about that before, and then I left; we'd had a discussion that was over. And then we met up about two or three weeks later, and he said to me, 'Last time we met I was terribly rude to you.' I said, 'No you weren't, you're never terribly rude, what are you talking about?' And he said, 'Well, while you were here I had to get rid of you, because I had to start writing, and there's a play for you downstairs.' And it was *Ashes to Ashes*. What we'd been talking about had triggered him off in some way. Something had pulled a tiny lever, and had started a play going. And I think *Ashes to Ashes* was a play that arrived fairly well formed in Harold's writing.

Would you mark your work with Pinter as significant in your career?

You know, I've designed for Zeffirelli, which is a wonderful experience, and he's a hugely talented man, but my work has been informed by working with Harold, who is not the most visual of people in lots of respects, who is not a designer himself, who doesn't have that sort of complexity of vision. And yet, his vision is closer to my heart, quite frankly.

You say he's not a designer – clearly he's never dabbled in stage design – do you find you're ever working with a kind of 'blindness' in him? That you are in effect contributing to his awareness of the work in hand?

It isn't a 'blindness'. Inevitably, because of what I do, I bring a visual quality to a verbal one. Sometimes you can surprise the author. I mean, it's interesting, authors don't necessarily know what people look like. Why would they? I mean Harold, you know – read his stage directions – there's nothing there. And yet there are other authors who tell you in hugely elaborate detail what people look like, which are usually wrong. Even novelists: the description of the female protagonist in *The French Lieutenant's Woman* is entirely different to what you see on the screen. That image of the woman standing there in a cloak on the Cobb is not what's in the book. In the book she's wearing a long military man's coat. And we decided that that was not the right image for that character. Authors don't necessarily know it all, and Harold of course doesn't try to in that I don't think he's ever told you what somebody looks like, or how somebody enters the room, or even what the room looks like. He might tell you where things are in the room, but that's about it. And usually you work that out for yourself anyway.

Many writers will dictate design and costume and so forth . . .

Yes, and usually it is dictation that you actually just chuck out straight away. I think it's padding very often. I think it's the sort of thing that often goes on in bad novels, you know, it's not helpful. I mean it's significant that Harold is a huge admirer of Beckett. I was lucky enough as a really young man to work on a production of *Waiting for Godot* that Beckett directed. A production at the Royal Court in the middle sixties, which was directed by Anthony Page, but was directed by Beckett as well. Beckett was there all the time. Beckett shared a quality with Harold in that he laughed a lot. And that's something people aren't always prepared for. They don't want to know that he was really happy sitting in a pub talking about football or cricket, and certainly laughing. It's interesting that Harold's film career as an actor seems to be moving along.

He seems to be embracing acting again, more and more this last decade.

I suspect he enjoys acting because in a sense it's less responsibility. The other thing that, of course, he enjoys about acting is the camaraderie. He enjoys being with actors, and I think he enjoys being just another actor. He gets nervous, very nervous, but he does enjoy it. The first preview we had of *The Collection* . . . the aisle seats of the Donmar are kept as house seats and I was sitting towards the back, Antonia Fraser was sitting two rows ahead of me, and at the very last minute, as the house lights were going down, Lauren Bacall slipped into the seat just ahead. We subsequently found out she'd actually been at a matinee of something else and had only just made it. She and Harold, of course, are friends. I knew that there were various points in that play where Harold stood on the stage at the edge of that aisle talking to a character who was standing in the aisle. So he had his wife and Lauren Bacall almost in his eyeline. Except, happily of course, he wasn't wearing his spectacles, so he couldn't see them. And that was his great bonus, because I think otherwise, especially at a preview, it might have turned him round completely. Because that theatre's so intimate. I wish I'd been able to do *One for the Road* with him, because they're going to be in New York, aren't they? Of course, Harold's relationship with America is not an easy one.

No. When last I met him, he was talking of how he'd be reviving his One for the Road, *and that he is going to play Nicolas in New York. And he kind of relished the prospect of causing disturbance there with that role, with that play.*

Well, that, and of course, I mean bombing Iraq doesn't exactly help, does it? And when all that stuff went on, what, two years ago now? And again a few weeks ago. Two years ago I said to Harold how glad I was that in his prominent position he'd be able to speak out and say stuff that almost nobody was saying, because it was pretty much a lone voice. I mean, obviously a lot of other people were thinking these things but not that much was being said. And a few weeks ago I wrote to him, because I absolutely agree. I mean I was furious that he had to say it, that this position had arisen.

Film

Joseph Losey

Harold Pinter's collaboration with the American film director Joseph Losey is a hugely important aspect of his career trajectory. Losey and Pinter first worked together on their film of Robin Maugham's The Servant *(1963). They then produced adaptations of Nicholas Mosley's* Accident *(1967) and L. P. Hartley's* The Go-Between *(1969). They had planned together an ambitious adaptation of Marcel Proust's* A la recherche du temps perdu *in 1972, but this was never filmed. This interview, with Michel Ciment, is taken from* Conversations with Losey *by Ciment (London: Methuen, 1985, pp. 239–42).*

MC: *What kind of collaboration did you have with Pinter on the three films you did together?*
JL: It was a progressively developing one. Immediately after *The Servant* I took *The Go-Between* to Harold and he wrote a screenplay of about fifty or sixty pages. In the middle of his work the project broke up because a man got hold of some subsidiary rights that blocked us. It was not revived until seven years later. And when we went back to that script, we found that we were not at all satisfied with it, which was a development simply of *The Servant* collaboration. So then, out of the Nicholas Mosley book, came a much more free collaboration and a much closer, much more exciting and interesting one because of the way we both saw the use of film. We got to understand each other very well and to trust each other com-

214

pletely. And I think it's the best and most useful collaboration I've ever had.

On *The Go-Between*, we decided very early on that the present should be the late 1950s – rather than the present present – because otherwise the span with 1900 was too great to make any of it work. If we had made it in 1970, then the old man would have been so old that it would have been meaningless. Initially, it was written with a great many more intercuts of the present and it was revised, and even in the shooting I shot certain things which I then left out in the cutting. But always with Harold's agreement or collaboration. I never did anything on any film that I worked on with him without consulting him. And this is generally what I do with my closest collaborators.

Originally we wanted to do *The Go-Between* with an unknown girl, because the girl really ought to have been about eighteen, nineteen years old, you know, to make it work the way it should have. It would have been better for the jealousy and the conflict with the mother; it would have been better in terms of the sentimental relationship with the little boy; it would have been more understandable in terms of the relationship with the farmer, and so on. The farmer too should have been very young. It really was a story of very young lovers who were using a little boy who was only slightly younger than they were. They were on opposite sides of adolescence, of pubescence, and that's the way I wanted to do it, but for reasons of finance we were quite unable to do it. We talked about all kinds of casting to try and satisfy backing.

The producer, Delfont, said he had to have one name, and so I conceded Julie Christie, whom I had tried to get initially in 1964, at which point she would have been almost the right age. And she had agreed at that point. And I must say, to her very great credit, because she's an extremely honest girl, she insisted that she was too old, which was true. But I did agree to go ahead with Julie because I thought she had a kind of freshness that would work. She refused. Later, she was persuaded to come back in, otherwise the whole thing would have fallen to pieces.

Which script raised the greatest problems of the three you did with Pinter?

I would think *Accident*. In many ways *Accident* was much more complex, too, because it moved around forward and back in time. There were many references to early shots, but when I go back to the kitchen, to the bedroom, to the car, I never use the same shots twice; almost, but not quite. It's slightly changed. So really, *Accident* was the critical time for us. *The Go-Between*, once we got through the money problems, was an absolute dream. Of course the money problems gave me many other problems too, because starting late meant that I lost the most valuable weather of the summer, and raised the question of lighting and jumping around in continuity in order to accommodate mostly rainy weather for the first month. Actually we made the picture eventually for about a million too, which is exactly half of what it was supposed to have cost two years before.

How do you work with Pinter?

I never stand over his shoulder. He wouldn't have it even if I wanted to work that way. And I wouldn't do it with any writer that I respected. We had lots and lots of discussion, lots of exchange of notes, marking up the book, getting relevant additional material from L. P. Hartley, the author of *The Go-Between*, finding ideas of the locations, looking for boys, in the case of *The Go-Between*, who were not going to be actorish, looking in the schools, auditioning, working with them.

I remember on *The Go-Between*, the day came for Harold to begin work on the script. He writes very fast when he's convinced he's ready to write. At eleven o'clock in the morning I got a phone call and he said, 'I'm in terrible trouble. I don't know what to do. I've been sitting here since eight o'clock this morning; my pencils are sharpened metaphorically, in fact they are on my desk, in a glass; my typewriter is also in front of me, and I've got lots of clean paper; my secretary is standing by if I want to dictate. I've got the book open with all of your marked notes on it, I've got your typed notes beside me, I've got my own notes, and I can't write a fucking word! What shall I do?' I said, 'Just start,' and he did. And I don't know how much longer, but let's say maybe three weeks later he called me and he said, 'I've got fifty pages,' and then I'd take them, study them, and make notes on them, and we'd get together and talk, and either go back and revise or go ahead.

If you look at his screenplays you will see that he never writes at length; they're very economical, and this is immensely helpful for me because his writing is always visually evocative, but at the same time it gives me a great deal of room. Mostly he works in master scenes and they are usually dialogue and, of course, he's superb at dialogue. And it's astonished many people because the dialogue in his writing of *The Go-Between* doesn't seem to bear much relationship to the dialogue he writes in his plays. Or even in *Accident*, for that matter. And I think that the screenplays that Harold has done with me – and I'm not leaving out Proust, which is the absolute height of his accomplishment – are absolutely different from anything that he's done for anybody else. His screenplays always have their personal stamp, there is no doubt about that. But if you look at some of the other films he's made, they are not the same films as the films that he makes with me.

Obviously there are very similar interests between you. What would you say you share with him?
I don't know. Observation of characters, a very acute awareness of class dynamics and contradictions. He does superbly evoke the visual for me, but I don't think he has any visual sense at all. I can't remember ever disliking anything that Harold wrote although I liked some things more than others. But I also don't remember one single production of any of Harold's plays in that period of time that I liked, or one single film written by Harold that I liked. Which is odd – very odd – but I think it's primarily a visual problem.

Adaptations

In recent years, Pinter has been happy to collaborate on two adaptations of his writing. In 1999, Di Trevis persuaded him that his Proust screenplay might effectively be adapted for the stage, and the National Theatre produced the adaptation in 2000. In 2003 Kerry Lee Crabbe undertook an adaptation of Pinter's only novel, The Dwarfs, *which was performed in 2003 at the Tricycle Theatre. The first extract, 'A Study in Time and Emotion' by Di Trevis, concerning the Proust, is taken from the* Daily Telegraph *(4 November 2000), and the second interview, 'Pinter Picture', between Kate Stratton and Kerry Lee Crabbe, is from* Time Out: London *(16–23 April 2003).*

Di Trevis in the *Daily Telegraph*

One day, unpacking cartons of books that had been sent from England, I came across a copy of a screenplay of *Remembrance of Things Past*, by Harold Pinter. [. . .] Thus I came to my first realisation of the full sweep of Proust's narrative – and a subtle and brilliant evocation of his meditations and epiphanies, his agonies and comic set-pieces – through a simple script of 455 shots [. . .]. I discovered that Joseph Losey had commissioned the screenplay and had struggled to raise the money to make the film, but that for various reasons it never materialised. I knew too that the writing of it had taken up an entire year of Pinter's life.

Then in 1996, Peter James, an English theatre director, and now principal of Lamda, asked me if there was an idea I would like to try out with a group of twenty-seven second-year students. I could work with them for four months – four afternoon sessions a week – investigating and devising a stage event that would be performed, if I felt the work had progressed enough, to an invited audience. As I drove to his office, the idea of Proust fell into my head in incredible detail. I told Peter I would be working on a version of *A la recherche du temps perdu*.

What followed was, to quote Brecht, nothing but confusion.

I went home, got out the screenplay and promptly had a panic attack. But I took a remark of Pinter's as my own motto: 'We knew we could in no sense rival the work but we could be true to it.'

What theatre does best is to evoke much from nothing: a kind of magic occurs. The actor carries the audience with his own belief. So first I decided on the simplest of stagings: the more varied the settings in the screenplay, the more ingenious we would be. In the end, I placed into the space twelve chairs and a piano, and from this and this alone, we evoked Proust's world. The action could then flow without interruption, switch from place to place within moments. Whatever images we used had to be expressible theatrically and capable of dissolving away effortlessly into narrative flow.

The architectural structure was based still on the two contrasting principles of which Harold Pinter writes: 'one a narrative movement towards disillusion, the other more intermittent moving towards the revelation of time lost being found in art'.

Four months later, the students performed the stage version and, for a further two, I worked at another draft.

Then came a nerve-racking moment. I finally went to Harold and told him what I had done. I had been working all this time without his knowledge. He listened to me in silence and then poured two glasses of white wine and said, 'This sounds pretty interesting.'

Another performance was arranged. This time, the students came to the National Theatre – it was the day that Trevor Nunn took over the directorship – and performed in a rehearsal room before an exalted, invited audience of about twenty-five including Harold Pinter, Trevor Nunn and Patricia Losey, Joseph Losey's widow. There was an atmosphere of intense concentration.

I thought I might die of nerves. But Pinter was enthusiastic. He rang me next day and said, 'You can certainly cut the mustard.'

Over the next months we worked on another draft, adding further scenes from the screenplay, refining, reordering, cutting, condensing. At the end of 1999, we heard that with the formation of a new ensemble at the National, the play could be presented. It was nearly three decades since Pinter had written it – in a year that was perhaps not *perdu* after all.

Kate Stratton in *Time Out: London*

'It's about friendship,' says Kerry Lee Crabbe. 'How our friendships function and what changes them. It's about that wonderful, painful stage of life where you're growing up and growing away; where your first friendships from school are beginning to be tested.' His eyes light up. 'It's like a 1950s East End version of the impact that Yoko had on the Beatles.'

He's talking about *The Dwarfs*, Harold Pinter's first and only novel, and the challenges of adapting 'Britain's greatest living playwright' for the stage. Penned in the early 1950s, before Pinter turned his hand to plays, it was put aside until 1960 when extracts were distilled into a radio play. Returning to the book in 1989, Pinter decided to revise and publish it, dismissing the radio version as 'quite abstract'. Last year he agreed to let Crabbe tackle the first full stage adaptation.

It's a formidable task for a man who's grown up on Pinter. 'He's been a shaping force,' says Crabbe, a writer and former producer at the BBC, 'since my early teens [. . .]. Harold has been very forthcoming about the links with his early life. The characters are based, in part, on people he knew; most of whom he's still in touch with. They were all would-be writers and extraordinary emotional intellectuals; hugely verbal, argumentative, feisty, passionate people.

'What's also interesting,' he continues, 'is the way that Pinter has characterised his life at that time as "immensely precarious" – the aftermath of WW2, Mosleyites in the East End, bomb sites, the Korean War – and full of the joy of living. The shadow of that context is palpable between all the lines.

'I have been devoutly minimalist about making any changes or additions. I wanted the attention to be as much as possible on the thing itself. And Harold's been wonderfully restrained. Yes, there've been a couple of cuts and one or two additions. But when the maestro comes in and says something, you jump at it. It's got to be worth your while.'

He lets the sentence hang, but he's not done yet. 'I absolutely believe it's a great work. Some of the scenes, I think, are among the best Harold has written. But of course, I would jump at anything that comes from his pen. There's no one like him. He has a unique poetic sensibility that fuses the two things I love: the profoundly comic and the profoundly disturbing. That seems to me to be the essence of the lives we lead.'

Notes

I EAST END TO WEST END

1 Both opening quotations are from *www.haroldpinter.org*.
2 John Fowles, 'Harold Pinter and Cricket', in Peter Rabey (ed.), *The Cambridge Companion to Harold Pinter* (Cambridge: Cambridge University Press, 2001), p. 261.
3 Ciaran Carty, 'Citizen Pinter', *Sunday Tribune* (Eire), 1 May 1994.
4 Joan Littlewood, *Observer*, 15 March 1959.
5 Harold Pinter to Ian Smith, in *British Theatre in the 1950s*, Dominic Shellard (ed.) (Sheffield: Sheffield Academic Press, 2000), p. 67.
6 John Osborne, *A Better Class of Person: an Autobiography 1929–1956* (London: Faber and Faber, 1982), p. 246.
7 Peter Brook, *The Empty Space* (London: Pelican, 1972), pp. 11–46.
8 Pinter to Geordie Greig, 'You talkin' to me?', *Tatler*, August 2004, p. 110.

2 1956 AND ALL THAT

1 B. Ifor Evans, *A Short History of English Drama* (Harmondsworth: Penguin, 1948), p. 158.
2 Richard Findlater, *The Unholy Trade* (London: Gollancz, 1952), p. 19.
3 Terence Rattigan, *Collected Plays, Volume Two* (London: Hamish Hamilton, 1953), p. xii.
4 Pinter to Smith, p. 75.
5 Pinter to Smith, p. 71.
6 'Au Babylone et au Lancry – Deux coups heureux sur le damier du théâtre', *Arts*, 16 January 1953.
7 Harold Hobson, *Sunday Times*, 7 August 1955.
8 Kenneth Tynan, *Tynan on Theatre* (Harmondsworth: Penguin, 1961), p. 31.

9 *The Encore Reader*, Charles Marowitz, Tom Milne and Owen Hale (eds.) (London: Methuen, 1965), pp. 40–41.

10 John Russell Taylor, *Anger and After* (London: Methuen, 1962), p. 37.

11 Osborne, *Almost a Gentleman: an Autobiography, Vol. II: 1955–1966* (London: Faber and Faber, 1991), p. 3.

12 Philip Roberts, *The Royal Court Theatre and the Modern Stage* (Cambridge: Cambridge University Press, 1999), pp. 47–8.

13 Hobson, *Sunday Times*, 5 January 1958.

14 Roberts, p. 49.

15 Pinter to Barry Davis, 'The 22 From Hackney to Chelsea: a conversation with Harold Pinter', *Jewish Quarterly*, no. 144, Winter 1991/92, p. 11.

16 Pinter, Letter to *Guardian*, 31 December 1999, p. 19.

3 FIRST STAGES

1 *Enfield Gazette and Observer*, 28 March 1958.

2 Respectively: Milton Shulman, *Evening Standard*, 20 May 1958, W. A. Darlington, *Daily Telegraph*, 20 May 1958 and M. W. W., *Manchester Guardian*, 21 May 1958.

3 Irving Wardle, 'The Birthday Party', *The Encore Reader*, p. 76.

4 Pugh Marshal, 'Trying to Pin down Pinter', *Daily Mail*, 7 March 1964, p. 8.

5 Pinter to John Sherwood, *The Rising Generation, no. 7*: 'A Playwright – Harold Pinter', BBC European Service, 3 March 1960.

6 Bamber Gascoigne, *Twentieth Century Drama* (London: Hutchinson, 1962), p. 207.

7 Alan Dent, *News Chronicle*, 20 May 1958.

8 Hobson, *Sunday Times*, 15 June 1958, p. 11.

9 Martin Esslin, *The Theatre of the Absurd*, third edition (London and New York: Penguin, 1980), p. 15.

10 Pinter to Philip Purser, *News Chronicle*, 28 July 1960.

11 Pinter to Sherwood.

12 Tynan, 'Ionesco – Man of Destiny', *Observer*, 22 June 1958 and Eugène Ionesco, 'The Playwright's Role', *Observer*, 29 June 1958.

13 Pinter, interviewed by Sherwood.

14 Tom Milne, 'Double Pinter', *Encore*, 24, 7, 2 (March–April 1960), p. 40.

15 Wardle, 'Comedy of Menace', *The Encore Reader*, p. 91.

4 AN ESTABLISHED WRITER

1 'The Black and White' and 'Trouble in the Works' were per-formed in the revue *One to Another* at the Lyric Hammersmith in July 1959, and 'The Last to Go', 'Request Stop' and 'Special Offer' were performed as part of *Pieces of Eight* at the Apollo Theatre in September of that year.

2 'Mr Pinter's Concession', *The Times*, 22 July 1960, p. 16.

3 Alan Pryce-Jones, *Observer*, 1 May 1960, p. 23.

4 Tynan, *Observer*, 5 June 1960.

5 Alan Brien, *Spectator*, 6 May 1960.

6 Reported by Charles Marowitz, *New York Times Magazine* 1 October 1967.

7 Pinter to Sherwood.

8 'Pinter replies', *Sunday Times*, 14 August 1960, p. 21.

9 Pinter, 'The Servant', *Collected Screenplays 1* (London: Faber and Faber, 2000), p. 70.

10 Pinter, 'An Interview with Lawrence M. Bensky', Marowitz and Trussler (eds.), *Theatre at Work* (London: Methuen, 1967), pp. 105–6.

11 Pinter to Kenneth Cavander, 'Harold Pinter and Clive Donner', Joseph F. McCrindle (ed.), *Behind the Scenes. Theatre and Film Interviews from the Transatlantic Review*, London: Pitman, 1971, p. 215.

12 Simon Trussler, *The Plays of Harold Pinter* (London: Victor Gollancz, 1973), p. 128.

13 Ann C. Hall, *'A Kind of Alaska': Women in the Plays of O'Neill, Pinter and Shepard* (Carbondale and Edwardsville: Southern Illinois University Press, 1993), p. 56.

14 William Packard, 'An Interview with Harold Pinter', *First Stage*, vol. 6, no. 2, p. 82.

15 Peter Hall, 'Directing Pinter', *Theatre Quarterly*, no. 16, 1974/1975, p. 6.

16 Pinter to Henry Hewes, 'Probing Pinter's Play', *Saturday Review*, vol. 50, 1967, p. 57.

5 TIME REGAINED

1 Pinter to Patricia Bosworth, 'Why Doesn't He Write More?', *New York Times*, 27 October 1968.

2 A. P. Hinchcliffe's *Harold Pinter* (New York: Twayne, 1967),

Ronald Hayman's *Harold Pinter* (London: Heinemann, 1968), J. R. Taylor's *Writers and their Work: Harold Pinter* (London: Longmans, 1969), J. R. Hollis's *Harold Pinter: the Poetics of Silence* (New York: Feffer & Simons, 1970) and Martin Esslin, *The Peopled Wound: the plays of Harold Pinter* (London: Methuen, 1971). Martin Esslin's book is currently in its sixth revised edition, retitled *Pinter the Playwright*.

3 Harold Pinter to Patricia Bosworth, 'Why Doesn't He Write More?', *New York Times*, 27 October 1968, section D, p. 3.

4 Pinter to Smith, p. 80.

5 This was in addition to his well-received adaptation of *The Caretaker* (1964), and his numerous original plays for television.

6 *The Basement*, though a new TV script for the BBC (broadcast in February 1967), was a rewriting of *The Compartment*, an unfilmed screenplay he had produced in 1963. It had been written as part of a projected triptych of films, alongside Eugène Ionesco's *The Hard-Boiled Egg* and Samuel Beckett's *Film*. Only Beckett's screenplay made it to production.

7 Pinter to Sydney Edwards, *Evening Standard*, 18 May 1970.

8 Pinter to Bosworth, p. 3.

9 Marcel Proust, *Letters of Marcel Proust*, Mina Curtis (trans.) (London: Chatto and Windus, 1950), p. 147.

10 Pinter, *The Proust Screenplay* (London: Faber, 1991), p. viii.

6 FRATERNITY AND BETRAYAL

1 Wardle, *The Times*, 14 November 1970.

2 Katherine Worth, 'Joyce via Pinter', *Revolutions in Modern English Drama* (London: G. Bells & Sons, 1973), p. 51.

7 THE DEAD

1 John Barber, *Daily Telegraph*, 23 June 1980.

2 John Elsom, *Listener*, 8 June 1980.

3 Pinter, *Radio Times*, 27 March 1982.

4 Pinter, 'Peace Studies', *The Times*, 24 January 1984.

5 Pinter to Nick Hern, 'A Play and its Politics', *One for the Road* (London: Methuen, 1985), p.13.

6 Giles Gordon, *Spectator*, 24 March 1984.

7 Quoted by Arthur Miller, *Echoes Down the Corridor* (London: Methuen, 2000), p. 218.

8 Pinter to John Tulsa, *Saturday Review*, BBC2, 28 September 1985.

9 Pinter, Channel 4 News, 9 January 1984.

10 Pinter to Hern, p. 8.

11 Marc Silverstein, *Harold Pinter and the Language of Cultural Power* (London and Toronto: Associated University Presses, 1993), p. 24.

12 Pinter to Bensky, p. 104.

13 Letter to *The Times*, 30 July 1971.

14 Pinter to Bensky, p. 104.

15 Pinter to Mark Batty, see p. 88

16 Pinter to Davis, p. 14.

17 Pinter to Kathleen Tynan, 'In Search of Harold Pinter. Part Two', *Evening Standard*, 29 April 1968.

18 Testimony given by Harold Pinter for his 1949 court appearance, reported in 'Teachers behind Pinter's First Political Lesson', *Guardian*, 30 December 1999, p. 3.

19 'The trial of Vladimir Bukovsky', Letters to the Editor, *The Times*, 31 January 1972.

20 Pinter to Smith, p. 69.

21 Pinter to Greig, p. 111.

22 Pinter to Bryan Appleyard, 'The New Light that Burns within Harold Pinter' *The Times*, 16 March 1984.

23 Pinter, 'Mountain Language', *Times Literary Supplement*, 7 October 1988.

24 Nigel Foxell, Letters, *Sunday Telegraph*, 13 November 1988.

25 *Daily Telegraph*, 14 January 1993.

26 Pinter to Davis, p. 17.

27 'Death', *War*.

28 'God Bless America', *War*.

8 PINTER VIEWS

1 On 16 February 2003 between 750,000 (police figures) and two million (organiser's figures) people marched through London to Hyde Park to participate in a 'Stop the War' rally against the planned attack on Iraq.

2 Pinter to Stephen Moss, *Guardian*, 4 September 1999.

3 Jay Rayner, 'Pinter of Discontent', *Observer*, 16 May 1999.

4 Pinter is referring to the US Tomahawk cruise missile strike on the Iraqi Intelligence Service of 29 June 1993.

5 In May 1985 this period was reduced to thirty days.

9 VIEWS ON PINTER

1 In recent months prior to this interview, Harold Pinter had
   revealed to his friends that he had been diagnosed with cancer of
   the oesophagus. This was not public knowledge at the time of
   this interview.

Select Bibliography

Primary Sources

(All published by Faber and Faber unless otherwise indicated.)

Plays and Screenplays

Poems and Prose, 1949–1977 (London: Eyre Methuen, 1978).

The Dwarfs (1990).

The Proust Screenplay (1991).

Plays One: *The Birthday Party, The Room, The Dumb Waiter, A Slight Ache, The Hothouse, A Night Out*, 'The Black and White' (short story), *The Examination* (1991).

Plays Two: *The Caretaker, The Dwarfs, The Collection, The Lover, Night School*, 'Trouble in the Works', 'The Black and White', 'Request Stop', 'The Last to Go', 'Special Offer' (1996).

Plays Three: *The Homecoming, Tea Party, The Basement, Landscape, Silence, Night, That's Your Trouble, That's All, Applicant, Interview, Dialogue for Three, Tea Party* (short story), *Old Times, No Man's Land* (1997).

Plays Four: *Betrayal, Monologue, One for the Road, Mountain Language, Family Voices, A Kind of Alaska, Victoria Station, Precisely, The New World Order, Party Time, Moonlight, Ashes to Ashes,* (1998).

Various Voices: Poetry, Prose and Politics 1948–1998 (1998).

Celebration and The Room (2000).

Harold Pinter and Di Trevis, *Remembrance of Things Past* (2000).

Collected Screenplays 1 (2000).

Collected Screenplays 2 (2000).
Collected Screenplays 3 (2000).
Press Conference (2002).
Kerry Lee Crabbe (adapter) *The Dwarfs* (2003).
War (2003)

Selected Speeches and Articles

'Aristotle University of Thessaloniki Degree Speech, 18 April
  2000', *The Pinter Review: Collected Essays 1999–2000*,
  Francis Gillen and Steven H. Gale (eds.), Florida: University
  of Tampa Press, 2000, pp. 103–4.
'Arthur Wellard (1902–1980): A Memoir by Harold Pinter',
  Observer, 24 April 1981.
'Cruel, Inhuman, Degrading', *New Internationalist*, no. 327,
  September 2000.
'The Knight has been Unruly – Memories of Sir Donald
  Wolfit', *Listener*, 18 April 1968, p. 501.
'The Kurds have Lifted the Veil', *Guardian*, 20 February
  1999, Review, p. 2.
'The NATO Action in Serbia', in Tariq Ali, *Masters of the
  Universe: NATO's Balkan Crusade*, London: Verso, 2000.
'Pinter Replies', *Sunday Times*, 14 August 1960.

Secondary Sources

Almansi, Guido, and Simon Henderson, *Harold Pinter*,
  London: Methuen, 1983. (Consideration of the significance
  of game-playing in Pinter's oeuvre.)
Atwood, Margaret, 'Pinteresque', in *The Pinter Review:
  Collected Essays 1999–2000*, Francis Gillen and Steven H.
  Gale (eds.), Florida: University of Tampa Press, 2000, p. 5.
Baker, William and Tabachnick, Stephen Ely, *Harold Pinter*,
  Edinburgh: Oliver Boyd, 1973. (A solid survey with useful
  consideration of Pinter's juvenilia and a summary chapter
  on the 1960s screenplays. Some contemplation of Pinter's

Jewishness amid the appraisal of the plays up to *Old Times*.)

Batty, Mark, *Writers and their Work: Harold Pinter*, Tavistock: Northcote House, 2001. (The ideal companion to this volume, providing a more detailed survey of Pinter's plays, with an emphasis on the development of thematic concerns.)

Billington, Michael, *The Life and Work of Harold Pinter*, London: Faber, 1996. (An indispensable biography, cataloguing the domestic, artistic and political contexts behind much of Pinter's writing.)

Bold, Alan (ed.), *Harold Pinter: You Never Heard Such Silence*, London: Vision Press, 1984. (A collection of essays, including a piece by Peter Hall on directing Pinter.)

Brook, Peter, *The Empty Space*, London: Pelican, 1972.

Brown, John Russell (ed.), *Modern British Dramatists: a Collection of Critical Essays*, New Jersey: Prentice-Hall, 1968.

Burkman, Katherine, *The Dramatic World of Harold Pinter: its Basis in Ritual*, Columbus, OH: University of Ohio Press, 1971. (The structures of ritual apparent in Pinter's plays are analysed.)

——, and John L. Kundert-Gibbs (eds.), *Pinter at Sixty*, Indianapolis: Indiana University Press, 1993. (A good collection of essays, with insight given on the screenplays and the recent politics of Pinter.)

Eslom, John, *Post-war British Theatre*, London: Routledge, 1981.

Esslin, Martin, *Pinter the Playwright*, sixth edition, London: Methuen, 1982. (A highly accessible and readable survey of Pinter's achievements. A useful companion to this book.)

——, *The Theatre of the Absurd*, third edition, London and New York: Penguin, 1980.

Evans, B. Ifor, *A Short History of English Drama*, Harmondsworth: Penguin, 1948.

Findlater, Richard, *The Unholy Trade*, London: Gollancz, 1952.

Fowles, John, 'Foreword', Harold Pinter, *The Screenplay of 'The French Lieutenant's Woman'*, London: Jonathan Cape, 1981, pp.vii–xv.

Gale, Steven H., *Harold Pinter: Critical Approaches*, London: Associated University Presses, 1986. (A good collection of academic essays, including consideration of media work other than stage plays.)

——, *Sharp Cut: Harold Pinter's Screenplays and the Artistic Process*, Lexington: University of Kentucky Press, 2003. (The definitive guide to Harold Pinter's screenwriting.)

Gascoigne, Bamber, *Twentieth Century Drama*, London: Hutchinson, 1962.

Gray, Simon, *An Unnatural Pursuit*, London: Faber & Faber, 1985. (Gray's witty prose gives insight into Pinter's directing processes on Gray's play *The Common Pursuit*.)

Gussow, Mel, *Conversations with Pinter*, London: Nick Hern Books, 1994. (An excellent collection of lengthy interviews with Pinter, given over twenty-two years, that cover much of his work and attitudes from 1971 to 1993.)

Hall, Ann C., *'A Kind of Alaska': Women in the plays of O'Neill, Pinter and Shepard*, Carbondale and Edwardsville: Southern Illinois University Press, 1993. (A chapter on Pinter's approach to female characters, considered through a spectrum of feminist readings, offers useful insight into how the plays might engage an audience.)

Hall, Peter, *Exposed by the Mask*, London: Oberon, 2000.

Klein, Joanne, *Making Pictures: the Pinter Screenplays*, Columbus, OH: State University Press, 1985. (Read in conjunction with Gale's and Renton's books, a useful guide to Pinter's Screenplays.)

Knowles, Ronald, *Understanding Harold Pinter*, Columbia, SC: University of South Carolina, 1995. (A very useful survey of Pinter's output by this highly respected Pinter scholar.)

Lahr, John and Anthea (eds.), *A Casebook on Harold Pinter's 'The Homecoming'*, New York: Grove Press, 1971. (A very

helpful collection of essays and interviews on this most
resilient of Pinter's works.)

Marowitz, Charles, Tom Milne and Owen Hale (eds.), *The Encore Reader*, London: Methuen, 1965.

Merritt, Susan Hollis, *Pinter in Play*, Durham and London: Duke University Press, 1990. (A survey of the variety of critical approaches that have been adopted by all the major Pinter scholars over the decades.)

Miller, Arthur, *Echoes Down the Corridor: Collected Essays 1944–2000*, London: Methuen, 2000.

Osborne, John, *A Better Class of Person: an Autobiography 1929–1956*, London: Faber and Faber, 1982.

——, *Almost a Gentleman: an Autobiography, Volume II: 1955–1966*, London: Faber and Faber, 1991.

Page, Malcolm (ed.), *File on Pinter*, London: Methuen, 1993. (A handy compilation of critical responses to Pinter's plays.)

Peacock, D. Keith, *Harold Pinter and the New British Theatre*, London and Westport, CT: Greenwood Press, 1997. (One of the best surveys of Pinter's work within the context of the developments of British Theatre, and the social and cultural contexts to the works.)

Proust, Marcel, *Letters of Marcel Proust*, Mina Curtis (trans.), London: Chatto and Windus, 1950.

Rabey, Peter (ed.), *The Cambridge Companion to Harold Pinter*, Cambridge: Cambridge University Press, 2001.

Rattigan, Terence, *Collected Plays, Volume Two*, London: Hamish Hamilton, 1953.

Renton, Linda, *Pinter and the Object of Desire: an Approach through the Screenplays*, Oxford: Legenda, 2002. (A highly useful Lacanian reading of Pinter's writing, approaching his work through film and concentrating on three screenplays; Renton demonstrates the shifts between desire and anxiety that both characters and audience are exposed to by Pinter's work.)

Roberts, Philip, *The Royal Court Theatre and the Modern Stage*, Cambridge: Cambridge University Press, 1999.

Sakellaridou, Elizabeth, *Pinter's Female Portraits*, London: Macmillan, 1988. (A valuable starting point for those wishing to consider Pinter from a feminist angle.)

Silverstein, Marc, *Harold Pinter and the Language of Cultural Power*, London and Toronto: Associated University Presses, 1993. (Taking the prompt from Austin Quigley, Silverstein convincingly applies critical theory to examine the language of *The Birthday Party*, *The Collection*, *The Homecoming* and *Old Times* and demonstrate how Pinter describes and decries a suffocating cultural order whilst offering modes of resistance to the prevailing ideologies of that order.)

Strunk, Volker, *Harold Pinter: Towards a Poetics of His Plays*, New York: Lang, 1989. (Pinter's distinctive style analysed.)

Taylor, John Russell, *Anger and After*, London: Methuen, 1962.

Thompson, David T., *Pinter: the Players' Playwright*, London and New York: Macmillan, 1985. (A study of Pinter's early career as an actor, and some hypothetical conjecture on the influence of that experience on him as a writer.)

Trussler, Simon, *The Plays of Harold Pinter*, London: Victor Gollancz, 1973. (Ultimately dismissive of much of Pinter's achievement, this book does provide useful analyses of the plays up to *Old Times*.)

Tynan, Kenneth, *Tynan on Theatre*, London: Penguin, 1961.

Worth, Katherine, 'Joyce via Pinter', *Revolutions in Modern English Drama*, London: G. Bells and Sons, 1973.

Published Interviews with Harold Pinter

(Listed by interviewer. Excludes those published in *Various Voices* and *Conversations with Mel Gussow*.)

Amette, Jacques-Pierre, *Le Point*, no. 1331, 21 March 1998, p. 92.

Anon., 'Mr Harold Pinter – Avant-Garde Playwright and Intimate Revue', *The Times*, 16 November 1959.

——, 'Pinterview', *Newsweek*, 23 July 1962, p. 69.

——, 'Two People in a Room', *New Yorker Magazine*, 25 February 1967.

——, *The American Film Theatre/Cinebill* (Simon Gray's *Butley*), January 1974.

Appleyard, Bryan, 'The New Light that Burns within Harold Pinter', *The Times*, 16 March 1984.

Baignères, Claude, 'Un portrait de Pinter', *Le Figaro*, 17 September 1971.

Bakewell, Joan, 'In an Empty Bandstand', *Listener*, 6 November 1969, p. 630.

Barber, John, 'Talking with Pinter . . .' *Daily Telegraph*, 23 June 1980, p. 11.

Bennetts, Leslie, 'On Film, Pinter's "Betrayal" Displays New Subtelties', *New York Times*, 27 February 1983, sec. 2, pp. 1 and 23.

Bensky, Lawrence M., 'Harold Pinter', in *Theatre at Work*, Charles Marowitz and Simon Trussler (eds.), London: Methuen, 1967, pp. 96–109.

——, 'Pinter: "Violence is Natural"', *New York Times*, sec. 2, 1 January 1967, pp. 1 and 3.

Billington, Michael, 'The Evil that Men do', *Guardian*, 30 June 2001.

Blow, David, 'Hackney's Empire', *Waterstone's New Books Christmas* 1990, pp. 46–7.

Bosworth, Patricia, 'Why Doesn't He Write More?', *New York Times*, 27 October 1968, section D, p. 3.

Canziani, Roberto, *Festival di Palermo* programme, 1997.

Carty, Ciaran, 'Citizen Pinter', *Sunday Tribune* (Eire), 1 May 1994.

——, 'This Empty Room', *Tribune Magazine* (Eire), 23 March 1997, p. 9.

Cavander, Kenneth, 'Harold Pinter and Clive Donner', Joseph F. McCrindle (ed.), *Behind the Scenes. Theatre and Film Interviews from the Transatlantic Review*, London: Pitman, 1971, pp. 209–21.

Ciment, Michel, 'Visually Speaking', *Film Comment*, vol. 25, no. 3, May/June 1989, pp. 20–22.

Cusac, Anne-Marie, *The Progressive*, March 2001.

Davis, Barry, 'The 22 from Hackney to Chelsea', *Jewish Quarterly*, no. 144, Winter 91/92, pp. 9–17.

Dean, Michael, 'Harold Pinter talks to Michael Dean', *Listener*, 6 March 1969, p. 312.

Edwards, David, 'Unthinkable Thoughts', Santa Monica Review, Spring 2000.

Edwards, Sydney, 'Pinter's Taxi to No Man's Land', *Evening Standard*, 11 July 1976.

——, 'To hell and back with Pinter', *Evening Standard*, 18 May 1979.

Farber, Stephen, 'Topical Relevance', *New York Times*, 10 May 1987, section 2, p. 25.

Ford, Anna, 'Radical Departures', *Listener*, 27 October 1988.

Gale, John, 'Taking pains with Pinter', *Observer*, 16 June 1962, p. 19.

Garis, Leslie, 'Translating Fowles into Film', *New York Times*, 5 October 1981, pp. 24, 48, 50, 52–3, 69.

Glanville, Brian, 'I am a Jew who writes', *Jewish Chronicle*, 11 March 1960.

Grahamyool, A., 'Blowing up the Media', *Index on Censorship*, vol. 21, no.5., May 1992, pp. 2–3.

Grant, Steve, 'Pinter: my plays, my polemics, my pad', *Independent*, 20 September 1993. (Also published as 'HP Source', *Time Out*, 15–22 September 1993.)

Greig, Geordie, 'You talkin' to me?', *Tatler*, August 2004, pp. 108–13.

Gross, Miriam, 'Pinter on Pinter', *Observer*, 5 October 1980, p. 25.

Hern, Nick, 'A Play and its Politics', *One for the Road*, London: Methuen, 1985, pp. 5–24.

Hewes, Henry, 'Probing Pinter's Play', *Saturday Review* (New York), 8 April 1967, pp. 57–8 and 96–7.

Johnson, B. S, 'Evacuees', *The Pinter Review: Collected*

Essays 1993–1994, Francis Gillen and Steven H. Gale (eds.), Florida: University of Tampa Press, 1994, pp. 8–13.

Jones, Edward T., 'Harold Pinter: a Conversation', *Literature/Film Quarterly*, vol. 21, no.1, 1993, pp. 3–9.

Langley, Lee, 'From *Caretaker* to *Servant*', *New York Herald Tribune Magazine*, 1 March 1964, p. 24.

——, 'Genius – A Change of Direction', *Daily Telegraph Magazine*, 23 November 1973.

Lister, David, 'Look, Justice!', *Independent*, 3 October 1997.

Marber, Patrick, *The Caretaker* programme, Comedy Theatre, London, November 2000.

Marshal, Pugh, 'Trying to Pin down Pinter', *Daily Mail*, 7 March 1964, p. 8.

Menick, Stephen, 'Remembrances of Things Future', *Village Voice* (New York), 12 December 1977, pp. 45–7.

Moher, Frank, 'Pinter on Woolf and Friendship', *Saturday Night Magazine*, 8 July 2000, pp. 28–31.

Moss, Stephen, *Guardian*, 4 September 1999.

O'Toole, Fintan, 'An Unflappable Gaze', *Irish Times*, 30 April 1994.

——, 'Walking into a Dark Room', *Irish Times*, 3 May 1994.

Owen, Michael, 'Funny, but Pinter and Cooney are Very Similar', *Evening Standard*, 6 October 1995, p. 18.

Packard, William, 'An Interview with Harold Pinter', *First Stage*, Summer 1967, vol. 6, no.2, p. 82.

Perrier, Jean-Louis, 'La corde raide', *Le Monde*, 15 October 1997.

Purser, Philip, 'A Pint with Pinter Helps Dispel the Mystery', *News Chronicle*, 28 July 1960.

Riddell, Mary, *New Statesman*, 8 November 1999.

Sakellaridou, Elizabeth, 'An Interview with Harold Pinter', *The Pinter Review: Collected Essays 1999–2000*, Francis Gillen and Steven H. Gale (eds.), Florida: University of Tampa Press, 2000, pp. 92–102.

Saunders, Kate, 'Pause for Thought', *Sunday Times*, 9 July 1995.

Sexton, David, 'Life in the Old Dog Yet', *Daily Telegraph*, 16 March 1995, p. 12.

Shiff, Stephen, 'Pinter's Passions', *Vanity Fair*, September 1990, pp. 219–22, 300–303.

Smith, Ian, 'Harold Pinter's Recollections of his Career in the 1950s', in Shellard, Dominic (ed.), *British Theatre in the 1950s*, Sheffield: Sheffield Academic Press, 2000.

Summers, Sue, 'Breaking the Silence', *London Daily News*, 19 June 1987, p. 19.

——, 'A Conscientious Objector', *Independent*, 18 October 1988. 1991/92, pp. 9–17.

Taylor, John Russell, 'Accident', *Sight and Sound*, Autumn 1966, vol. 35, no. 4, pp. 179–184.

Thébaud, Marion, 'Harold Pinter: retour au politique', *Le Figaro*, 19 March 1998.

Thompson, Harry, 'Harold Pinter Replies', *New Theatre Magazine*, January 1961, vol. 2, no. 2, pp. 8–10.

Tynan, Kathleen, 'In Search of Harold Pinter', *Evening Standard*, 28 and 29 April 1968

Walsh, John, 'That Nice Mr Pinter', *Independent*, 8 February 1999, pp. 1, 8.

Zampa, Fabrizio, 'Tanto tempo fa', *Il Messaggero*, 11 May 1973.

Selected Radio and TV Interviews with Harold Pinter

Allen, Paul, BBC Radio 3, 7 October 1990.

Channel 4 News, 9 January 1984.

Kitchin, Lawrence, *New Comment*, BBC Home Service, 5 October 1963.

Mayersberg, Peter, 'The Author in Search of Collaborators', BBC Third Programme, (Pinter, Losey), 26 February 1964.

Oakes, Philip, 'On Films', BBC Third Programme, 6 October 1963.

Sherwood, John, *Rising Generation*, no.7, 'A Playwright – Harold Pinter', BBC European Service, 3 March 1960.

Tulsa, John, *Saturday Review*, BBC2, 28 September 1985.
Tynan, Kenneth, 'Interview with Harold Pinter', BBC Home
  Service, 28 October 1960.

Other Interviews

(Listed by interviewee)

Blakely, Colin, 'Old Times', *Plays and Players*, vol. 18, no. 10,
  July 1971, pp. 22–4.
Crabbe, Kerry Lee, to Kate Stratton, 'Pinter Picture', *Time
  Out: London*, 16–23 April 2003.
Duncan, Lindsay, to Kate Bassett, 'Pinter's Women', *Daily
  Telegraph*, 18 March 2000.
Hall, Peter, to Catherine Itzin and Simon Trussler, 'Directing
  Pinter', *Theatre Quarterly*, vol. 4, no. 16, 1974/75,
  pp. 4–17.
——, 'A Director's Approach', John and Anthea Lahr (eds.), *A
  Casebook on Harold Pinter's 'The Homecoming'*, London:
  Davis, Poynter, 1974, pp. 9–25.
Hodge, Douglas, to Heather Neill, 'When Pinter met Hodge
  [long pause] . . .', *Independent*, 12 November 2000, p. 7.
Leveaux, David, to Georgina Brown, 'Because it's not quite
  Cricket', *Independent*, 1 September 1993.
Losey, Joseph, to Michel Ciment, *Conversations with Losey*,
  London: Methuen, 1985, pp. 239–42.
Schneider, Alan, 'If you Didn't Know it was by Pinter', *New
  York Times*, 1 October 1967, section 2, pp. 1, 3.
Trevis, Di, 'A Study in Time and Emotion', *Daily Telegraph*,
  4 November 2000.
——, to Paul Taylor, 'The Play of the Film of the Novel',
  Independent, 22 November 2000, p. 10.
Williams, Lia, to Kate Bassett, 'Pinter's Women', *Daily
  Telegraph*, 18 March 2000.
Woolf, Henry, to Jasper Rees, 'Pinter's Old Pal Act', *Evening
  Standard*, 15 March 2000.

Acknowledgements

I am extremely grateful to Harold Pinter and his personal assistant Ros Fielden for their help and advice in compiling this book. Thanks also to Richard Boon, Philip Roberts, Juliette Taylor and Dinah Wood for their support and their advice on the various drafts of the manuscript, and on other matters regarding its compilation. I am grateful also to Nick Hern for his advice. Many thanks to those who were happy to chat with me about their work with Harold Pinter: Andy de la Tour, Eileen Diss, Lindsay Duncan, Dani Everett, Mick Hughes, Gari Jones, Tom Rand, Lia Williams and Henry Woolf. My gratitude also goes to the small group of students who transcribed my various interviews: Josie Bamforth, Lauren Bracewell, Catherine Browne and Hannah Taylor. Thanks also to Chris Eckersley for kindly translating an interview from Dutch and a nod to Dan Rabellato for my borrowing of his title. I am grateful to those who have helped in tracking down the numerous interviews that Pinter has given during his career, especially Els Boonen at the BBC Written Archives Centre and Susan Hollis-Merrit. Thanks to my friends and colleagues in the Workshop Theatre and School of English at Leeds, especially Tracy Hargreaves, Francis O'Gorman and John McLeod, all of whom add congeniality to the working environment at Leeds. Thanks to Ewan Jeffrey, who gave me insight into Pinter's developing representation of family, and whose considered thoughts are borrowed and brutally diluted in this work. Thanks also to the generations of my *Theatricalities* students, who continue to open up fresh perspectives for me in Pinter's writing.

For permission to reprint copyright material the publishers gratefully acknowledge the following:

MARGARET ATWOOD: 'Pinteresque', *The Pinter Review: Collected Essays 1999–2000*, Gillen, Francis and Gale, Steven H., eds., Florida: University of Tampa Press, 2000, 5 © Margaret Atwood; LAWRENCE M. BENSKY: 'Harold Pinter', in *Theatre at Work*, Marowitz, Charles and Trussler, Simon, eds., London: Methuen, 1967, 96–109; DAVID BLOW: 'Hackney's Empire', *Waterstone's New Books Christmas 1990*, 46–7 © David Blow; GEORGINA BROWN, 'Because it's not quite Cricket', interview with David Leveaux, *Independent*, 1.9.93 KENNETH CAVANDER: 'Harold Pinter and Clive Donner', in McCrindle, Joseph F., ed., *Behind the Scenes. Theatre and Film Interviews from the Transatlantic Review*, London: Pitman, 1971, 209–21; CIARAN CARTY: 'This Empty Room', *Tribune Magazine* (Eire), 23.3.97, 9; MICHEL CIMENT: *Conversations with Losey*, London: Methuen, 1985, 239–42; KERRY LEE CRABBE: to Kate Stratton, 'Pinter Picture', *Time Out: London*, 16–23.4.03; BARRY DAVIS: 'The 22 from Hackney to Chelsea', *Jewish Quarterly*, No. 144, Winter 91/92, 9–17; ANNA FORD: 'Radical Departures' *Listener*, 27.10.88; LESLIE GARIS: 'Translating Fowles into Film', *New York Times*, 5.10.81, 24–69; STEVE GRANT: 'Pinter: my plays, my polemics, my pad', *Independent*, 20.9.93; NICK HERN: 'A Play and its Politics', *One for the Road*, London: Methuen, 1985, 5–24 © Nick Hern and Harold Pinter; CATHERINE ITZIN AND SIMON TRUSSLER to Peter Hall, 'Directing Pinter', *Theatre Quarterly*, Vol. 4, No. 16, 1974/75, 4–17 © Peter Hall; B.S. JOHNSON: 'Evacuees', in *The Pinter Review: Collected Essays 1993–1994*, 8–13; LEE LANGLEY: 'From *The Caretaker* to *The Servant*', *New York Herald Tribune Magazine*, 1.3.64, 24; PATRICK MARBER: *The Caretaker* programme, Comedy Theatre, London, November 2000 © Patrick Marber and Harold Pinter;

ACKNOWLEDGEMENTS

STEPHEN MENICK: 'Remembrances of Things Future', *Village Voice* (New York), 12.12.77, 45–7; PHILIP PURSER: 'A pint with Pinter helps dispel the mystery', *News Chronicle*, 28.7.60; HAROLD PINTER: 'The NATO Action in Serbia', in Tariq Ali, *Masters of the Universe: NATO's Balkan Crusade*, London: Verso, 2000 © Harold Pinter; KATE SAUNDERS: 'Pause for Thought', *Sunday Times*, 9.7.95; SUE SUMMERS: 'Breaking the Silence', *London Daily News*, 19.6.87, 19; SUE SUMMERS: 'A Conscientious Objector', *Independent*, 18.10.88; 'Accident', by John Russell Taylor, *Sight & Sound*, published by the BFI, Autumn 1966, (vol.35, no.4, pp.179–184); MARION THÉBAUD: 'Harold Pinter: retour au politique', *Le Figaro*, 19.3.98; HARRY THOMPSON: 'Harold Pinter Replies', *New Theatre Magazine*, January 1961, Vol. 2, No. 2, 8–10; DI TREVIS: 'A Study in Time and Emotion', *Daily Telegraph*, 4.11.00 © The Daily Telegraph; KENNETH TYNAN: 'Interview with Harold Pinter', BBC Home Service, 28.10.60 reproduced with the permission of the BBC Written Archives Centre; HENRY WOOLF: 'Pinter and I were Kings of the World', *Guardian*, 14.1.02 © Henry Woolf; 'Two People in a Room', *New Yorker Magazine*, 25.2.67; 'Mr. Harold Pinter – Avant-Garde Playwright and Intimate Revue', *Times*, 16.11.59.

Index

INDEX